THE LEAGUE OF YOUTH
A DOLL'S HOUSE
THE LADY FROM THE SEA

HENRIK IBSEN was born at Skien, Norway, in 1828. His family went bankrupt when he was a child, and he struggled with poverty for many years. His first ambition was medicine, but he abandoned this to write and to work in the theatre. Of his early verse plays, *The Vikings at Helgeland* is now best remembered. In the year of its publication (1858) he married Susannah Thoresen, a pastor's daughter.

A scholarship enabled Ibsen to travel to Rome in 1864. In Italy he wrote *Brand* (1866), which earned him a state pension, and *Peer Gynt* (1867), for which Grieg later wrote the incidental music. These plays established his reputation. Apart from two short visits to Norway, he lived in Italy and Germany until 1891.

From *The League of Youth* (1869) onwards, Ibsen renounced poetry and wrote prose drama. Though a timid man, he supported in his plays many crucial causes of his day, such as the emancipation of women. Plays like *Ghosts* (1881) and *A Doll's House* (1879) caused critical uproar. Other plays included *The Pillars of the Community*, *The Wild Duck*, *The Lady From the Sea*, *Hedda Gabler*, *The Master Builder*, *John Gabriel Borkmann* and *When We Dead Wake*.

Towards the end of his life Ibsen, one of the world's greatest dramatists, suffered strokes which destroyed his memory for words and even the alphabet. He died in 1906 in Kristiania (now Oslo).

A Note on the Translator

PETER WATTS was born in 1900 and went to school in Canada. He originally trained as a doctor at Cambridge and St Thomas' Hospital, but then turned to journalism and the theatre. In the twenties he stage-managed the Old Vic for eight years. He then travelled about Europe and the Middle East, and after a period as a literary agent and then as a wine merchant he returned to the theatre in 1938 as a producer. When the theatres closed at the beginning of the war, he went to the Admiralty as a King's Courier, but left in 1941 when the BBC offered him a post as a drama producer. He remained with them for nearly twenty years, working both in radio and in television. He produced most of his translations of Ibsen and Strindberg on the Third Programme. Peter Watts died in 1972.

Henrik Ibsen

THE LEAGUE OF YOUTH
A DOLL'S HOUSE
THE LADY FROM THE SEA

TRANSLATED BY
Peter Watts

PENGUIN BOOKS

Penguin Books Ltd, Harmondsworth, Middlesex, England
Viking Penguin Inc., 40 West 23rd Street, New York, New York 10010, U.S.A.
Penguin Books Australia Ltd, Ringwood, Victoria, Australia
Penguin Books Canada Ltd, 2801 John Street, Markham, Ontario, Canada L3R 1B4
Penguin Books (N.Z.) Ltd, 182–190 Wairau Road, Auckland 10, New Zealand

—

This translation first published 1965
Reprinted 1967, 1969, 1970, 1971, 1973, 1974 (twice),
1975, 1976, 1977, 1978, 1979, 1980, 1981,
1982, 1983, 1984, 1985 (twice)

—

—

Made and printed in Great Britain
by Richard Clay (The Chaucer Press) Ltd,
Bungay, Suffolk
Set in Monotype Bembo

All applications to perform the plays in
this volume should be made to A. P. Watt & Son,
26/28 Bedford Row, London WC1R 4HL

CONTENTS

INTRODUCTION

The three plays in this book, written at ten-year intervals, show three very different sides of Ibsen's talent. *The League of Youth* (1869) was Ibsen's first play in colloquial prose, and is a realistic comedy; *A Doll's House* (1879) comes from his great 'middle period' and is perhaps his most popular play; *The Lady from the Sea*, written in 1888 when he was sixty, was the first of six final plays in which, having finished his 'plays of protest', he enlarged on themes that he had already dealt with in his controversial works.

The League of Youth marks a great turning-point in Ibsen's development; to appreciate its importance, it might be helpful to run quickly over his life up to that time. His first forty years (for he was forty when he wrote that essentially youthful play *Peer Gynt*) were a fight against poverty and failure. He was born into a wealthy family who, when he was four, moved into an even larger house where they entertained lavishly. Ibsen can have remembered little about those early glories, though he must have heard of them from his mother, just as Åse recalls to Peer the parties given by 'the wealthy Jon Gynt'. By the time Ibsen was six, Knud Ibsen was bankrupt, and the family had moved out of their home town of Skien to a farm that was all that was left of his fortune. Daniel Hejre in *The League of Youth* is a merciless portrait of Ibsen's father as he remembered him – and incidentally one of the best acting parts for a man that Ibsen ever wrote.

Ibsen was the solitary, eldest child of a large family. For the sake of peace he used to shut himself up in a disused pantry away from his brothers' teasing, drawing caricatures of them as dogs and monkeys and bursting into ungovernable rages if ever they interfered with his papers or touched his toy theatre. Only for his sister Hedwig, whose name he was to use for the heroine of *The Wild Duck*, did he feel any real warmth, and in later life she was the only one of his family with whom he kept in any sort of touch.

Ibsen had set his heart on becoming a doctor, but though his father often boasted of the promising young men whom he had helped through college in the past, there was now no money for his own son's education. The nearest that Ibsen could get to his ambition was to be apprenticed to an apothecary in Grimstad, some fifty miles

7

away. Here he spent six unhappy years, not able even to afford a
room to himself, but having to share with the chemist's small boys.
In his loneliness he turned to a servant-girl ten years older than himself, and for the next fourteen years he had to pay maintenance for
their child. (He was to remember this when Peer Gynt meets the
Woman in Green with her Ugly Brat.)

At first he went back to Skien once or twice a year to visit his
family, but soon he gave up even that, and thirty years later it was
from a newspaper that he learned of his father's death.

It would be wrong, though, to think of the years in Grimstad as
completely barren and gloomy. He wrote poems and lampoons, drew
caricatures, and got up to pranks and mischief with his friends
Christopher Due and Ole Schulerud. In 1849 he wrote his first full-
length play, *Cataline*, a verse play about Roman history. The Kristiania Theatre praised it but turned it down; the publishers merely
turned it down. Schulerud paid for it to be published, and it appeared
in 1850. The critics gave it guarded praise, and two days later Ibsen
and Schulerud left Grimstad for the University at Kristiania. Though
for the moment they lived in a garret, Ibsen would write two or three
plays a year and they would soon both be rich. But of the edition of
250, 205 were left. These remaindered copies did eventually bring
the boys some comfort; they sold them to a grocer for wrapping
paper, 'and for a few days', as Ibsen wrote afterwards, 'we wanted
for none of the necessities of life'.

That winter, his play *The Warrior's Tomb* was staged, and was
given three performances, which, in the repertory system of those
days, by no means implies such a failure as it would today. During
the summer he took his examinations and failed in Greek and mathe-
matics. However, Ole Bull of the Bergen Theatre offered him the
post of Resident Poet – which seems in practice to have meant a sort
of assistant to the assistant stage manager – at twenty Specie dollars a
month (about £60 a year). He was a conscientious worker – some of
his very neat property plots and scene plans still exist – but he was too
shy with actors – and especially with actresses – to have much authority over them. A Danish member of the company at the time described him as 'a tight-lipped little Norwegian with alert eyes'. He
felt his poverty keenly, and dressed as elaborately as he could to hide
it.

Ibsen stayed at the Bergen Theatre for seven years, writing plays in verse based on old Norse folk ballads and legends. At this time, the man who was to become known as 'The Great Realist' could write: 'In Art there is no place for mere Reality – what is wanted is illusion.' *St John's Night*, *Lady Inger of Østråt*, *Olaf Liljekrans* and the rest are little more than names today, but his bright and cheerful *Feast at Solhaug* was given six performances and had the students singing under his window. It was his first taste of success, and it gave him, as he says, his first happy day in Bergen. It has one important conse-quence, it brought him an invitation to the house of Pastor Thoresen. Fru Thoresen afterwards described him as 'a shy little marmot, more quaint than handsome, with something nervous and ungainly in his movements, who seemed terrified of making a fool of himself or being laughed at'. Here he met the Thoresen's nineteen-year-old daughter Susannah, plain, rather dumpy, and a bit of a tomboy, but with beautiful hair that let down almost to her ankles. In June 1858 they were married.

In 1857 he had signed on for another year at the Bergen Theatre, but almost immediately the National Theatre at Kristiania (now Oslo) offered him a post at almost twice the salary. Bergen released him from his contract and he moved to the capital in September 1857. He was then aged thirty, and he was to stay at this theatre till he was thirty-five.

Up till this time, the theatre in Norway had been dominated by Danes and nearly all its actors were Danish – the Norwegian and Danish languages being about as nearly identical as those of Devon-shire and Surrey. The National Theatre was founded to present Norwegian drama and to develop a national style. At first the theatre was successful, and it brought many new and distinctively Norwegian plays into its repertory – including in its first winter Ibsen's *Warriors at Helgeland*. But there were not enough of the right kind of plays available, and, after the first enthusiasm had cooled, they found, like many an English provincial repertory company today, that they had to fill out with farces. Ibsen, as usual, was before his time; during his years at Bergen he had been writing nationalistic plays, but now that there was some demand for them, he found that they no longer satis-fied him, and though he made a start on the play that we now know as

The Pretenders, he soon shelved it. He took to painting again and to writing poems; his best-known poem, *On the Fells*, dates from this time.

In 1862, the theatre, having limped along uneasily for the past few years, finally failed and Ibsen was left unemployed. Although he made a little money by journalism and poetry, the Ibsens, now with a four-year-old son, were wretchedly poor. He had run even more deeply than usual into debt when at last the university gave him a small grant to travel over the country collecting folksongs and legends, as he had done during his holidays at Bergen. Now he started a new play in prose which he called *Love's Comedy*, but he found prose too difficult, and soon returned to his usual rhymed couplets. The play was published on the last day of 1862, and was so fiercely denounced by both Press and pulpit as an attack on marriage that it did not get a stage production.

When, the following year, Ibsen applied for a Poet's Stipend, *Love's Comedy* had offended too many people, and though his friend and rival Bjørnson was awarded a stipend of four hundred dollars, the Storthing (the Norwegian parliament) rejected Ibsen's application.

Ibsen continued his experiments with prose drama, and he now succeeded in finishing his historical play *The Pretenders*. It was published in the autumn of 1863 and produced on the stage the following January. Although it ran for five hours – which Ibsen later cut to four – and must have been a great strain for actors working under repertory conditions, it was given eight successful performances in the next two months.

Meanwhile, thanks to Bjørnson's help, Ibsen was awarded a grant for foreign travel, and in April 1864 he sailed for Copenhagen. The Danes were fighting heroically in their war with Prussia, and Ibsen, deeply stirred by their courage, wrote many poems and articles to try to rally all Scandinavia to their aid. The Norwegian and Swedish governments decided to remain neutral, and the Danes were finally defeated at Dybbøl. Ibsen felt bitterly ashamed of his country, and a little later, when he passed through Berlin and saw the trophies of the defeated Danes carried through the city 'when we had stood by and done nothing', he took it as a personal betrayal, and felt that he could never return to Norway. He moved on to Rome, revelling in the sun after the dark northern winters where, as he made *Brand* complain in his next play, he

> '. . . never saw a sunlit sky
> From leaf-fall until cuckoo-cry.'

In *Brand* he was moved to show his countrymen as they should have been. He wrote quickly for once, working right through the day. The only other time in his life when he could write so fluently was twenty years later when, also inspired by anger, he wrote *A Public Enemy*. In his self-imposed exile Ibsen became aggressively Norwegian; he wrote *Brand* in the Norwegian vernacular and evolved a nationalistic spelling.

The play was finished in October 1865, but during this time the Ibsens were often penniless. Money that should have come from home often arrived late; once the news came that a friend, thinking with some justification that the Ibsens would never come back, had paid their creditors by selling all the furniture and belongings (including Susannah's family silver) that Ibsen had left in store at the Kristiania Theatre. Then there was a delay over the publication of *Brand*; Ibsen could reasonably have expected it to be on sale by Christmas – since publishers worked somewhat faster then than they do to-day – when in fact it did not appear till March. In one of his letters at this time, sent unstamped to his publisher, he writes: 'Please debit my account with the postage on this letter; it works out cheaper that way than if I stamp it here.' In spite of all this, when the Kristiania Theatre wrote to offer him the post of director, he declined, saying: 'Up there I could not write freely and without reserve, which is the same as saying that I couldn't write at all.'

When *Brand* appeared, Ibsen was for once in tune with the feeling of the time. The play touched the nation's conscience, still guilty at having failed Denmark, and it ran into four editions that year. Now, too, Ibsen was granted his Poet's Stipend, thanks to Bjørnson's efforts on his behalf and the lucky accident that the churchman who had opposed it most violently was away ill on the day of the crucial meeting.

During the winter of 1865, the Norwegian colony had voted Ibsen their shabbiest countryman in Rome. Now he suddenly appeared in a smart black velvet jacket with a new shirt and kid gloves. The bitter years were over and he was now accepted as a great national poet. Success had come to Ibsen at last.

THE LEAGUE OF YOUTH

After a month or two spent in revising old plays and struggling with the enormous and turgid play that was to become *Emperor and Galilean*, Ibsen turned to *Peer Gynt*. If Brand was the Norwegian as he should have been, the gay feckless Peer, created in the sunny lighthearted atmosphere of Sorrento, was the Norwegian as he is. It was published at the end of 1867 and the first large edition was quickly sold out. But if *Peer Gynt* was Ibsen's greatest play in verse, it was also his last. He was determined to conquer the technique of writing a play in the realistic contemporary prose that had defeated him in *Love's Comedy*. The play was written in Berchtesgaden and Dresden, but the scene, like that of all Ibsen's plays except for the two unsuccessful excursions into Roman history, was set in Norway, though he spent nearly the whole of his life as a dramatist abroad.

As often happened, Ibsen's new play sprang from ideas that had been touched on in the play before, and *The League of Youth* has been described as 'Peer Gynt in politics'. But this time there are no trolls, no Bøjg, no Button-Moulder; the characters were realistic flesh and blood, and most of them, and many of the incidents, came from memories of Skien and Grimstad. He based his central figure on a politician named Herman Bagger who arrived in Skien in the 1830s, dabbled in local journalism to further his political ends, and in 1839 became Member for the Bratsberg division. There was even some rather questionable trafficking with an I.O.U. which became the basis of the note-of-hand episode in the latter part of the play.

Much as Ibsen had disliked his father, from seven hundred miles away in Dresden he could draw in Daniel Hejre a surprisingly affectionate portrait of the waspish old reprobate.

At least one other portrait comes from Ibsen's youth; Aslaksen's name and a good deal of his character comes from N. F. Axelsen, the printer of the paper *The Man* which Ibsen edited for the nine months of its unsuccessful life. (He reappears in *A Public Enemy* twelve years later, but by this time Ibsen had forgiven Axelsen enough to turn him from the whining tippler of *The League of Youth* into a pillar of the Temperance Society.)

In October 1868 Ibsen wrote to Hegel his publisher:

> My new play is forging ahead; I have been wrestling with it all the summer . . . and now . . . the first act is finished. It is to be in prose, yet it will be in every way suitable for the stage. The title is *The League of Youth, or The Almighty & Co.*

Hegel wisely persuaded him to drop the alternative title, which was an allusion to the habit of Norway's Liberal politicians of continually dragging God into their speeches. In February 1869 he wrote:

> I hope and believe that you'll like this peaceful play. . . . It will fill about two hundred pages of print.

But by June he must have had justifiable doubts about the word 'peaceful', for he wrote to Lorentz Dietrichsen:

> The play is a simple comedy and nothing more. In Norway they'll probably say that I have portrayed actual people and incidents. That isn't true, though of course I've used models, which are as necessary to a writer of comedy as they are to a sculptor.

The League of Youth was published at the end of September 1869, with a second edition nine months later. For the third edition Ibsen rewrote the play in his 'New Norwegian' spelling.

Its first stage performance, a fortnight after publication, went splendidly, with loud applause after each of the first three acts. In Act Four, when Bastian spoke his line about the Nation, there was some whistling from students in the gallery, but there were many curtain calls at the end, and the papers gave the play excellent notices. But Ibsen's prophesy was right; before the second performance, which was Ibsen's benefit, the Liberals had decided that it was a Conservative attack on their party, while the Conservatives took it as an attack on themselves. Both sides came to the theatre prepared to make trouble, and the whistling broke out before Lundestad had finished his quite harmless opening speech. The curtain was lowered and the manager came out to appeal for quiet so that the play could proceed. Even so there were continual interruptions, and at the end the uproar went on for so long that the gas had to be turned out before the auditorium could be emptied, and the battle went on in the foyer and in the street outside.

Worst of all, the Liberal leaders Sverderup, Ole Richter, and Bjørnson were deeply offended, particularly as they had all worked hard to get Ibsen his Poet's Stipend. Bold as Ibsen was on paper, one of his less endearing traits was his readiness with an excuse when trouble threatened in real life, but he was probably sincere in claiming that he had meant to caricature not Bjørnson and the other leaders, but the florid style of some of their less gifted followers. Ibsen heard of the rumpus, when he was in Egypt as the guest of the Khedive at the opening of the Suez Canal. He wrote to Hegel:

I'm delighted with the way *The League of Youth* was received; I was expecting opposition, and I should have been disappointed if the play hadn't aroused some.

(How does he square this with the description 'peaceful' in his earlier letter?) He goes on:

But rumour has it that Bjørnson is taking it as a personal attack. I didn't expect that. Is it really true? Surely he must see that it was not he whom I had in mind, but that I'd taken my models from the pernicious clique that surrounds him.

Be that as it may, Bjørnson wrote a poem of condolence to Sverderup, calling the play a *snigmord* – a 'sneak-murder' or stab in the back.

Ibsen was genuinely sorry to have offended Bjørnson, and he wrote offering to dedicate the new edition of *The Pretenders* to him. But he withdrew the offer two days later, explaining that he had heard that Bjørnson was making himself very unpopular in Norway, and he was afraid this might harm the sales of the book. It was eleven years before the breach was healed.

Although Ibsen was forty when he wrote this play, his craftsmanship is still immature. He often springs a situation on us that would have been more effective if he had prepared us for it; yet he works up gradually to incidents that might have come better as a surprise (though we must remember that he was writing for an audience rather slower in the uptake than those of today). Characters sometimes appear on the scene rather too conveniently, and the long chains of duologue upon duologue are the mark of a prentice dramatist. He has not yet learned when to bring down the curtain, and some drastic cutting after Stensgård's last entrance would have helped to make the end more effective. But if today *The League of Youth* hardly strikes us as experimental drama, when we read the other plays of that date in the European theatre we see that Ibsen was in fact making some most adventurous experiments in technique. As he wrote to Georg Brandes:

I have accomplished the feat of doing without any soliloquies, and in fact without a single aside.

It is noteworthy, too, how in his striving for realistic dialogue Ibsen found it necessary to reassure his publisher, in the letter already quoted, that although the play was to be in prose, it would still be 'in every way suitable for the theatre'.

The change from verse to prose was a great step in Ibsen's development, and one from which he was never to turn back. When in 1863 a famous Norwegian actress asked him to write a prologue in verse for her, he replied:

I cannot – my artistic principles would not allow it. . . . Verse has done incalculable harm to the art of acting, and any actor who is concerned with the drama of today should be on his guard against delivering even a single line of verse. I believe that in the theatre of the future verse will hardly be used at all; it is irreconcilable with the aims of the drama, and so it will die out. Art forms become extinct just as the unreasonable animal forms of prehistory became extinct when they had had their day. For the past seven or eight years I have hardly written a single line of verse, confining myself to the much more difficult task of truthfully portraying the fluent speech of everyday life.

And in 1874 he wrote to Edmund Gosse:

You feel that drama should be in verse, and that this play would have been improved if I had so written it. I must disagree. It is, as you must have seen, a realistic play, and I wanted to make the reader feel that he was sharing in something that really happened. . . . Since it was human beings that I wanted to draw, I could not let them speak the language of the gods.

Towards the end of his life he relented so far as to admit that he had played with the idea of reverting to verse for his last play 'if only one could know which is to be the last'. But when the time came, he found that he could no longer write verse. He was overwhelmed with guilt at what he held to be his wasted talent, and what was in fact his last play, *When We Dead Wake*, is an apology and a symbolic penance for his betrayal of his Muse.

Although *The League of Youth* is still popular in Norway, it has hardly ever been staged outside Scandinavia. In England there was a solitary performance by the Stage Society on a Sunday night in 1900 (when Granville Barker played Erik, the veteran radio actor Robert Farquharson was Bastian, and the playwright Edward Knoblock a waiter), but it is full of amusing incidents and neat character drawing, and it would be interesting to see it on the stage. Daniel Hejre is a part to delight any character actor, a little cutting of some of the repetitions would strengthen it enormously, and with its clear-cut types and straightforward situations, it should be well within the reach of an adventurous amateur society.

A DOLL'S HOUSE

In Act Four of *The League of Youth*, Selma has a little outburst that is rather out of keeping with the rest of the play. It was an afterthought of Ibsen's while he was making the fair copy. With his experience of repertory theatres, he saw that while Thora would fall to the *ingénue* and Madam Rundholmen to the character woman, there would be nothing for the leading lady of the company but the rather colourless part of Selma, so he wrote in this little 'purple patch' for her. We can only hope that Fru Gundersen, who created the part, was grateful. When Georg Brandes saw the play he wrote to Ibsen that in this one speech there was an idea for a whole play. Ten years later, Ibsen wrote it.

He had become interested in women's independence, and already in *The Pillars of Society* he had drawn Lona Hessel and Dina Dorf, both of whom had minds of their own. He had also been much impressed by a book by his friend Camilla Collett on the status of women, and at the Scandinavian Club in Rome he had sponsored a proposal that its women members should be allowed to vote at the club meetings. When this motion was soundly defeated he had stamped out of the Club in a rage. (Typically, he returned some months later at the Club's anniversary celebrations, wearing all his many decorations.)

We first hear of *A Doll's House* in May 1878, six months after *The Pillars of Society* appeared, when, in a letter to Hegel, Ibsen speaks of working on 'a play of modern life'. After that, we hear no more about it till September when he writes that he is going to Rome, where he hopes to finish the play. Meanwhile, the Ibsens had a visit in Munich from Laura Kieler. Ibsen had known her ten years before as Laura Petersen, when she had the temerity to write a sequel to *Brand* which she called *Brand's Daughters*. Now she was married to a Danish schoolmaster named Kieler, and the marriage was not going well. Fru Kieler was far from being the doll that Ibsen makes of Nora, in fact she was beginning to make a name for herself as a writer. Indeed it might be more accurate to claim that Torvald was a portrait of Kieler rather than that Nora was founded on Laura. At any rate, their visit had a great influence on Ibsen when he was planning the play.

His first notes are dated 'Rome, 19 x. 78': in the following May he reported to Hegel that the play was nearly finished, and that he hoped to send him the MS. in July. But like most authors, his mind ran ahead of his pen. In June he wrote:

It's getting hot in Rome, and next week we're going to Amalfi, where it'll be cooler as it's on the sea, and where we'll have a chance to bathe. There I mean to finish the new play that I'm working on.

And it was at the Albergo della Luna at Amalfi that the greater part of *A Doll's House* was written.

Ibsen, as his stage directions (which became more and more detailed as he grew older) show, always visualized his characters and their movements minutely, though he once said that at first he saw them in a mist from which they gradually emerged with a clear outline. One day he said to his wife:

'I saw Nora today. She came and put her hand on my shoulder as I was writing.'

'How was she dressed?' asked Fru Ibsen.

'In a plain blue woollen frock,' Ibsen replied.

In the middle of June he wrote that he wanted to perfect the dialogue, telling Hegel: 'It's highly unlikely that you will hear anything from me till August, but that will still leave you plenty of time' (presumably to get the play on the bookstalls by Christmas). In all, he went over the dialogue three times before he was satisfied with it, and it was not until early September that he began sending off the MS. piecemeal, act by act. As he told Hegel in a covering letter:

I may say quite definitely that I can't remember any of my other books giving me such great pleasure to evolve as this did while I was working on it.

A Doll's House appeared in an edition of 8,000 at the beginning of December 1879. It was produced at the Theatre Royal Copenhagen three weeks after its publication, and it is hard for us today to appreciate the sensation that it caused. To nineteenth-century Europe, the idea of a woman not only forsaking her marriage vows, but also displaying a mind of her own and renouncing her duty of unquestioning obedience to her husband, was almost indecent; that she should also make him look small was scandalous. But as Ibsen had said:

I revel in adverse criticism. . . . My enemies have been a great help to me – their attacks have been so vicious that people come flocking to see what all the shouting was about.

The book was reprinted in January 1880 and again in March.

In Germany, the theme was so unpalatable that when the play was performed in March 1880 Ibsen was forced to write a different ending. He described it as 'an act of barbarous violence against the play', but he preferred to write it himself rather than let anyone else lay hands on his work. In it, Helmer forces Nora to look at her sleeping children; she finds herself unable to leave them, drops her travelling bag, and sinks to the ground as the curtain falls with masculine supremacy restored and Woman relegated to her proper sphere of '*Kirche, Küche und Kinder*'.

It was ten years before *A Doll's House* was played outside Scandinavia and Germany, though in 1884 Henry Arthur Jones's play *The Breaking of a Butterfly* 'founded on Ibsen's *Nora*' was put on at the Prince of Wales Theatre in London, with Tree playing the equivalent of Krogstad. It was five years more before Janet Achurch played Nora at the Novelty Theatre, and not till 1894 did it reach Paris with Réjane. Yet with all this delay, it was *A Doll's House* more than any other of his plays that first made Ibsen widely known outside Scandinavia.

THE LADY FROM THE SEA

When Ibsen had finished *Rosmersholm*, he told Brandes: 'Now I shall write no more controversial plays.' At the time, Brandes remarked

'Good heavens, what's to become of the man?' though, recalling the incident after Ibsen's death, he had to admit that in his six last plays Ibsen had kept his word. *The Lady from the Sea*, ending as it does in unaccustomed peace and sunshine, was the first of these plays.

Actually, in 1880, as soon as he had finished *A Doll's House*, Ibsen started to make notes for a new play very much on the lines of *The Lady from the Sea*, but he soon set it aside, and there were *Ghosts*, *A Public Enemy*, *The Wild Duck*, and *Rosmersholm* to be written before the idea appealed to him again. In 1885, after *Rosmersholm*, now that he was internationally famous, he dared to visit Scandinavia again. He was fêted in Kristiania, students sang under his hotel windows, and the Kristiania Theatre put on *Love's Comedy*, the play that they had rejected over twenty years before. But there was one thing above all that Norway could give him; in all the years that he had spent in Germany he had never seen the sea. As he had written to Hegel from Munich in 1880, 'Of all that I miss down here, I miss the sea most of all; that is the loss that I find it hardest to reconcile myself to', and now he went to stay by the sea at Molde, a rose-growing town that he described as 'a place of great natural beauty, with quiet peaceful citizens'. Fru Ibsen was less pleased, finding that there were no pleasant walks thereabouts; and so it was that when the Ibsens went north again two years later, they went to Sæby 'by the soft quiet Danish sea'. From here Ibsen wrote to William Archer that he was 'preparing some tomfoolery for next year'. Both Sæby and Molde have claimed to be the setting for this 'tomfoolery' which became *The Lady from the Sea*, though neither really fits, and it seems most likely that, just as Ellida was founded on several women, so both towns, as well as Grimstad, served as joint models for the setting.

While in Molde, Ibsen had been impressed with the story of a local pastor's wife who had been so fascinated by 'the troll-craft in a Finnish stranger's eyes' that she had left her home and children for him. He also noted the story of a local sailor who was believed drowned but who came home years later to find his wife married to another man. But several incidents from Ibsen's own experience seem to have contributed to the story. The episode of the two rings is said to be taken from an early love affair in Grimstad; and Ibsen's mother-in-law, Magdelene Thoresen, could hardly bear to be away from the sea, and, even as an old lady, used, like Ellida, to bathe every day.

She too, as a girl in Jutland, had fallen disastrously in love and had run away from it to Norway where she later married Pastor Thoresen. In the early drafts of the play Ibsen called his heroine 'Thora', which suggests a connexion with 'Thoresen'. Ellida also contains something of Camilla Collett, sister of the poet Wergeland, and the strange influence that her brother's rival poet Welhaven had over her. There is a letter from Ibsen to her thanking her most sincerely for her understanding of the play: 'I was perfectly certain that I could rely on you more than on anyone else for some such understanding.'

Finally, in Sæby, a young Danish woman, Engelke Wulff, has described how as a girl of nineteen she had met 'a little stocky man with grey muttonchop whiskers who stood looking out to sea and would then lean on his stick while he wrote things in a book'. When she got to know him, he told her that he was putting her in his next play, and he called her 'my Hilde'. She might not have been so flattered if she had known more about Hilde's character.

Ibsen went back to Munich in October 1887 and brooded over his play for the next eight months. In July 1888 he started his first rough draft. He worked quickly and the play was published in November, in Ibsen's sixtieth year. It was played at the Kristiania Theatre in February 1889, and productions in Denmark, Sweden, and Germany soon followed; Ibsen himself saw the opening night at the Schauspielhaus in Berlin in March 1889 and was particularly impressed with the actor who played the Stranger. The first production in London was at Terry's Theatre in May 1891, with Janet Achurch as Ellida. The part was a favourite with Eleneora Duse.

THE TRANSLATION

Although Ibsen's plays are universal in their content, in detail they are essentially Norwegian, so that a translation that is really a transplantation is bound to bristle with improbabilities and inconsistencies. If the action could not have taken place outside Norway – or at any rate outside Scandinavia – neither would it have been possible except in the late nineteenth century, and a translator who used up-to-date colloquial English would confront his readers with innumerable small anachronisms in a world without cigarettes, cars, or telephones, and among nineteenth-century manners and morals. On the other hand, one has only to try to read Henry Arthur Jones today (or even the otherwise excellent translations of Ibsen by Archer) to find that the authentic stage language of the period is almost unreadably stilted. I have therefore tried to use a simple undated English that is not unduly modern and yet that does not seem out of keeping with the period costumes that the speakers would wear in the theatre.

I have deliberately retained words that help to underline the Norwegian setting, speaking, for example, of the Storthing rather than of Parliament, and where names are common to both languages, I have tried to use a spelling that would suggest the Norwegian rather than the familiar English pronunciation. I should have liked to use 'Herr' rather than 'Mr' (not that 'Herr' is specifically Norwegian, but because 'Mr' is aggressively English), but this would have meant using the too unfamiliar 'Fru' and 'Frøken' for the wives and daughters. It is hard to be strictly logical, but where a custom might puzzle a reader or an audience without striking them as particularly Norwegian – such as the usage by which a woman addresses a man, and even her husband, by his bare surname – I have tried to use something that would strike us as less outlandish.

On one minor point I have taken liberties with the original. From our Viking invaders we have inherited the custom of using certain words in pairs – 'free and easy', 'well and good', and that dreadful cliché 'this day and age', and so on – but to nothing like the same extent as the Scandinavians do. An accurate translation of this idiom is apt to seem woolly and repetitive, so that where I could find a single English word to convey the whole sense, I have tended to use it.

P.W.

THE LEAGUE OF YOUTH

A Comedy in Five Acts

CHARACTERS

CHAMBERLAIN BRATTSBERG, an ironmaster[1]
ERIK BRATTSBERG, his son, a merchant and student of law
THORA, the Chamberlain's daughter
SELMA, Erik's wife
DR FJELDBO, Medical Officer at the ironworks
STENSGÅRD, a lawyer
MONSEN, a landowner at Storli
BASTIAN MONSEN, his son
RAGNA, his daughter
HELLE, a student, resident tutor at Storli
RINGDAL, Works Manager
ANDERS LUNDESTAD, a farmer
DANIEL HEJRE
MADAM RUNDHOLMEN, widow of a local tradesman
ASLAKSEN, a printer
A maid at the Brattsberg's
A waiter
A maid at Madam Rundholmen's
Countryfolk, guests at the Chamberlain's, etc., etc.

*The action takes place near a market town
in southern Norway*

ACT ONE

An open space in the Chamberlain's grounds; evening. A public fête to celebrate Independence Day.[2]
There are coloured lamps in the trees, and music and dancing in the background.
In the centre, set rather far back, is a dais.
To the right is the entrance to a large refreshment tent, with a table and forms outside it.
In the foreground on the opposite side is another table, decorated with flowers and surrounded by comfortable chairs.

[*A large crowd of people.* LUNDESTAD,[3] *with a steward's rosette in his buttonhole, is on the dais.* RINGDAL, *the Works Manager, also with a rosette, is at the table to the left.*]

LUNDESTAD: – and so, fellow parishioners, here's to our freedom! It's come down to us from our fathers, and we'll preserve it for ourselves and for our children! Three cheers for Independence Day! Three cheers for May the seventeenth!

THE CROWD: Hurrah! Hurrah! Hurrah!

RINGDAL [*as* LUNDESTAD *gets down*]: And now a cheer for old Lundestad!

[*There are a few hisses, but they are drowned by many voices shouting:* 'Hurrah for old Lundestad! Long live Lundestad! Hurrah!' *The crowd disperses.* MONSEN *and his son* BASTIAN, *with* STENSGÅRD *and* ASLAKSEN, *make their way forward through the crowd.*]

MONSEN: I'm blessed if he isn't getting past it.

ASLAKSEN: It was 'our local conditions' he was talking about.[4] Ha ha!

MONSEN: He's made that same speech every year for as long

25

as I can remember. Let's sit *here*. [*He makes for the decorated table.*]

STENSGÅRD: No, no – not there, Mr Monsen. And we've completely lost your daughter.

MONSEN: Oh, Ragna'll soon find us again.

BASTIAN: She's all right, young Helle is with her.

STENSGÅRD: Helle?

MONSEN: Yes, Helle. [*Nudging him familiarly*] But you've got *me*, you know, and here we are, all together! So come along, and we'll sit here, away from the common herd. And we can have another little talk about – [*during this, he has sat down at the table on the left*].

RINGDAL [*coming up*]: Excuse me, Mr Monsen, that table's reserved.

STENSGÅRD: Reserved? Who for?

RINGDAL: For the Chamberlain's party.

STENSGÅRD: Oh, the Chamberlain's party! Well, there's none of them here yet.

RINGDAL: No, but we're expecting them any minute.

STENSGÅRD: Then they can sit somewhere else. [*He takes a chair.*]

LUNDESTAD [*taking hold of the chair*]: No, this table's taken – as he says.

MONSEN [*getting up*]: Come on, Mr Stensgård, there's other places just as good. [*He goes over to the right.*] Waiter! Hm – no waiters either! The Entertainment Committee ought to have seen to that. Hey, Aslaksen, you go in and fetch us four bottles of champagne – get the most expensive – tell 'em Monsen's paying!

[ASLAKSEN *goes into the tent, the other three sit down.*]

LUNDESTAD [*going quietly across to them and speaking to* STENSGÅRD]: No offence meant . . .

MONSEN: Offence? We aren't offended – far from it.

LUNDESTAD [*still to* STENSGÅRD]: Because it isn't my doing – it was the Committee that decided –

MONSEN: Of course. The Committee says the word and we've got to obey. . . .

LUNDESTAD [*to* STENSGÅRD, *as before*]: We *are* on the Chamberlain's land here. He's been good enough to throw open his park and gardens for this evening, so we felt –

STENSGÅRD: We're quite comfortable here, Mr Lundestad, if only we can be left in peace – by the crowd, I mean.

LUNDESTAD [*amicably*]: Ah well, just as you please. [*He goes to the back.*]

ASLAKSEN [*coming out of the tent*]: The waiter's bringing the wine. [*He sits.*]

MONSEN: A table to himself – by special orders of the Committee! And on Independence Day too! There you are, you see how things stand!

STENSGÅRD: But good lord, you're honest men – why do you put up with it?

MONSEN: It's the old-established custom, you see.

ASLAKSEN: You're new to the district, Mr Stensgård; if only you knew a bit more about 'our local conditions', then –

WAITER [*bringing the champagne*]: Was this the table that ordered . . . ?

ASLAKSEN: Yes, of course. Well, open it.

WAITER [*drawing the cork*]: And I was to put it down to you, Mr Monsen?

MONSEN: Yes, all of it; that's all right. [*The waiter goes. *MONSEN *touches glasses with* STENSGÅRD.] You're very welcome here, Mr Stensgård; I'm glad to have met you, and I must say it's an honour for the district that a man like you should settle here. We've read a lot about you in the papers – at meetings and things. You've got a fine knack of speechifying, Mr Stensgård, and you've got the common good at heart. I hope you're going to bring all your energies to bear on – well, on –

ASLAKSEN: On 'our local conditions'.

MONSEN: Ah yes, our local conditions. Let's drink to that.
  [*They drink.*]
STENSGÅRD: I shall certainly not spare my energies.
MONSEN: Bravo! Hear hear. Another glass to that promise!
STENSGÅRD: No, stop ... I've already had –
MONSEN: Nonsense! One more, to seal the bargain.
  [*They touch glasses again. During the following,* BASTIAN
  assiduously refills the glasses.]
Still, while we're on the subject, I may as well tell you, it
isn't the Chamberlain who's got everything under his
thumb. No, the one that stands in the background and
manages everything is old Lundestad, and that's a fact.
STENSGÅRD: Yes, I've heard that from several sources. I can't
  understand how a Liberal like him –
MONSEN: Lundestad? D'you call Anders Lundestad a Liberal?
  Oh yes, he called himself one in his young days, when it'd
  help him to get on. But then he came into his father's seat
  on the Storthing.[5] Good Lord, everything goes by inheritance here, these days.
STENSGÅRD: But surely there's some way of putting a stop
  to all these abuses?
ASLAKSEN: Yes, damn it – just put a stop to them, Mr
  Stensgård.
STENSGÅRD: I don't say that *I* ...
ASLAKSEN: Yes, you! You're just the man. You've got the
  gift of the gab, as the saying goes. What's more, you're a
  clever writer. My paper's at your disposal, you know.
MONSEN: Well, if there's anything to be done, it's got to
  be done quickly – the Preliminary Election's in a day or
  two.[6]
STENSGÅRD: And if you were elected, all your private inter-
  ests wouldn't stand in the way?
MONSEN: Oh, I daresay my private interests would suffer,
  but if it looked as if it'd help the common good, of course
  I'd put personal considerations aside.

STENSGÅRD: Ah, that's splendid. And I've noticed that you have a party to back you already.

MONSEN: I flatter myself that most of the energetic younger folk –

ASLAKSEN: Ahem! Here comes that popinjay!

HEJRE [coming from the tent, he peers shortsightedly, then approaches]: Ah, might I beg the loan of a spare chair? I should like to sit over there.

MONSEN: The seats are fastened down, as you see. But won't you sit at this table?

HEJRE: Here – at your table? Why, certainly. [Sitting] Well, well – champagne, surely?

MONSEN: Yes, will you have a glass with us?

HEJRE: Thank you, no – the champagne that Madam Rundholmen keeps isn't. . . . Ah well, just half a glass, to keep you company . . . that is, if I had a glass.

MONSEN: Bastian, go in and get one.

BASTIAN: Oh, Aslaksen, go in and get a glass.

[ASLAKSEN goes into the tent. Pause.]

HEJRE: I'm not disturbing you gentlemen? I shouldn't like . . . Thank you, Aslaksen. [With a bow to STENSGÅRD] Ah, a strange face – a new arrival! Mr Stensgård, if I'm not mistaken?

MONSEN: That's right. [Introducing them] Mr Stensgård, the lawyer – Mr Daniel Hejre –

BASTIAN: – the capitalist!

HEJRE: Ex-capitalist, to be accurate – that's a thing of the past. I've got through it, as you might say. Not that I'm bankrupt – no, damn it, you mustn't think that.

MONSEN: Drink up, drink up – while there's still some sparkle to it.

HEJRE: There was sharp practice, you know – trickery and so on . . . enough said! Ah well, let's hope it'll be only temporary. Once I get some outstanding law-suits and a few other little matters off my hands, then my goodness, our aristocratic friend Mr Slyboots will have to look out. Let's drink to that. What – won't you?

STENSGÅRD: First I should want to know who your aristocratic friend Mr Slyboots is.

HEJRE: Tee-hee! No need to look so embarrassed; you surely never thought I meant Mr Monsen? You could hardly call *him* aristocratic! No, my dear young friend, it's Chamberlain Brattsberg.

STENSGÅRD: What? Surely the Chamberlain's perfectly honest in business matters?

HEJRE: D'you think so, young fellow? Hm – enough said! [*Drawing nearer*] Twenty years ago I was worth a packet – came into a fortune from my father. You must have heard of my father? What, not old Mads Hejre? They called him Golden Mads. He was a shipowner – made his pile in the good old days. Had his doorposts and window frames gilded – that's why they called him Golden Mads.

ASLAKSEN: Didn't he gild his chimney pots, too?

HEJRE: No, that was just a journalist's lie – long before *your* time, though. Ah, he got some fun out of his money – and so did I. What my trip to London cost me . . .! You'll have heard of my trip to London? I took a regular retinue with me . . . have you really not heard about it – eh? And what I haven't spent on the Arts and Sciences . . .! And the number of promising young men I've helped to get on . . .

ASLAKSEN [*rising*]:[7] Well, thank you, gentlemen . . .

MONSEN: What, are you leaving us?

ASLAKSEN: Yes, I'll just stretch my legs. [*He goes.*]

HEJRE [*dropping his voice*]: There goes one of them – and he repays me just the same as the others, tee-hee! D'you know, I kept him at College for a whole year?

STENSGÅRD: Really? Was Aslaksen at College?

HEJRE: Just like young Monsen here. He never came to anything – also like . . . but enough said. What I was going to tell you was that I had to drop him – soon noticed his unfortunate taste for spirits. . . .

MONSEN: But you're getting off the point; you were going to tell Mr Stensgård about the Chamberlain.

HEJRE: Ah, that's a very involved story: when my father was at the height of his glory, things were going downhill for the old Chamberlain – this chap's father, you understand, for he was a Chamberlain, too –

BASTIAN: Of course; everything goes by inheritance here.

HEJRE: Including charm of manner. Enough said. Well, falling values, thriftlessness, extravagances that he fell into in the year 1816 or thereabouts, forced him to sell some of his land –

STENSGÅRD: And your father bought it?

HEJRE: Bought and paid for it. Well, what happened? I come into the property – I make improvements by the thousand –

BASTIAN: Naturally.

HEJRE: Your health! – improvements by the thousand, as I was saying; I thin out the woods. . . . The years pass, and along comes my Mr Trickster – the present one, I mean – and repudiates the bargain!

STENSGÅRD: But my dear Mr Hejre, surely you could have stopped that.

HEJRE: Not so simple. A few small formalities had been omitted – or so he maintained. And just then I chanced to find myself in temporary financial difficulties – which later happened to become permanent – and how far can you get nowadays without capital . . .?

MONSEN: Yes, by God, you're right. And in some matters you can't get far *with* capital, either! That's what I keep finding. Why, even my innocent children –

BASTIAN [*thumping the table*]: Ugh, Father – if only I had certain people here now!

STENSGÅRD: Your children, you were saying . . .?

MONSEN: Well, yes. Look at Bastian. Wouldn't you say he'd had a good education?

HEJRE: He's had three! First he tries for the University, then he tries to be an artist, and then he tries to be – no, that's right, this time he really *is* – a civil engineer.

BASTIAN: Yes, damn it all, I am.

MONSEN: Yes, he is, and I've got his diploma – and his bills – to prove it. But who gets all the work for the local council? Who's had all the contracts for the roads hereabouts – for the past two years at any rate? Why, foreigners – or strangers, anyway – fellows, in fact, that nobody knows anything about.

HEJRE: Yes, the whole thing's a disgrace. At the beginning of this year, they wanted a manager for the Savings Bank. They passed over Mr Monsen, and chose an individual who only knows – ahem – who only knows how to keep the purse strings tight – which our munificent host manifestly doesn't. And it's just the same when it's a question of a position of trust in the town. Never Monsen – always someone who enjoys the confidence of the bigwigs. Well, *commune suffragium*, as they say in Roman Law, is more like *naufragium* in local politics,[8] that it is. The devil take it. Your health.

MONSEN. Thanks. But, changing the subject, how are all your lawsuits going?

HEJRE: They're all still pending – that's all I can say for the moment. Yes, and what sharp practice I've come up against in *that* quarter! Next week, I'm sorry to say, I shall have to summon the whole Town Council before a Conciliation Court.[9]

BASTIAN: Is it true what they say – that you once summoned yourself before a Conciliation Court?

HEJRE: Myself? Yes, but I didn't appear.

MONSEN: Aha! You didn't, eh?

HEJRE: I had a legitimate excuse. Had to cross the river, and unfortunately that was the year that Bastian built the bridge. And you know what happened. Splash! Down it went!

BASTIAN: Well, damn it all –

HEJRE: Take it easy, young fellow. Plenty of people round here bend the bow till it breaks – and a bridge is a kind of bow, you know. Everything runs in families – enough said.

MONSEN: Ha ha! Enough said indeed. Drink up and shut up! [*To* STENSGÅRD] You see, Mr Hejre is licensed to say what he likes.

HEJRE: Yes, free speech is the only civic right that I really value.

STENSGÅRD: What a shame that the law restricts it.

HEJRE: Tee-hee! Is our legal friend's mouth watering for an action for slander? You keep your hands off me, my dear sir – I'm an old hand, I am.

STENSGÅRD: Especially at slander?

HEJRE: I beg your pardon, young man – your indignation does you credit. Please forgive an old fellow for sitting here and talking openly about your absent friends.

STENSGÅRD: Absent friends?

HEJRE: The son's quite a worthy fellow, of course . . . enough said. So's the daughter. And if I did happen to throw a little mud at the Chamberlain's reputation . . .

STENSGÅRD: The Chamberlain? Are you saying the Chamberlain's my friend?

HEJRE: Well, a fellow doesn't go visiting his enemies, does he?

BASTIAN: Visiting?

MONSEN: What's this?

HEJRE: Oh dear, oh dear! I seem to have let out something that –

MONSEN: Have you been visiting the Chamberlain?

STENSGÅRD: Nonsense – a complete distortion.

HEJRE: Really a most unfortunate slip! But how was I to know that it was a secret? [*To* MONSEN] Besides, you

33

mustn't take my words too literally – when I said 'visiting', I only meant a formal call – frock-coat and yellow gloves, you know.

STENSGÅRD: I tell you, I've never exchanged a single word with the family.

HEJRE: Honestly? Weren't they in the second time, either? I know that the first time they said they weren't at home.

STENSGÅRD [to MONSEN]: I had some documents to deliver from a third person in Kristiania, that's all.

HEJRE [rising]: Now that's a disgraceful thing, I'm damned if it isn't. Here's a young man, trustful but inexperienced in the ways of life, who goes to call on an experienced man of the world at his house; he goes to this man, who lives in the lap of luxury, to ask for ... but enough said. The man of the world slams the door in his face – he's 'not at home'! Well, people are never at home when it's a question of ... enough said. [Indignantly] But it's shocking bad manners, all the same!

STENSGÅRD: Oh, let the wretched thing drop!

HEJRE: 'Not at home'! From him, who goes about saying 'I'm always at home to respectable people'.

STENSGÅRD: Does he say that?

HEJRE: It's only a figure of speech. He's never at home to Mr Monsen either. But I can't understand why he should hate you so. Yes, I say 'hate', because do you know what I heard yesterday?

STENSGÅRD: I don't want to know what you heard yesterday.

HEJRE: Full stop, then. All the same, the words didn't surprise me – coming from Chamberlain Bratsberg. It's just that I can't imagine why he should have added 'Charlatan' ....

STENSGÅRD: Charlatan?

HEJRE: Well, since you force me, I must confess that the Chamberlain called you a fortune-hunter and a charlatan.

STENSGÅRD [springing up]: What?

HEJRE: Charlatan and fortune-hunter ... or fortune-hunter and charlatan. I couldn't swear to the order.

STENSGÅRD: And you heard this?

HEJRE: *I*? If I'd been present, Mr Stensgård, I should certainly have stood up for you as you deserve.

MONSEN: There, you see what comes of –

STENSGÅRD: How dare he have the impertinence to –

HEJRE: Now, now, now! Not so hasty! It wasn't meant literally, I'll stake my neck on that. Just a playful expression. Tomorrow you'll be able to ask for an explanation – because you'll be at the big luncheon party, won't you?

STENSGÅRD: I'm not going to any luncheon party.

HEJRE: Two calls, and yet no invitation ...!

STENSGÅRD: Charlatan and fortune-hunter! What could he have meant?

MONSEN: Look over there! Talk of the devil ...! Come on, Bastian.

[MONSEN *and* BASTIAN *go.*]

STENSGÅRD: What could it have meant, Mr Hejre?

HEJRE: I really can't imagine. Does it upset you? Give me your hand, young fellow. Forgive me, I'm afraid my frankness has wounded you. Believe me, you'll come across many worse things on your way through life. You're young, you're trustful, and you think well of people. That's splendid – it's even rather touching, but – but ... Trustfulness is silver, but experience of the world is golden – that's a proverb of my own invention, my boy. God bless you. [*He goes.*]

[CHAMBERLAIN BRATTSBERG, *his daughter, and* DR FJELDBO *come from the left.*]

LUNDESTAD [*at the dais, striking the bell*]: Silence for Mr Ringdal.

STENSGÅRD [*shouting*]: Mr Lundestad, I demand to be heard!

LUNDESTAD: Later.

STENSGÅRD: No, now – at once!

LUNDESTAD: You can't speak now, Mr Ringdal has the floor.

RINGDAL [*from the rostrum*]: Ladies and gentlemen, we have the honour at this moment to see in our midst the warmhearted and generous man whom we have looked up to as a father for so many years – the man who is always ready to help us, both in word and deed – whose door is never closed to any respectable man among us – who – who – But our guest of honour does not care for long speeches, so I merely call for three cheers for Chamberlain Brattsberg and his family. Long may they live! Hip – hip –

THE CROWD: Hurrah! Hurrah! Hurrah!

[*Great applause; they crowd round* BRATTSBERG, *who thanks them, shaking the hands of those nearest.*]

STENSGÅRD: May I speak now?

LUNDESTAD: Certainly. The platform is yours.

STENSGÅRD [*leaping on the table*]: I'll choose my own platform!

YOUNG MEN [*crowding round him*]: Hurrah!

BRATTSBERG [*to* DR FJELDBO]: Who is this obstreperous fellow?

FJELDBO: It's Stensgård, the lawyer.

BRATTSBERG: Oh, him!

STENSGÅRD: Listen to me, my happy brothers and sisters![10] Listen to me, you who have the joyful music of Independence in your hearts, though you yourselves are in bondage! I am a stranger among you –

ASLAKSEN: No!

STENSGÅRD: I thank you for that 'No'! I take it as a token of your longings and aspirations. But, indeed, a stranger I am; though I swear to you that as I stand here, my heart beats with a great and vital sympathy with your sorrows and with your joys – your victories and your defeats. Had I any power to alter things –

ASLAKSEN: You have – you have!

LUNDESTAD: No interruptions, please. You haven't the right to speak.

STENSGÅRD: And you still less! I abolish the Committee! Freedom on the Day of Freedom, boys!

YOUNG MEN: Hurrah for Freedom!

STENSGÅRD: They want to deny us our freedom of speech! You heard that. They want to stop your mouths. Down with such tyranny! I'll not stand here addressing a muzzled herd! Oh, I shall speak – but you shall speak too. And we shall speak from our hearts!

THE CROWD [*with mounting enthusiasm*]: Hurrah!

STENSGÅRD: Let us have no more of these empty celebrations in our Sunday best! From now on, a golden harvest of deeds shall spring from our Independence Day! For May is the season of growth, when the year is in the full maidenly blush of youth. On the first of June, I shall have been among you for just two months – and in that time, what greatness and what pettiness, what beauty and what ugliness have I not seen here?

BRATTSBERG: Just what is he talking about, Doctor?

FJELDBO: Aslaksen says it's about local conditions.

STENSGÅRD: I've seen shining virtue among the Masses, but I've also seen the spirit of corruption stifling that virtue and bringing it to nought! Yes, I've seen warm, trusting young hearts flocking to meet together – and I have seen the doors shut in their faces!

THORA: Oh dear!

BRATTSBERG: What does he mean by that?

STENSGÅRD: Yes, my brothers and sisters in Freedom, in the air about us there is a Power – a spectre from the bad old days – which spreads oppression and gloom where there should be airiness and light. Back to its grave with that spectre!

THE CROWD: Hurrah! Hurrah for Independence Day!

THORA: Come away, Father.

BRATTSBERG: What the devil's this spectre he's talking about, Doctor?

FJELDBO [*hastily*]: Oh, it's ... [*He whispers a few words.*]¹¹

BRATTSBERG: Aha! So *that's* it?

THORA [*quietly*]: Thank you.

STENSGÅRD: If no one else will slay the dragon, I will. But we must stand together, boys!

MANY VOICES: Yes, yes!

STENSGÅRD: We are the young! The Present is ours, but we also belong to the Present. Our right is our duty. Elbow-room for all with ability – for all who have the will and the strength. Listen to me: we will found a League. Moneybags shall no longer rule in these parts.

BRATTSBERG: Bravo! [*To the* DOCTOR] Moneybags, he said; so he really *did* mean –

STENSGÅRD: Yes, my lads, we – we are the wealth of the land if only there is metal in us. Our will is the ringing coin that shall pass from man to man – War to the death against all who would hinder our minting!

THE CROWD: Hurrah!

STENSGÅRD: A sarcastic 'Bravo' has been flung in my face this evening –

BRATTSBERG: No.

STENSGÅRD: No matter! Neither flattery nor threats count with a man who knows his own mind. And we have God on our side! Yes, for it is His voice that bids us, the Young, go confidently about our task. Let us go into the tent – this very day will we found our League!

THE CROWD: Hurrah! Carry him – shoulder-high!

[*They chair him.*]

VOICES: Go on! More! More!

STENSGÅRD: Unity, I say! Providence is on the side of our League of Youth! It is in our power to rule the world – here in this District!

[*They carry him into the tent amid wild enthusiasm.*]

MADAM RUNDHOLMEN [*wiping her eyes*]: Ah, what a speaker he is! Don't you feel you could kiss him, Mr Hejre?

HEJRE: Kiss him? Well, not really.

MADAM: Oh, *you*! I should think not.

HEJRE: Perhaps *you'd* like to kiss him, Madam Rundholmen?

MADAM: Oh, you *are* wicked! [*She goes into the tent, followed by* HEJRE.]

BRATTSBERG: 'Spectre, and dragon, and Moneybags' . . . Abominably rude – but well deserved.

LUNDESTAD [*approaching*]: I'm really very sorry, sir –

BRATTSBERG: Yes, and you're supposed to be a judge of character! Well, well, we all make mistakes. Good night, Mr Lundestad, and many thanks for a pleasant evening. [*Turning to* THORA *and the* DOCTOR] Upon my soul, I've been very rude to that nice young man.

FJELDBO: How?

THORA: When he called, you mean?

BRATTSBERG: He called twice. It's really Lundestad's fault – telling me he was a fortune-hunter or – or something, I forget what. Well, luckily I can remedy that.

THORA: How?

BRATTSBERG: Come along, Thora, we'll do it at once.

FJELDBO: Oh, is it really worth while, Chamberlain?

THORA [*quietly*]: Sh!

BRATTSBERG: When you've wronged someone, you must put it right – that's only fair. Good night, Doctor; I've spent an amusing hour – which is more than *you've* provided me with today.

FJELDBO: I, Chamberlain?

BRATTSBERG: Yes, yes, yes . . . you and the rest of them.

FJELDBO: But may I ask what I . . .?

BRATTSBERG: Now, Doctor, ask no questions. . . . I never do. And now, for goodness sake, let's say good night.

[*The* CHAMBERLAIN *and* THORA *go out to the left;*
FJELDBO *looks thoughtfully after them.*]

ASLAKSEN [*coming from the tent*]: Hey, waiter – pen and ink!
Ah, things are moving, Doctor.

FJELDBO: What's moving?

ASLAKSEN: He's founding the League. It's practically
founded.

LUNDESTAD [*quietly, as he comes up to them*]: Have many of
them signed in there?

ASLAKSEN: We've got about thirty-seven so far – not counting widows and such like. Pen and ink, I say! No waiters
anywhere! All the fault of our local conditions. [*He goes off
behind the tent.*]

LUNDESTAD: Phew, it's been warm today!

FJELDBO: I'm afraid there'll be hotter days to come.

LUNDESTAD: Do you think the Chamberlain was very angry?

FJELDBO: Oh, not a bit, you could see that. But what do you
say to the new League?

LUNDESTAD: Hm – I don't say anything. What is there to say?

FJELDBO: It's the beginning of a struggle for power here in
the District.

LUNDESTAD: Well, there's a lot to be said for a fight. He's a
very gifted man, this Stensgård.

FJELDBO: And a man who means to get on.

LUNDESTAD: Young fellows always mean to get on. I did
when I was young – there's no harm in that. But perhaps
we might just go inside. . . .

HEJRE [*coming from the tent*]: Well, Mr Lundestad, you going
in to heckle him, eh? Form an opposition? Tee-hee! You'll
have to be quick.

LUNDESTAD: Oh, I'll be in plenty of time!

HEJRE: You're too late, old chap – unless you're going to
stand godfather.

[*Cheering from the tent.*]

There, the choir is singing Amen – the christening's over.

LUNDESTAD: I suppose we're allowed to listen – I intend to hold my tongue. [*He goes in.*]

HEJRE: There goes one of the falling trees! More and more of them will come down now – the place'll begin to look like the forest after a storm. Amusing – very amusing indeed!

FJELDBO: Tell me, Mr Hejre, how can it interest you personally?

HEJRE: Interest me? I'm not a person who gets interested, Doctor. If I'm pleased about this, it's on my fellow citizens' behalf; there'll be life here – purpose – meaning. Personally – good heavens, it's all the same to me. I say, as the Grand Turk said of the Emperor of Austria and the King of France: 'It's all the same to me whether the pig eats the dog or the dog eats the pig.' [*He goes out at the back, to the right.*]

THE CROWD [*in the tent*]: Long live Stensgård! Three cheers! Hurrah! Hurrah for the League of Youth! Hey – Hey . . . Wine – punch – beer! Hurrah!

BASTIAN [*coming from the tent*]: God bless him – God bless all of them! [*With a catch in his voice*] Oh, Doctor, I feel so inspired this evening – I must *do* something!

FJELDBO: Don't mind me! What do you want to do?

BASTIAN: I think I'll go down to the dance hall and thrash a couple of my friends. [*He goes out behind the tent.*]

STENSGÅRD [*coming out of the tent, greatly excited and without his hat*]: Ah, my dear Fjeldbo . . .

FJELDBO: At your service, Mr Popular Leader. I suppose you've been chosen –

STENSGÅRD: Naturally, but –

FJELDBO: And what will you get out of it? What important job in the District? Bank Manager, perhaps, or –

STENSGÅRD: Oh, don't say that sort of thing to me. You don't mean it, you know. You're not as detached and cold-hearted as you like to make out.

FJELDBO: What's coming now?

STENSGÅRD: Fjeldbo, can't we be friends like we used to be? A coldness seems to have come between us. You've become so unkind – keeping me at arm's length with your jokes and sneers. No, I shouldn't have said that? [*Putting an arm round his shoulders*] Oh God, how happy I am!

FJELDBO: You too? So am I, so am I.

STENSGÅRD: Yes, I'd be the meanest wretch on earth – shouldn't I? – if all this good fortune didn't make me kind and noble. What have I done to deserve it? What has a scallywag like me done to be so richly blessed?

FJELDBO: Here's my hand. Upon my soul, this evening I quite like you.

STENSGÅRD: Thank you. Be a true friend, as I shall be to you. Oh, I can't tell you what a wonderful feeling it is to be able to sway all those people like that! How can anyone fail to become good, out of sheer gratitude? How can anyone fail to love all his fellow creatures? I feel as if I could take them all in my arms and beg them, with tears in my eyes, to forgive me because God has been so unfair as to give me more than He's given them.

FJELDBO [*quietly*]: Yes, one man can have so very much. . . . Tonight I couldn't even tread on a worm, or crush a green leaf in my path.[12]

STENSGÅRD: You?

FJELDBO: That's all – don't let's talk about it. I only wanted to show you that I understand how you feel.

STENSGÅRD: What a wonderful night! Music and laughter ringing out over the meadows, yet down there – how still it is! Yes, a man who doesn't re-consecrate his life at a time like this, doesn't deserve to live on God's earth!

FJELDBO: Yes, but now tell me, what are you going to make of it – tomorrow, and in all the days to come?

STENSGÅRD: To make? First, it's a matter of tearing down.

... You know, Fjeldbo, I once dreamed – or perhaps I really saw it ... no, it was a dream – but very vivid. It seemed as if Judgement Day had come to the world. I could see the whole round Earth – there was no sun, only a threatening yellow glow. Then a storm came tearing from the west and sweeping everything before it – first the dead leaves, then the men – though the men somehow kept on their feet. Their cloaks were blown tightly round their legs, so that they seemed to be carried along sitting! First they looked like townspeople running after their hats in a gale, but as they came nearer they became kings and emperors, and what they were running after and reaching for – and seemed on the point of grasping, but never grasped – were their crowns and sceptres. Oh, there were hundreds and hundreds, of every kind, and none of them knew what it all meant. Many of them cried out and asked where this terrible storm had come from. Then the answer came: 'One Voice spoke, and such were the echoes of that single Voice that the storm arose!'

FJELDBO: When did you dream this?

STENSGÅRD: Oh, sometime ... I don't remember when. Many years ago.

FJELDBO: There'd been an upheaval somewhere in Europe, and you'd been reading the papers after a heavy dinner!

STENSGÅRD: This evening I felt the same thrill – the same shiver down my back. I *shall* fulfil my destiny – I shall be the Voice. ...

FJELDBO: Listen, my dear Stensgård, just stop and think things over. You say you'll be the Voice. All right. But *where* will you be the Voice? Here in this parish? Or, at the most, here in this county? And who will be the echo that will raise the storm? People like Monsen or Aslaksen, or that fat-headed genius Bastian? And instead of the fleeing emperors and kings, shall we see Farmer Lundestad running after his seat in the Storthing? What will it all amount to?

It'll become what it first looked like in the dream – small townspeople in a wind.

STENSGÅRD: To begin with, yes. But who knows how far a storm may blow?

FJELDBO: Oh, to blazes with you and your storm! When it comes to it, what you'll do – blind and gullible and bewildered as you are – will be to turn your weapons against the ablest and most honourable men among us –

STENSGÅRD: That's not true.

FJELDBO: It *is* true. Old Monsen of Storli got hold of you as soon as you came here, and if you don't shake him off it'll be the ruin of you. Chamberlain Brattsberg is a man of honour, you can depend on that. Do you know why Monsen hates him? Why, because –

STENSGÅRD: I won't hear another word – not one word against my friends!

FJELDBO: Think carefully, Stensgård – is Mr Monsen really your friend?

STENSGÅRD: Mr Monsen has very kindly opened his doors to me –

FJELDBO: To the best people here, he opens them in vain.

STENSGÅRD: Whom do you call the best people? *I* know – a few stuck-up officials. But as far as I'm concerned, I've been received at Storli with such hospitality and appreciation that –

FJELDBO: Appreciation, yes – unfortunately that's just the point.

STENSGÅRD: Not at all! I can look at things impartially. Mr Monsen's an able man; he's well read, he has an instinct for public affairs –

FJELDBO: Able? Ye-es, in his way. Well read? He takes the papers, and he's noticed the speeches you've made and the articles you've written. ... As for the instinct for public affairs, of course he's proved that by agreeing with your speeches and newspaper articles.

STENSGÅRD: Look, Fjeldbo, you're showing the worst side of yourself again. Can't you ever shake off that cynical habit of mind? Why must you always credit people with mean or ridiculous motives? Ah, you don't really mean it . . . now you look your old trusty self again, so I'll tell you the best thing of all – the real heart of the matter. Do you know Ragna?

FJELDBO: Ragna Monsen? Yes – at second-hand, anyway.

STENSGÅRD: Yes, she sometimes goes to the Chamberlain's.

FJELDBO: On the quiet. She and Miss Brattsberg are old school-friends.

STENSGÅRD: And what do you think of her?

FJELDBO: Well, from all I've heard, she must be a very charming girl.

STENSGÅRD: Ah, you should see her at home; she thinks of nothing but her two little sisters.[13] And how she must have looked after her mother. You know that her mother was out of her mind for the last few years of her life?

FJELDBO: Yes indeed, I was their doctor at one time. But tell me, my dear fellow, do you really mean . . .?

STENSGÅRD: Yes, Fjeldbo, I don't mind telling *you* – I really love her. Oh. I quite realize it must be a surprise to you; you must think it odd that so soon after . . . You know, of course, that I was engaged in Kristiania?

FJELDBO: Yes, so I heard.

STENSGÅRD: It was all a great disappointment. I *had* to break it off – it was the best thing for both of us. Oh, you can't imagine what I went through at the time – it was torture! However, it's all over now, thank goodness. But that was the reason I left the capital.

FJELDBO: And you're quite sure of yourself about Ragna Monsen?

STENSGÅRD: Oh, I certainly am; there couldn't possibly be any mistake.

FJELDBO: Well, then, for goodness sake go ahead with it. It's a great piece of luck. There's a lot I could tell you –

STENSGÅRD: Could you really? Has she said anything? To Miss Brattsberg, perhaps?

FJELDBO: Ah, that isn't what I mean. . . . But how can you possibly go and get mixed up in political orgies in the middle of all this? That a mind like yours should interest itself in petty local affairs –

STENSGÅRD: Why not? Man isn't simply a machine – I'm not, at any rate. Besides, it's through these party squabbles that I shall find my way to her.

FJELDBO: A damned trivial way.

STENSGÅRD: I'm ambitious, Fjeldbo – you know that. I mean to get on in the world. When I think that I'm thirty and still at the bottom of the ladder, I feel my conscience gnawing me.

FJELDBO: Yes, but not with its wisdom teeth!

STENSGÅRD: It's no good talking to you – you've never been hounded by a driving need like this. You've spent your whole life drifting and idling – at school, at College, then abroad, and now here.

FJELDBO: Well, perhaps – but at any rate I've enjoyed it. And there's no reaction afterwards, such as you feel when you leave the table after –

STENSGÅRD: That's got nothing to do with it, and I'm blessed if I'll stand for it. You're doing me a bad turn talking like this – you're robbing me of my enthusiasm.

FJELDBO: Well, you know, if you can lose your enthusiasm as easily as *that* . . .

STENSGÅRD: Stop it, I tell you! What right have you to interfere with my happiness? Do you think I'm not in earnest?

FJELDBO: Good heavens, I'm quite sure you are!

STENSGÅRD: Then why do you go on making me feel cheap and worthless – dissatisfied with myself?

[*Shouts and cheers from the tent.*]

Listen, they're drinking my health. If a thing can take such a hold on them, God knows, there *must* be some truth in it.

[MISS BRATTSBERG, MISS MONSEN, *and young* HELLE *come in from the left and cross the centre.*]

HELLE [*to* MISS BRATTSBERG]: Look, there's Mr Stensgård.

THORA: Well, I won't come any farther. Good night, Ragna. Good night.

HELLE AND RAGNA: Good night. [*They go out to the right.*]

THORA [*approaching*]: I'm the Chamberlain's daughter, I have a letter for you from my father.

STENSGÅRD: For me?

THORA: Yes, here it is. [*She starts to go.*]

FJELDBO: May I see you home?

THORA: No, don't bother, thank you. Good night. [*She goes out to the left.*]

STENSGÅRD [*reading by the light of a Chinese lantern*]: What on earth . . .?

FJELDBO: Well, my dear chap, what does the Chamberlain say?

STENSGÅRD [*bursting out laughing*]: I certainly never expected this!

FJELDBO: Well, tell me!

STENSGÅRD: Chamberlain Brattsberg's a terrible fellow!

FJELDBO: Don't you dare –

STENSGÅRD: An absolute rascal – and you can say I said so! Well, never mind the rest of it. . . . [*Putting the letter away*] This is between ourselves.

[*The crowd comes out of the tent.*]

MONSEN: Where's our President? Where's Mr Stensgård?

THE CROWD: There he is – hurrah!

LUNDESTAD: You forgot your hat, Mr Stensgård [*giving it to him*].

ASLAKSEN: Some punch, Mr Stensgård – we've got a whole bowl!

STENSGÅRD: No more, thank you.

MONSEN: And remember, Members, we meet tomorrow at my house at Storli, to –

STENSGÅRD: Tomorrow? No, it wasn't tomorrow, surely?

MONSEN: Yes, to draw up the Manifesto that –

STENSGÅRD: No, I really can't manage tomorrow. I'll see about it the day after tomorrow – or the day after that. Well, good night, gentlemen. I'm most grateful for what you've done today – and here's to the Future!

THE CROWD: Hurrah! Let's escort him home!

STENSGÅRD: Thank you – thank you ... but you really mustn't –

ASLAKSEN: We'll all escort him.

STENSGÅRD: Good night, Fjeldbo. You won't be coming with us?

FJELDBO: No ... but I must tell you that what you said about the Chamberlain –

STENSGÅRD: Sh! Sh! That was an exaggeration, I withdraw it. Well, friends, if you're coming, let's go. I'll lead the way.

MONSEN: Give me your arm, Stensgård.

BASTIAN: A song! Strike up! Something really patriotic!

[*They play and sing a national song as they march out at the back to the right.*]

FJELDBO [*to* LUNDESTAD, *who has remained behind*]: A splendid following.

LUNDESTAD: Ah, but he's a splendid leader.

FJELDBO: Then where are you going, Mr Lundestad?

LUNDESTAD: Me? I'm going home to bed.

[*He bows and goes.* FJELDBO *remains alone at the back.*]

The curtain falls

ACT TWO

The garden-room at the Chamberlain's. It is elegantly furnished, with a piano, flowers, and hothouse plants.
There is an entrance at the back.
To the left, a door leads to the dining-room; to the right, several french windows lead out to the garden.

[ASLAKSEN *is standing at the entrance. A maid is crossing the room, carrying two dishes of fruit into the dining-room.*]

MAID: Yes, but I tell you they're still at lunch. You'll have to come back later.

ASLAKSEN: I'd sooner wait, if I may.

MAID: All right, if you'd rather. You can sit *there* for the time being.

[*She goes into the dining-room.* ASLAKSEN *sits by the door. Pause.* DR FJELDBO *comes in from the back.*]

FJELDBO: Well, hullo, Aslaksen, *you* here?

MAID [*coming back*]: Oh, Doctor – you *are* late!

FJELDBO: I was called out to a case.

MAID: The Master and Miss Brattsberg have both been asking about you.

FJELDBO: Oh?

MAID: Yes, will you go in, sir? Or shall I say –?

FJELDBO: No, never mind; I can always get something to eat later on. I'll wait here for the time being.

MAID: Yes, they won't be long. [*She goes out at the back.*]

ASLAKSEN [*after a moment*]: And you can miss a lunch party like that! With good wine and plum pudding and all sorts of good things.

FJELDBO: Yes, damn it, you're more likely to suffer from too many good things here, than too few.

ASLAKSEN: I can't agree with you there.

FJELDBO: Hm! Tell me, are you waiting for someone?

ASLAKSEN: Yes, I'm waiting for someone.

FJELDBO: And is everything going reasonably well at home? Is your wife . . .?

ASLAKSEN: She's in bed, as usual. Wasting away with her cough.

FJELDBO: And that second child of yours?

ASLAKSEN: Oh, he's quite crippled now – you know that. What the devil's the use of talking about it? – that's the way things are with us.

FJELDBO: Let me have a look at you, Aslaksen.

ASLAKSEN: Well, what do you want to see?

FJELDBO: You've been drinking today.

ASLAKSEN: And yesterday, too.

FJELDBO: Ah, yesterday was excusable. But today and –

ASLAKSEN: What about them in there? They'll be drinking, too.

FJELDBO: Yes, my dear Aslaksen, in a way, you're right. But in this world, circumstances differ so.

ASLAKSEN: I didn't choose my circumstances.

FJELDBO: No, God chose them for you.

ASLAKSEN: *That* he didn't! Men chose them. Daniel Hejre chose them when he took me out of my printing-house and educated me. And Chamberlain Brattsberg chose them when he ruined Daniel Hejre and I had to go back to the printing-house again.

FJELDBO: Now, you know better than to talk like that. Chamberlain Brattsberg never ruined Daniel Hejre – Daniel Hejre ruined himself.

ASLAKSEN: All right. But how dare Daniel Hejre ruin himself when he had a responsibility like that to me? Obviously God's to blame, too – why did He give me my talent and ability? I might have used them as an honest craftsman, but along comes that old windbag –

FJELDBO: That's no way to talk! Daniel Hejre had the best of intentions in all he did for you.

ASLAKSEN: And a lot of good his intentions have been to me! In there, where they're sitting clinking glasses and drinking healths, I used to sit once – dressed in good clothes like the rest of them. That was just right for me, that was; I'd read a lot, and I'd always longed to have a share in all the good things of life. Then – crash! How long did Hassan stay in luxury?[14] One two three – out goes he! And all my fine hopes were smashed to 'pie' – as we printers say.

FJELDBO: Ah well, you weren't really so badly off – you did have your trade to fall back on.

ASLAKSEN: That's a nice way to talk! After a thing like that, your job isn't your job any longer! They took the solid ground from under my feet and put me on a sheet of ice – and then I have to put up with abuse because I stumble.

FJELDBO: Well, I certainly don't want to judge you too harshly . . .

ASLAKSEN: And nor you should! It's a funny mess! Daniel Hejre and Providence, and the Chamberlain and Force of Circumstance . . . and then there's me! I've sometimes thought of disentangling it and writing a book about it, but it's all such a confounded muddle that – [Looking towards the door on the left] Hullo, they're getting up from lunch.

[The guests, both ladies and gentlemen, gaily chattering, cross from the dining-room to the garden. Among them is STENS-GÅRD, with THORA on his left arm and SELMA on his right. DR FJELDBO and ASLAKSEN stay by the door at the back.]

STENSGÅRD: Well ladies, I'm a stranger here, so you must tell me where to take you.

SELMA: Oh, out of doors – you must see the garden.

STENSGÅRD: Oh yes, that would be delightful.

[They go out to the right through the nearest french window.]

FJELDBO: Good Lord, surely that was Stensgård!

ASLAKSEN: Yes, he's the one I'm waiting to see. I'd been looking for him everywhere, and then luckily I met Daniel
Hejre and –
[HEJRE and ERIK BRATTSBERG *come from the dining-
room.*]

HEJRE: Tee-hee! Upon my word that was an excellent sherry.
Haven't had anything like it since I was in London.

ERIK: Good, isn't it? Puts some life into a chap.

HEJRE: Ah well, it's nice to see one's money so well spent.

ERIK: What? [*Laughing*] Ah yes, I see what you mean!
[*They go out to the garden.*]

FJELDBO: You say you want to speak to Stensgård?

ASLAKSEN: Yes, I do.

FJELDBO: On business?

ASLAKSEN: Of course – the account of the fête for the paper.

FJELDBO: Well, I tell you what – you'd better wait out there
for the moment.

ASLAKSEN: Out in the passage?

FJELDBO: In the hall, yes. This isn't the time or place . . .
But look, I'll see if I can get Stensgård alone for a moment.

ASLAKSEN: Very well, I'll wait for my chance. [*He goes out
at the back.*]
[*The* CHAMBERLAIN, LUNDESTAD, RINGDAL, *and one
or two other men come in from the dining-room.*]

BRATTSBERG [*talking to* LUNDESTAD]: Excessive, you think?
Well, I certainly can't defend the manner of the speech, but
I can assure you there were some gems in it.

LUNDESTAD: Oh well, if you're satisfied, Chamberlain, I
suppose I must be.

BRATTSBERG: I think you should. Ah, here's the Doctor –
and on an empty stomach, I expect.

FJELDBO: It doesn't matter, Chamberlain. It's not far to the
dining-room, and I feel quite at home in this house.

BRATTSBERG: Well, well, do you? You shouldn't be in too
much of a hurry.

FJELDBO: What? You don't mind, do you? You said yourself that I might –

BRATTSBERG: What I said, I said. Ah well, make yourself at home, and see if you can find your way to the dining-room. [*He pats him on the shoulder and turns to* LUNDESTAD.] Now *there's* someone you might call a fortune-hunter and a . . . I can't remember what the other thing was.¹⁵

FJELDBO: But Chamberlain . . .

LUNDESTAD: No, I assure you . . .

BRATTSBERG: No arguments after dinner – it's bad for the digestion. There'll be coffee outside at any minute. [*He goes out to the garden with the other guests.*]

LUNDESTAD [*to* FJELDBO]: I've never known the Chamberlain behave so oddly before, have you?

FJELDBO: I noticed it last night.

LUNDESTAD: Imagine; he will insist that I called Mr Stensgård a fortune-hunter or something.

FJELDBO: Oh well, Mr Lundestad, what if you did? Excuse me, I must go and pay my respects to the ladies. [*He goes out to the right.*]

LUNDESTAD [*to* RINGDAL, *who is arranging a card-table*]: How does Stensgård come to be here?

RINGDAL: I wish you could tell me; he wasn't on the original list of guests.

LUNDESTAD: Added later, then? After the dressing-down the Chamberlain got last night?

RINGDAL: Yes, can you understand it?

LUNDESTAD: Understand it? Ah well . . .

RINGDAL [*dropping his voice*]: You think the Chamberlain's afraid of him.

LUNDESTAD: I think he's cautious, that's what I think.
    [*Still talking, they go out through the back and then into the garden. At the same time,* SELMA *and* STENSGÅRD *come in through the nearest french window.*]

SELMA: Yes, look – over those tree-tops we can see the church tower and all the higher parts of the town.

STENSGÅRD: So you can – I should never have believed it.

SELMA: It's a lovely view, don't you think?

STENSGÅRD: Everything's lovely here – the garden, the view, the sunlight, and the people. . . . My goodness, how lovely it all is! And do you spend all the summer here?

SELMA: No, my husband and I don't – we come and go. We have a fine big house in town – much finer than this. You must come and see it.

STENSGÅRD: I suppose your family lives in the town?

SELMA: Family? Whom do you mean by my family?

STENSGÅRD: Well, I didn't know if –

SELMA: We fairy princesses have no family.

STENSGÅRD: Fairy princesses?

SELMA: At the most, we just have a wicked stepmother. . . .

STENSGÅRD: A witch, yes. So you're a princess?

SELMA: Princess of the Castles under the Sea, where you hear music on Midsummer Eve. Dr Fjeldbo thinks it must be a most delightful life, but . . . well, let me tell you –

ERIK [*coming in from the garden*]: Ah, young woman, so I've found you at last!

SELMA: Yes, this young woman's been telling Mr Stensgård the story of her life.

ERIK: Oho! And what part does the husband play in the story?

SELMA: Why, fairy prince, of course. [*To* STENSGÅRD] You know there's always a prince who comes and breaks the spell so that it all ends happily. Then there's mirth and rejoicing in the world, and that's the end of the story.

STENSGÅRD: Ah, but it was too short.

SELMA: Perhaps . . . in a way. . . .

ERIK [*putting an arm round her*]: But there was a sequel to the fairy tale – the princess became a queen.

SELMA: On the same conditions as real princesses?

ERIK: What conditions?

SELMA: They have to go away to a foreign land.

ERIK: A cigar, Mr Stensgård?

STENSGÅRD: Not just now, thank you.

[DR FJELDBO *and* THORA *come in from the garden.*]

SELMA [*going to them*]: Ah, there you are, Thora dear. You're not ill, are you?

THORA: I? No.

SELMA: Oh, but you must be – you're always consulting the Doctor these days!

THORA: No, I assure you.

SELMA: Nonsense – let me feel your forehead. It's on fire! Dear Doctor, do you think this fever will pass off?

FJELDBO: In its own time. . . .

THORA: It's better than freezing.

SELMA: No, a steady normal temperature . . . that's what my husband thinks, too.

BRATTSBERG [*coming from the garden*]: All the family engaged in private session? That's not very polite to the guests.

THORA: I'm just going, Father dear.

BRATTSBERG: Ah, I see! All the ladies paying court to Mr Stensgård? I shall have to look into this!

THORA [*quietly to* FJELDBO]: Wait. [*She goes out to the garden.*]

ERIK [*offering* SELMA *his arm*]: If My Lady has no objection . . .

SELMA: Come on. [*They go out to the right.*]

BRATTSBERG [*looking after them*]: It's quite impossible to get those two apart.

STENSGÅRD: It would be a shame to try.

BRATTSBERG: Well, fortune favours fools. . . . [*Calling*] Thora! Thora, keep an eye on Selma. Take her a shawl, and don't let her run about so – she'll catch cold. We men are short-sighted, Doctor; do you know any cure for that complaint?

FJELDBO: Yes – bitter experience. Try some of that, and you see much better next time.

BRATTSBERG: Oh dear! Thank you for the advice. Well, since you feel yourself so much at home here, oughtn't you to be looking after the guests, too?

FJELDBO: Ah, yes ... Stensgård, shall we –?

BRATTSBERG: Oh no, my dear fellow; there's my old friend Hejre out there. . . .

FJELDBO: Yes, he feels himself at home here, too.

BRATTSBERG: Ha ha ha! So he does, yes.

FJELDBO: Well, he and I will join forces and do our best. [*He goes out to the garden.*]

STENSGÅRD: Chamberlain, you mentioned Daniel Hejre. . . . I must say I was surprised to see him here.

BRATTSBERG: Were you? Mr Hejre and I were at school and college together. And since then, we've been through a great many of life's vicissitudes together.

STENSGÅRD: Yes, Mr Hejre gave us the benefit of some of those encounters last night.

BRATTSBERG: Hm!

STENSGÅRD: If it hadn't been for him, I certainly shouldn't have boiled over as I did in my speech last night. But he has a way of talking about people and things that ... Well, to put it plainly, he has a wicked tongue in his head.

BRATTSBERG: My dear young friend, Mr Hejre is my guest – you mustn't forget that. My house is Liberty Hall – but with one reservation: there must be no unchivalrous talk about the people I invite here.

STENSGÅRD: I do beg your pardon.

BRATTSBERG: Well, well, you belong to the younger generation, who don't value these things so much. As to Mr Hejre – I doubt if you know him very well. At any rate, he's a man to whom I owe a great deal.

STENSGÅRD: Yes, so he said. But I never thought to hear you -

BRATTSBERG: I owe him the greater part of our family happiness, Mr Stensgård – I owe him my daughter-in-law. Yes, I really do. Daniel Hejre looked after her when she was a child. She was a little prodigy – she was giving concerts when she was only ten years old. You must have heard her name – Selma Sjöblom. . . .

STENSGÅRD: Sjöblom? Ah, I see, her father was Swedish?

BRATTSBERG: A music teacher, yes. He came here years ago. Musicians, you know, don't make much of a living as a rule, and their way of life isn't always suitable for – Well, Mr Hejre has always been on the lookout for talent – he took an interest in the child, and had her sent to Berlin. Then, after her father died, and when Hejre's fortunes were rather changed, she came back to Kristiania, where naturally she was soon taken up by the best people. So, you see, it became possible for her and my son to meet.

STENSGÅRD. Yes, in that way, old Daniel Hejre was certainly the instrument . . .

BRATTSBERG: That's how one thing leads to another in this life. We're all instruments, including you – who, I should say, are an instrument of destruction.

STENSGÅRD: Oh, Chamberlain, please . . . I'm so ashamed of myself . . .

BRATTSBERG: Ashamed?

STENSGÅRD: Yes, it was extremely ill-mannered . . .

BRATTSBERG: Perhaps here and there the form might have been open to objection, but the intention was good. And I do beg you that in future when you have anything on your mind, you'll come and talk it over frankly with me – freely and without reserve. You see, we all want to act for the best, and it's my duty to –

STENSGÅRD: You'd really let me speak frankly to you?

BRATTSBERG: Heaven knows I would. Do you think I didn't see long ago that, in some ways, things have been taking a not very desirable turn here? But what could I do?

In the late King's time, I lived mostly in Stockholm.[16] I'm an old man now, and it isn't in my nature to institute reforms, or to involve myself personally in public upheavals. You, on the other hand, Mr Stensgård, have all the qualifications for them . . . so we should join forces.

STENSGÅRD: Thank you, Chamberlain, thank you.

[RINGDAL and DANIEL HEJRE *come in from the garden.*]

RINGDAL: But I tell you it must be a misunderstanding.

HEJRE: Oh, indeed? That's rich! Would I misunderstand my own ears?

BRATTSBERG: Is this something new, Hejre?

HEJRE: Only that Anders Lundestad's on the point of going over to Monsen's side.

BRATTSBERG: Ah, you're joking.

HEJRE: Excuse me, my dear sir, I have it from his own lips. Lundestad means to retire into private life on the grounds of ill health. One can guess the rest.

STENSGÅRD: You have this from his own lips?

HEJRE: Indeed, yes. He proclaimed the momentous news to an enthralled circle out there – tee-hee!

BRATTSBERG: But my dear Ringdal, what can this mean?

HEJRE: Well, it isn't hard to imagine.

BRATTSBERG: But not with any certainty. This is a serious thing for the district. Come with me, Ringdal, we must certainly have a word with the man.

[*He and* RINGDAL *go out to the garden.*]

FJELDBO [*coming through the french window*]: Has the Chamberlain gone out?

HEJRE: Sh! The wise men are in conclave! Great news, Doctor: Lundestad's resigning his seat in the Storthing.

FJELDBO: Impossible!

STENSGÅRD: Can you understand it?

HEJRE: Well, now there'll be a fine to-do! It's the League of Youth starting to work, Mr Stensgård. D'you know what you ought to call yourselves? Well, I'll tell you later!

STENSGÅRD: Do you really think that it's our League . . .?

HEJRE: Without a shadow of doubt! Well, now we're to have the pleasure of sending Squire Monsen off to the Storthing! I wish he were there already – I'd gladly give him a lift! Enough said – tee-hee! [*He goes out to the garden.*]

STENSGÅRD: Tell me, Fjeldbo, what do you make of all this?

FJELDBO: There's something else that's even harder to understand – what are you doing here?

STENSGÅRD: Me? I was invited, of course, like everyone else.

FJELDBO: Yes, last night, so I hear – after your speech.

STENSGÅRD: Well?

FJELDBO: And you accepted the invitation?

STENSGÅRD: Well, what the devil was I to do? I couldn't insult such decent people.

FJELDBO: Oh? Couldn't you? You did in your speech.

STENSGÅRD: Nonsense. It was principles I was attacking in my speech, not individuals.

FJELDBO: And how do you explain the Chamberlain's invitation?

STENSGÅRD: My dear chap, there's only one possible explanation.

FJELDBO: Namely, that the Chamberlain's afraid of you?

STENSGÅRD: God knows he shall have no cause to be. He's a man of honour.

FJELDBO: He is.

STENSGÅRD: And isn't it rather touching that the old fellow should take it like this? And how charming Miss Brattsberg looked when she brought me his letter. . . .

FJELDBO: But tell me – has anyone here said anything about last night's scene?

STENSGÅRD. Not a word – they're all too well-bred to do anything of the sort. It's rather on my conscience, and later on I want to make an apology –

FJELDBO: Oh, I really do advise you not to do that. You don't know the Chamberlain.

STENSGÅRD: Very well, then my actions shall speak for me.

FJELDBO: You're going to break with the Monsen faction?

STENSGÅRD: I'll bring about a reconciliation. I have my League, and it's a power already, as you can see.

FJELDBO: Yes, but while I think of it, there's one thing . . . your feelings about Miss Monsen – I advised you to go ahead with it –

STENSGÅRD: Oh well, we can always –

FJELDBO: No, listen – I've been thinking it over. You'd better put the whole idea out of your head.

STENSGÅRD. Yes, I think you're right. If you marry into that class of people, you find that you've practically married the whole family!

FJELDBO: Yes – and there are other reasons, too.

STENSGÅRD: Monsen *is* lower class – I can see that now.

FJELDBO: He's not exactly out of the top drawer.

STENSGÅRD: He certainly isn't! He goes and speaks ill of people who are guests in his house – that's unchivalrous. And all the rooms at Storli reek of stale tobacco –

FJELDBO: But my dear fellow, hadn't you noticed the smell of tobacco before?

STENSGÅRD: It's the contrast that does it. I made a wrong start when I first came – I got into the hands of a party clique who filled my head with all sorts of nonsense. Well, I've done with all that. I'm not going to waste my life being a tool for vulgar, self-centred stupidity.

FJELDBO: What will you use your League for, then?

STENSGÅRD: There's no need for the League to change – it's founded on a pretty broad basis. That's to say, it was formed to fight evil influences – now I'm beginning to see which quarter those influences come from.

FJELDBO: But do you think 'Youth' will see things in the same light?

STENSGÅRD: They shall! I can surely expect fellows like that to rely on my better judgement.

FJELDBO: But supposing they won't?

STENSGÅRD: Then they can go their own way – I don't need them any longer. Are you suggesting that, out of wilful blindness and for the sake of some stupid consistency, I should let my whole future go astray, and never reach my goal?

FJELDBO: And what do you mean by your goal?

STENSGÅRD: A life that gives scope to my talents, and that fulfils all my needs.

FJELDBO: No vague phrases! What do you mean by your goal?

STENSGÅRD: Well, I don't mind telling you. . . . When I say 'my goal', I mean getting into the Storthing one day – even becoming a Privy Councillor. And being happily married into a rich and respectable family.

FJELDBO: Well, well . . . And you think that with the Chamberlain's influence . . .?

STENSGÅRD: I mean to get there by my own efforts. It'll happen – it *must* happen . . . but entirely by myself. Yes, it's a long way off, but never mind that. Meanwhile, I want to enjoy life here, where there's beauty and light.

FJELDBO: Here?

STENSGÅRD: Yes, here. Here life's gracious and refined; the floors here seem to be laid to be trodden only by patent leather; here there are deep armchairs for lovely ladies to sit in; here conversation is tossed lightly and elegantly like a shuttlecock, and no clumsy remark strikes the company dumb. Oh, Fjeldbo – here for the first time I've realized what breeding is. Yes, we have an aristocracy after all – an aristocracy of breeding – a small circle, and I mean to belong to it. Here a man becomes refined – don't you feel that yourself? Don't you feel that wealth, here, is quite a different thing? When I think of Monsen's wealth, I picture it as

great bundles of greasy banknotes and beer-stained mort-
gages. But here – here it's pure shining silver! And it's the
same with the people. Look at the Chamberlain – what a
fine, courtly old chap he is!

FJELDBO: He certainly is.

STENSGÅRD: And his son – firm, forthright, and capable.

FJELDBO: Quite so.

STENSGÅRD: And the daughter-in-law too. She's a jewel –
heavens, how rich and rare her personality is.

FJELDBO: So is Thora's – Miss Brattsberg.

STENSGÅRD: Yes – but, you know, I don't find her so striking.

FJELDBO: Ah, you don't know her. You don't know what
depths there are in that quiet integrity of hers.

STENSGÅRD: But the daughter-in-law! So straightforward –
reckless, almost – and yet so sensitive, so attractive. . . .

FJELDBO: I really believe you're in love with her!

STENSGÅRD: A married woman? My dear fellow, you're
mad! What would be the use of that? All the same, I *am*
falling in love – I feel sure of it. Yes, there really *are* depths
in that quiet integrity of hers.

FJELDBO: Whose?

STENSGÅRD: Miss Brattsberg's, of course.

FJELDBO: What? You're surely not thinking of –

STENSGÅRD: Yes, I am indeed.

FJELDBO: But I assure you, you haven't a chance.

STENSGÅRD: Oho! Will-power's a great force in this world,
my friend. We'll see if I have a chance!

FJELDBO: But this is completely irresponsible! Yesterday it
was Miss Monsen –

STENSGÅRD: Yes, well that *was* rather hasty. Besides, you
warned me yourself –

FJELDBO: I warned you – in no uncertain terms – not to think
of either of them.

STENSGÅRD: Oh? Perhaps you're thinking of proposing to one of them yourself?

FJELDBO: I? No, I assure you –

STENSGÅRD: Well, even if you were, it wouldn't have stopped me. When anyone gets in my way and tries to upset my plans, I'm quite ruthless.

FJELDBO: Be careful I don't say the same!

STENSGÅRD: You? What right have you to set yourself up as the Brattsberg family's guardian and defender?

FJELDBO: At any rate, I have the right of a friend.

STENSGÅRD: Pooh! That sort of nonsense doesn't impress me. The only right you have is sheer self-interest. It satisfies your petty vanity to be part of the furniture in this house, so I'm to keep away!

FJELDBO: Yes, that would be the best thing you could do. You're on very shaky ground here.

STENSGÅRD. Am I really? Many thanks. Then the best thing I can do is to try to build firmer foundations.

FJELDBO: You can try. But I warn you they'll give way.

STENSGÅRD: Aha! So you've got something up your sleeve? I'm very glad to hear it. Now I know that you're my enemy – the only one I have here.

FJELDBO: Oh no I'm not.

STENSGÅRD: You are! You always have been, ever since we were at school. Just look how everyone round here appreciates me, although I'm a stranger. But you, on the other hand, although you know me, you've never appreciated me. That's your great failing – you can never appreciate anyone. In Kristiania you used to go round all the teaparties retailing silly gossip. That sort of thing hits back at you, you know. It blunts your feeling for everything that's really worth while in life, till, in the end, you become good for nothing.

FJELDBO: So I'm good for nothing?

STENSGÅRD: Have you ever been able to appreciate me?

FJELDBO: What is there for me to appreciate?

STENSGÅRD: My will-power, if nothing else. Everyone else appreciates it – all the people at the fête yesterday, and the Chamberlain and his family –

FJELDBO: And Monsen and his ditto, and . . . Damn it, that reminds me – there's someone out there waiting to see you.

STENSGÅRD: Who?

FJELDBO: Someone who appreciates you. [*Going to the back, he opens the door and calls*] Come in, Aslaksen.

ASLAKSEN [*appearing*]: Ah, at last!

FJELDBO: *Au revoir!* I don't want to come between friends. [*He goes to the garden.*]

STENSGÅRD. What the devil do you want here?

ASLAKSEN: I *must* speak to you. Yesterday you promised me an account of the founding of the League, and –

STENSGÅRD: You can't have it now – it must wait till some other time.

ASLAKSEN: But it can't, Mr Stensgård – the paper comes out first thing tomorrow.

STENSGÅRD: I can't help that. The whole thing'll have to be altered. The position has changed – there are fresh influences at work. What I said about Chamberlain Brattsberg must be drastically edited before you can use it.

ASLAKSEN: But the bit about the Chamberlain is already set up.

STENSGÅRD: Well, then it must come out again!

ASLAKSEN: Come out!

STENSGÅRD: Yes. I won't have it printed as it stands. It's no good staring at me. D'you think I don't know how to manage the League's affairs?

ASLAKSEN: Oh, of course you do. But I must just say –

STENSGÅRD: No excuses, Aslaksen – I won't have that sort of thing.

ASLAKSEN: Mr Stensgård, do you realize that you're taking what little bread I have out of my mouth?

STENSGÅRD. No, I don't realize anything of the kind.

ASLAKSEN: Well, you are. Last winter, before you came here, my paper was gaining ground. I was editing it myself, and I may say, I was editing it on principle.

STENSGÅRD: You?

ASLAKSEN: Yes, me. I said to myself, it's the general public that supports a paper, but the general public is a vulgar public – that's thanks to local conditions – and this vulgar public wants a vulgar paper. So I edited the paper –

STENSGÅRD: Vulgarly! Yes, there's no denying that.

ASLAKSEN: Yes, and I did very nicely out of it. Then you came, and introduced ideas into the district, and the paper had to take a different tone, so that all Anders Lundestad's friends stopped taking it. The ones that are left simply don't pay. . . .

STENSGÅRD: But it's become a good paper.

ASLAKSEN: How can I live off a good paper? There was to be trouble brewing here – things were to go the way you promised yesterday. The high-and-mighty were to be pilloried, there were to be things in the paper that everybody would want to read. And now you back out!

STENSGÅRD: Ah, you expect me to provide you with scandals? No, thank you, my good man!

ASLAKSEN: Don't drive me too far, Mr Stensgård, or you'll regret it.

STENSGÅRD: What do you mean by that?

ASLAKSEN: I mean that I might try another way to make my paper pay. Lord knows I don't want to. Before you came, I made an honest living out of unfortunate accidents and suicides, and harmless things like that – things that sometimes hadn't even happened . . . and now you've upset everything. People want something different –

STENSGÅRD: Well, all I'll say to you is this: if you take it on yourself to go a single step beyond what I tell you, or if you try to use the Movement for your own dirty ends, I'll go to another printer and start an opposition paper. We've got the money, you know. And your rag would be ruined in a fortnight!

ASLAKSEN [*blenching*]: You wouldn't do that!

STENSGÅRD: I certainly would. I'm just the man to run a paper that would take away your 'general public' from you.

ASLAKSEN: Then I'm going straight to Chamberlain Brattsberg –

STENSGÅRD: You? What business have you there?

ASLAKSEN: What business have *you* here? D'you think I don't know why he's asked you? It's because he's afraid of you and what you might do – and that's what you're counting on. But if he's afraid of what you might do, then he'll be afraid of what I might print, and *I*'m counting on that!

STENSGÅRD: You'd never dare – a rat like you!

ASLAKSEN: Yes, I'll show you. If your speech is to be kept out of the paper, then the Chamberlain's going to pay me for keeping it out.

STENSGÅRD: You dare! Just you dare! You're drunk, man.

ASLAKSEN: Only moderately. But I'm like a lion if anyone tries to take my miserable crust away from me. You wouldn't believe what my home life is like – a bedridden wife, a crippled child –

STENSGÅRD: Get out of here! Do you want to drag me down to your level? What have your overworked wives and misshapen brats to do with me? If you dare to stand in my way, or to oppose a single one of my projects, you'll find yourself in the workhouse before the year's out.

ASLAKSEN: I'll wait just one day. . . .

STENSGÅRD: Ah, so you're beginning to come to your senses again.

ASLAKSEN: I'll get out a special edition to say that, as the result of an indisposition contracted at the fête, the Editor has –

STENSGÅRD: Yes, yes, do that. Later, I daresay we can come to some arrangement.

ASLAKSEN: I hope so. But remember, Mr Stensgård, that this paper is my ewe-lamb. [*He goes out at the back.*]

LUNDESTAD [*coming through the farthest french window*]: Well, Mr Stensgård?

STENSGÅRD: Well, Mr Lundestad?

LUNDESTAD: Are you alone? If it's convenient, I should like a word with you.

STENSGÅRD: With pleasure.

LUNDESTAD: In the first place, I want to say that if you've heard that I may have said anything derogatory about you, you mustn't believe it.

STENSGÅRD: About me? What could you have said?

LUNDESTAD: Nothing, I assure you. But there are a lot of idle people here who simply go round making trouble.

STENSGÅRD: Yes, taking it all round, the position between us is a little unfortunate.

LUNDESTAD: It's a very natural position, Mr Stensgård. It's the position of the old with regard to the new; it's always like this.

STENSGÅRD: Oh come, Mr Lundestad, you're not as old as all that.

LUNDESTAD: Oh yes, yes, I'm getting old. I've sat in the Storthing since 1839. I'm beginning to feel that the time may have come for my relief.

STENSGÅRD: Relief?

LUNDESTAD: Times change, you know. Fresh problems arise, and they need fresh minds to solve them.

STENSGÅRD: Tell me frankly, Mr Lundestad, will you really make way for Monsen?

LUNDESTAD: Monsen? No, I'm not retiring for Monsen's sake.

STENSGÅRD: But didn't I understand . . .?

LUNDESTAD: Suppose I did retire in Monsen's favour, do you think he'd have any chance of being elected?

STENSGÅRD: It's hard to say. The Preliminary Elections are the day after tomorrow, and public opinion hasn't been properly prepared yet, but –

LUNDESTAD: I don't think it's likely. My party – the Chamberlain's party – won't vote for him. When I say 'my party', that's only a figure of speech; I mean the men of property, the old families whose homes are here and who are rooted in their land. They won't have anything to do with Monsen; he's an interloper – no one really knows anything about him and his affairs. And to clear a place for himself, he's had to do a good deal of hacking down – families as well as trees, you might say.

STENSGÅRD: Well, then, if you don't think he has a chance –

LUNDESTAD: Hm. You're a most gifted man, on the whole, Mr Stensgård. Heaven has treated you very generously, but there's one little thing it should have added.

STENSGÅRD: What's that?

LUNDESTAD: Tell me, why do you never think of *yourself*? Why haven't you any ambition?

STENSGÅRD: Ambition? Me?

LUNDESTAD: Why do you keep squandering your talents on other people's behalf? In short, why don't you go into the Storthing yourself?

STENSGÅRD: I? You're not serious?

LUNDESTAD: You're eligible, I hear;[17] and if you don't seize this chance, someone else *will* – and once he's firmly in the saddle, it won't be easy to turn him out.

STENSGÅRD: But, good heavens, Mr Lundestad, do you really mean what you're saying?

LUNDESTAD: This is getting us nowhere. Of course, if you're not willing –

STENSGÅRD: Not willing? I don't mind telling you that I'm

not so lacking in ambition as you think. But do you really believe it'd be possible?

LUNDESTAD: Of course it would. I'd do all I could, and so would the Chamberlain – he knows what a good speaker you are – the young people are on your side, and –

STENSGÅRD: My goodness, Mr Lundestad, you're a real friend.

LUNDESTAD: Ah, you can't really mean that; if I were your friend, you'd take the burden off my shoulders. Yours are younger, they could so easily carry it.

STENSGÅRD: I'm at your disposal. I shan't fail you.

LUNDESTAD: Then you agree . . .?

STENSGÅRD: Here's my hand on it.

LUNDESTAD: Thank you! Believe me, Mr Stensgård, you'll never regret it. But we must go about it cautiously. We must both be careful to get on the College of Electors – I, so that I can propose you as my successor, and question you a little in the Assembly; and you, so that you can put forward your views –

STENSGÅRD: Oh, if we can get as far as that, we're safe – in the Assembly, you're invincible.

LUNDESTAD: Oh, there is a limit to my power; naturally, you'll have to use your gifts as a speaker to explain away anything that might seem awkward or obstructive.

STENSGÅRD: You surely don't mean that I must break with my party?

LUNDESTAD: Now, just look at things reasonably. What does it mean, having two parties here? It means that, on the one hand, we have certain people or families enjoying the ordinary advantages of citizenship – I mean property, independence, and a share of power – that's the party I belong to. On the other hand, there are plenty of our younger fellow-citizens who would like to acquire these advantages – that's your party. But you will quite naturally and properly pass out of that party when you acquire a share of power and establish yourself securely as a man of property – and of course that's essential, Mr Stensgård.

STENSGÅRD: Yes, I quite agree. But time's short, and one can't attain a position like that with a wave of the hand.

LUNDESTAD: No, indeed one can't. But it would be a help to you if only you had some prospects.

STENSGÅRD: Prospects?

LUNDESTAD: Would you have any great objection to considering a good marriage, Mr Stensgård? There are rich heiresses in the neighbourhood; a man like you, with a future before him – a man who can count on reaching the highest office. . . . Believe me, no one will refuse you if you play your cards rightly.

STENSGÅRD: Then for heaven's sake, help me to play them! You've opened a great prospect before me – a vision! Everything that I'd hoped and longed for – to walk among the people as a free man – all the distant things I'd dreamed of are here before me now in the flesh!

LUNDESTAD: Well, we'll keep our eyes open, Mr Stensgård. I can see that your ambition is stirring already – that's a good thing; the rest will come of itself. In the meantime – thanks! I shall never forget that you were ready to take the burden of power from my old shoulders.

[*The guests and the family come gradually in from the garden. During the following, two maids bring lamps and hand round refreshments.*]

SELMA [*going towards the piano at the back*]: You must join us, Mr Stensgård, we're going to play forfeits.

STENSGÅRD: Thank you, there's nothing I should like more. [*He goes to the back with her to discuss arrangements, place chairs, and so on.*]

ERIK [*quietly*]: What the dickens is this that my father's talking about, Mr Hejre? What was this speech that Stensgård made up here last night?

HEJRE: Tee-hee, don't you know about it?

ERIK: No, we townspeople had our Dinner and Ball down at the Club. But Father says that Mr Stensgård made a complete break with the Storli crowd, and said some extremely rude things about Monsen –

HEJRE: About Monsen? No, my dear sir, you must have misunderstood.

ERIK: Well, there was such a crowd round him that I couldn't hear it all, but I certainly heard him say that –

HEJRE: Enough said. Wait till tomorrow, you'll get the whole story at breakfast in Aslaksen's paper. [*He drifts away.*]

BRATTSBERG: Well, my dear Lundestad, are you still sticking to that absurd idea of yours?

LUNDESTAD: It's not so absurd, Chamberlain. When you're in danger of being pushed out, it's best to retire of your own accord first.

BRATTSBERG: What a way to talk! Who's thinking of pushing you out?

LUNDESTAD: I'm an old weather-prophet, and there's change in the air. . . . Well, I've found a successor – Mr Stensgård is ready to –

BRATTSBERG: Stensgård?

LUNDESTAD: Yes, wasn't that what you meant? I took it as a hint, when you said that he was a man we ought to join with and support.

BRATTSBERG: Well, I meant in his stand against all the jobbery that goes on at Storli.

LUNDESTAD: But how could you have been so sure that he would break with those people?

BRATTSBERG: My dear fellow, surely that was obvious last night.

LUNDESTAD: Last night?

BRATTSBERG: Yes, when he talked about Monsen's pernicious influence in the district.

LUNDESTAD [*open-mouthed*]: About *Monsen's* . . .?

BRATTSBERG: Yes, when he was up on the table.

LUNDESTAD: On the table, yes.

BRATTSBERG: He was extremely rude – called him 'money-bags', and a basilisk or a monster or something of the sort. Ha ha – it was most amusing.

LUNDESTAD: You found it amusing?

BRATTSBERG: Yes, I don't mind admitting, Lundestad, that I enjoyed seeing those people get a trouncing. But now we must support him, because after a savage attack like that –

LUNDESTAD: Like yesterday's, you mean?

BRATTSBERG: Yes, of course.

LUNDESTAD: From the table?

BRATTSBERG: Yes, from the table.

LUNDESTAD: On Monsen?

BRATTSBERG: Yes, on Monsen and his crew. Naturally they'll try to get their revenge – you can't really blame them. . . .

LUNDESTAD [*decisively*]: Mr Stensgård must be supported, that's obvious.

THORA: Father dear, you must come and play.

BRATTSBERG: Oh, nonsense, my dear.

THORA: Oh, you must – Selma wants you to.

BRATTSBERG: Ah well, I suppose I must give in. [*Quietly, as he goes*] I'm quite worried about Lundestad, I really think his brain's going. Just imagine, he hadn't the least idea what Stensgård –

THORA: Oh, do come along – we're starting the game! [*She pulls him into the circle where the game is in full swing among the young people.*]

ERIK [*calling from his place*]: Mr Hejre, you've been appointed Forfeits Judge.

HEJRE: Tee-hee! It's the first appointment I've ever held.

STENSGÅRD [*also from the circle*]: It's thanks to all your experience in the Courts, Mr Hejre!

HEJRE: My dear young friends, I should be delighted to pronounce sentence on you all, but . . . enough said.

STENSGÅRD [*under his breath to* LUNDESTAD, *who is standing in front to the left*]: You were talking to the Chamberlain; what was it about? Anything to do with me?

LUNDESTAD: I'm afraid so – about last night.

STENSGÅRD [*wincing*]: Damnation!

LUNDESTAD: He says he thinks you were extremely rude.

STENSGÅRD: Do you think I'm not upset about that?

LUNDESTAD: Now's your chance to put it right.

ERIK [*calling*]: Mr Stensgård, it's your turn.

STENSGÅRD: Coming! [*Hurriedly, to* LUNDESTAD] How can I do that?

LUNDESTAD: Find an opportunity to apologize to the Chamberlain.

STENSGÅRD: Yes, by Jove, I will!

SELMA: Hurry! Hurry!

STENSGÅRD: I'm coming, Mrs Brattsberg. . . . Here I am.
[*The game goes on with happy laughter. To the right, a few older men are playing cards.* LUNDESTAD *sits to the left, with* DANIEL HEJRE *by him.*]

HEJRE: That puppy says I have experience of the Courts!

LUNDESTAD: I must admit he rather lets his tongue run away with him.

HEJRE: That's why the whole family goes and fawns on him. Tee-hee, it's pitiful to see how afraid they are.

LUNDESTAD: No, you're wrong there, Mr Hejre – the Chamberlain isn't afraid.

HEJRE: No? My dear sir, do you think I'm blind?

LUNDESTAD: No, but . . . look, can you keep a secret? Good, then I'll tell you how things really stand. The Chamberlain thinks it was Monsen that he was talking about last night!

HEJRE: Monsen? Impossible!

LUNDESTAD: I assure you, Mr Hejre. Either Ringdal or Miss Thora must have put the idea in his head. . . .

HEJRE: So off he goes and invites him to his big luncheon party! Well, upon my word, that's rich! Well, you know, I can't keep *that* a secret!

LUNDESTAD: Sh! Sh! Remember your promise! The Chamberlain's an old school-friend of yours, and even if he has been a little hard on you –

HEJRE: Tee-hee! I'll pay him back with interest!

LUNDESTAD: Be careful – the Chamberlain's powerful. Don't twist the lion's tail!

HEJRE: Brattsberg a lion? Pooh, he's a fool, old chap – and I'm not. Oh, this'll provide me with some lovely taunts and gibes and pinpricks when I once get our big lawsuit under way.

SELMA [*calling from the circle*]: Judge, what shall the owner of this forfeit do?

ERIK [*surreptitiously to* HEJRE]: It's Stensgård's – find something amusing.

HEJRE: That forfeit? Tee-hee! Let me see. . . . He might perhaps . . . enough said. He must make a speech!

SELMA: It's Mr Stensgård's!

ERIK: Mr Stensgård must make a speech!

STENSGÅRD: Oh no! Let me off! I did quite badly enough last night.

BRATTSBERG: You did very well, Mr Stensgård – and I know a little about speech-making.

LUNDESTAD [*to* DANIEL HEJRE]: I hope to goodness he doesn't make a bloomer.

HEJRE: A bloomer? Tee-hee! You're a crafty one, you are! A perfect inspiration! [*Quietly to* STENSGÅRD] If you showed up badly last night, you can put everything right today.

STENSGÅRD [*struck with a sudden idea*]: Lundestad, here's my chance!

LUNDESTAD [*evasively*]: Play your cards well! [*He reaches for his hat, and makes unobtrusively for the door.*]

STENSGÅRD: Very well, I'll make a speech.

THE LADIES: Bravo! Bravo!

STENSGÅRD: Take your glasses, ladies and gentlemen. I'm going to begin my speech with a fairy-tale, because in this company I seem to breathe the spirit of fairyland and its ways.

ERIK [*to the ladies*]: Listen . . .

[*The* CHAMBERLAIN *takes up his glass and remains standing by the card-table.* RINGDAL, DR FJELDBO, *and a few other men come in from the garden.*]

STENSGÅRD: Once upon a time in the spring, a young cuckoo came flying over the hills. The cuckoo is a fortune-hunter, and there was a great gathering of birds in the smooth meadow below him, and both the wild and the tame birds were flocking to it. They came tripping out from the hen-runs, and waddling up from the duckponds. Down from Storli there swept a tough old grouse[18] with a low swaggering flight; he settled, and ruffled his feathers and flapped his wings to make himself look bigger than he really was, and he kept crowing: 'Kowk-ouk-ouk' as much as to say 'I'm the cock of the walk from Storli, I am!'

BRATTSBERG: Magnificent! Hear hear!

STENSGÅRD: Then there came an old woodpecker. He bustled up and down the tree-trunks, probing with his sharp beak, gobbling up the grubs and all the things that you find where there's rottenness. On every side you could hear 'tap tap tap', and that was the woodpecker –

ERIK: Wait a minute, wasn't it a stork or a –[19]

HEJRE: Enough said!

STENSGÅRD: It was an old woodpecker. Then there was a stir in the flock – they'd found someone they could cackle abuse about. They clustered together and cackled in chorus, till at last the young cuckoo began to cackle with them –

FJELDBO [*unobtrusively*]: For God's sake shut up, man!

STENSGÅRD: Now this was all about an old eagle who sat in solitary grandeur on a steep crag.[20] They were all agreed about him. 'He's a menace to the district!' said a hoarse old raven. But the eagle swooped down in a great curve and picked up the cuckoo and carried him up to the summit, where he won his heart. From those heights, the fortune-hunting bird had a glorious view out over the plain; there was sunshine and peace, and there he learned to judge the rabble from the hen-runs and the squalid fields –

FJELDBO [*loudly*]: Curtain! Curtain! Strike up the band!

BRATTSBERG: Sh! Don't interrupt him.

STENSGÅRD: Mr Brattsberg – that is the end of my fairy-tale, and I stand before you in the presence of everyone here, to ask your forgiveness for last night.

BRATTSBERG [*taken aback*]: Mine?

STENSGÅRD: Thank you for the way you have revenged yourself for my thoughtless speech. From now on, you have in me a faithful champion. And so, ladies and gentlemen, here's a health to the eagle on the crag – to Chamberlain Brattsberg.

BRATTSBERG [*feeling for the table*]: Thank you, Mr Stensgård.

THE GUESTS [*most of them painfully embarrassed*]: The Chamberlain! Chamberlain Brattsberg!

BRATTSBERG: Thank you, ladies and gentlemen. [*Quietly*] Thora –

THORA: Yes, Father.

BRATTSBERG: Oh, Doctor, Doctor, what have you done?

STENSGÅRD [*glass in hand, beaming with happiness*]: And now – back to our game! Hi, Fjeldbo, come and join us – join this League of Youth. It's a wonderful game!

HEJRE [*in front, to the left*]: A wonderful game, upon my word! [LUNDESTAD *slips out by the door at the back.*]

The curtain falls

ACT THREE

An elegant ante-room, with an entrance at the back.
To the left is a door to the Chamberlain's study, and farther back a
door to the drawing-room.
To the right is a door to the Works Manager's office, and farther
forward a window.

[THORA *is sitting crying on a sofa to the left, while the*
CHAMBERLAIN *is pacing angrily up and down.*]

BRATTSBERG: Yes, now we have the Epilogue! Sobs and
tears . . .

THORA: I wish to goodness we'd never seen the man.

BRATTSBERG: What man?

THORA: That awful Mr Stensgård, of course.

BRATTSBERG: It'd be more to the point if you said you
wished to goodness we'd never seen that awful doctor.

THORA: Dr Fjeldbo?

BRATTSBERG: Yes, Fjeldbo, Fjeldbo. Wasn't it he who filled
me up with lies?

THORA: No, dear, darling Father, it was I.

BRATTSBERG: You? Well, the pair of you, then! Conspiring
behind my back. . . . Charming!

THORA: Oh, Father, if only you knew –

BRATTSBERG: I know quite enough . . . more than enough –
much more.

[FJELDBO *comes in from the back.*]

FJELDBO: Good morning, Chamberlain – good morning,
Miss Brattsberg.

BRATTSBERG [*still pacing up and down*]: Oh, it's you, is it, you
bird of ill omen?

FJELDBO: Yes, it was certainly a most unfortunate business.

77

BRATTSBERG [*looking out of the window*]: Oh, you think so, do you?

FJELDBO: You surely must have noticed how I was keeping an eye on Stensgård the whole evening. When I heard they were going to play forfeits, I'm afraid I thought there was no more danger.

BRATTSBERG [*stamping his foot*]: To be made a laughing-stock by a windbag like that! What must my guests have thought of me? That I was petty enough to want to buy off this creature, this – this – whatever it was that Lundestad called him.

FJELDBO: Yes, but –

THORA [*unseen by her father*]: Don't say anything.

BRATTSBERG [*after a moment, turning to* FJELDBO]: Tell me frankly, Doctor – am I really sillier than most people?

FJELDBO: How can you ask that, Chamberlain?

BRATTSBERG: But how was it that I was probably the only person there who didn't realize that the confounded speech was aimed at me?

FJELDBO: Shall I tell you?

BRATTSBERG: I wish you would.

FJELDBO: It's because you see your position here in the district differently from the way other people see it.

BRATTSBERG: I see my position in exactly the same way as my father did. No one would ever have dared to treat *him* like that.

FJELDBO: Your father died in about the year 1830. . . .

BRATTSBERG: Oh yes, things have changed a great deal since his day. After all, it's my own fault; I've mixed too freely with these people, and now I find myself treated on a par with Lundestad.

FJELDBO: Well, frankly, I don't see any disgrace in that.

BRATTSBERG: You know quite well what I mean. Of course, I don't give myself airs about social distinctions or titles or anything of that sort. But what I do respect – and what I expect others to respect – is the integrity that's been handed down in our family for generations. What I mean is that when a man like Lundestad goes into politics, he can't keep his character and his conduct entirely spotless. Lundestad must expect to have mud thrown at him. But they should leave me alone. . . . I stand outside all their Parties.

FJELDBO: Not altogether, Chamberlain – at any rate, you were delighted as long as you thought it was Monsen who was being attacked.

BRATTSBERG: Don't talk to me about Monsen! It's he who's lowered the whole moral tone of this district. Unfortunately, he's turned my son's head, too.

THORA: Erik?

FJELDBO: Your son?

BRATTSBERG: Yes, why should he get himself involved in trade? No good will come of that.

FJELDBO: But, my dear Chamberlain, he must live. . . .

BRATTSBERG: If he were careful, he could live very well on the money his mother left him.

FJELDBO: He could live on it, perhaps, but what would he have to live *for*?

BRATTSBERG: To live for? Well, if he *must* have something to live for, he's a qualified lawyer, why can't he live for his profession?

FJELDBO: He couldn't do that, it's against his nature. For one thing, he could never hope to get any public appointment. This property you've always managed yourself; and he has no children to bring up. So, in the circumstances, when he sees tempting instances all round him – of men who started with nothing and now are making their half-million –

BRATTSBERG: A half-million? Oh come, let's stay in the hundred thousand range! But neither that half-million nor the hundred thousand are scraped together with entirely clean hands. I don't mean in the eyes of the world – heaven knows it's easy enough to keep within the law – but in their own consciences. Naturally, my son would never stoop to anything of that sort – so don't worry, the firm of Brattsberg won't amass any half-millions!

[SELMA, *in walking dress, comes in from the back.*]

SELMA: Good morning. Isn't Erik here?

BRATTSBERG: Good morning, child. Are you looking for your husband?

SELMA: Yes, he said he'd be out here. Mr Monsen came to see him early this morning, and –

BRATTSBERG: Monsen? Does Monsen come to your house?

SELMA: Now and then – usually on business – But, Thora dear, what's the matter? Have you been crying?

THORA: Oh, it's nothing.

SELMA: Oh, yes, it is! Back at home, Erik was peevish, and now *here* – I can see it in your faces, something's wrong – what is it?

BRATTSBERG: Oh well, it's nothing that need upset you, at any rate. You're too delicate to carry burdens, Selma dear. Go into the drawing-room for the time being; if Erik said he was coming, he'll be here.

SELMA: Come along, Thora – and don't let me get in a draught! [*Putting an arm round her*] Oh, Thora darling, I could hug you! [*The two girls go out to the left.*]

BRATTSBERG: So the two speculators are getting together! They ought to go into partnership. . . . Monsen and Brattsberg – it sounds charming!

[*There is a knock on the door.*]

Come in.

[STENSGÅRD *enters.* BRATTSBERG *recoils a step.*]

BRATTSBERG: What on earth?

STENSGÅRD: Yes, I'm here again, Chamberlain.

BRATTSBERG: So I see.

FJELDBO: Are you off your head, man?

STENSGÅRD: You went off early yesterday, sir. By the

time Fjeldbo had explained the situation to me, you'd already –

BRATTSBERG: Please! Any explanation would be superfluous.

STENSGÅRD: Of course. You mustn't think that's why I've come.

BRATTSBERG: No? Why, then?

STENSGÅRD: I know I've insulted you –

BRATTSBERG: So do I. And before I have you thrown out, perhaps you'll tell me why you've come here.

STENSGÅRD: Because, Chamberlain, I love your daughter.

FJELDBO: What!

BRATTSBERG: What was that he said, Doctor?

STENSGÅRD: Ah, you can't take it in. You're an old man, Chamberlain; you have nothing to fight for. . . .

BRATTSBERG: And you presume to –

STENSGÅRD: I've come to ask for your daughter's hand, Chamberlain.

BRATTSBERG: You . . . you . . .? Won't you sit down?

STENSGÅRD: Thank you, I'd rather stand.

BRATTSBERG: Doctor, what do you say to this?

STENSGÅRD: Oh, Fjeldbo's on my side; he's my friend – the only true friend I have.

FJELDBO: No, man, no – never in this world, since you –

BRATTSBERG: Was that why my doctor got me to invite him to this house?

STENSGÅRD: You only know me from my performances of yesterday and the day before, and that's not enough. What's more, I'm not the same man today that I used to be. Mixing with you and your family has been like an April shower to me – the buds have sprouted in a single night! You can't cast me back into misery! I've never really known the gracious things of life till now – they've always been as far out of my reach as the birds on the housetops.

BRATTSBERG: And my daughter . . .?

STENSGÅRD: Oh, I shall win her.

BRATTSBERG: Indeed? Hm!

STENSGÅRD: Yes, because that is what I want. Remember what you told me yesterday: you weren't happy about your son's marriage – and look how well that's turned out. You should learn from experience, as Fjeldbo said.

BRATTSBERG: Was *that* what he meant?

FJELDBO: Far from it. My dear Chamberlain, let me have a word with him alone.

STENSGÅRD: Nonsense – there's nothing I want to talk to you about. Look, Chamberlain, be reasonable – be sensible . . . a family like yours needs new blood, or the stock deteriorates.

BRATTSBERG: No, this is too much!

STENSGÅRD: Sh! sh! Don't lose your temper. Get rid of all these tiresome ideas about rank. Why, damn it, what are they after all but frippery? You'll see how proud you'll be of me when you get to know me. Yes, you *shall* be proud of me – both you and your daughter. I shall make her –

BRATTSBERG: What do *you* think, Doctor?

FJELDBO: I think he's mad.

STENSGÅRD: Yes, for you it would be madness, but you know, *I* have a mission to fulfil here on God's fair earth – I'm not going to be deterred by stupid prejudices.

BRATTSBERG: Mr Stensgård, there is the door!

STENSGÅRD: You're showing me . . .?

BRATTSBERG: – the door!

STENSGÅRD: Don't do that!

BRATTSBERG: Get out! You *are* a fortune-hunter and a – a – Oh, confound it – You're a –

STENSGÅRD: A what?

BRATTSBERG: You're the other thing . . . oh, it's on the tip of my tongue. . . . But that's what you are!

STENSGÅRD: Be careful how you thwart my destiny!

BRATTSBERG: Why?

STENSGÅRD: Because I'll hound you – attack you in the

Press, malign you, undermine your reputation in every way I can. You shall howl under the lash. You shall crouch in terror with your arms around your head to shield you from the blows. On your knees you shall crawl to shelter –

BRATTSBERG: Crawl to shelter yourself – in a madhouse, where you belong.

STENSGÅRD: Ha! That's a cheap retort, Chamberlain, but you can't find a better. Let me tell you this: I am a vessel of God's wrath; it is His will that you are opposing. He meant me for the light – do not shade it! Well, I see that I'm making no progress with you today, but no matter. All I ask is that you speak to your daughter. Prepare her. Give her the chance to choose. Look around yourself here, and just consider. Where can you hope to find yourself a son-in-law among these louts and blockheads! Fjeldbo says she has depths in that quiet integrity of hers. . . . Well, now you know it all. Good-bye, Chamberlain. You can have me either as a friend or an enemy. Good-bye. [*He goes out at the back.*]

BRATTSBERG: So it's come to this. That's how they dare to treat me in my own house.

FJELDBO: Stensgård dares – no one else would.

BRATTSBERG: He today, others tomorrow!

FJELDBO: Let them come! I'll fend them off – I'd go through fire and water for you!

BRATTSBERG: You? Why, you're to blame for the whole thing! Hm, that Stensgård is the most impudent scoundrel I've ever met . . . and yet, after all, there's something – what the devil is it? – something that I can't help liking.

FJELDBO: There *are* possibilities in him.

BRATTSBERG: There's forthrightness in him, Doctor. He doesn't go playing tricks behind one's back, like so many other people; he – he –

FJELDBO: It isn't worth arguing about; just be firm, Chamberlain. . . . No, and again no, to Stensgård.

BRATTSBERG: Oh, keep your advice to yourself! You can be quite sure that neither he nor anyone else –

RINGDAL [*coming in from the right*]: Excuse me, sir, could I have a word with you? [*Whispers.*]

BRATTSBERG: What? In your office?

RINGDAL: He came to the back door, and asked most urgently if he could see you.

BRATTSBERG: Ha! . . . Doctor, would you go in to the ladies for a moment, there's someone who . . . But don't say anything to Selma about Stensgård or his visit – she must be kept out of this. As to my daughter, I'd prefer it if you said nothing to her, either, but . . . Oh, I don't like this! Well, if you wouldn't mind leaving me . . .

[FJELDBO *goes into the drawing-room. Meanwhile,* RINGDAL *has gone back to his office and after a moment* MONSEN *comes in.*]

MONSEN [*in the doorway*]: I do hope you'll excuse me, Chamberlain –

BRATTSBERG: Well, come in – come in.

MONSEN: I hope all your family are well.

BRATTSBERG: Thank you. Is there something you want?

MONSEN: I wouldn't put it that way. Thank god I'm a man who *has* pretty well everything he wants.

BRATTSBERG: Indeed? That's quite a large claim.

MONSEN: But I've worked for it, Chamberlain. Oh, I know you don't think much of the *way* I've worked.

BRATTSBERG: My opinion hasn't had much influence on the way you've worked.

MONSEN: Well, who knows? Anyway, now I'm thinking of retiring from business.

BRATTSBERG: Indeed?

MONSEN: I don't mind telling you, I've been lucky. I've got on as far as I want, and I think this might be the moment to start gradually winding things up, and –

BRATTSBERG: I congratulate you – and a great many other people, too.

MONSEN: And if I could do you a good turn at the same time . . .

BRATTSBERG: Me?

MONSEN: When the woods at Langerud came up for auction five years ago, you made a bid –

BRATTSBERG: Yes, but you outbid me, and they were knocked down to you.

MONSEN: You can have them now – sawmills and all.

BRATTSBERG: After the wicked way you've been hacking them down –

MONSEN: Oh, they're still worth quite a bit; and, with what you know about forestry, in a year or two they'll –

BRATTSBERG: Thank you, I'm afraid I can't consider the idea.

MONSEN: But you'd do well out of it, Chamberlain. As for me . . . well, I'll tell you: I've got a big gamble on, and there's a lot at stake. What I mean is, I stand to make a hundred thousand or so!

BRATTSBERG: A hundred thousand? That is certainly a considerable sum.

MONSEN: Aha! Quite a nice bit to rake in and add to the pile! But when you're going into battle, you need your reserves, as they say. There isn't a lot of ready money hereabouts – all the backers whose names are worth anything have been used to death. . . .

BRATTSBERG: Yes, certain people have seen to that.

MONSEN: Oh, what's sauce for the goose . . .! Well, Chamberlain, shall we do a deal? You can have the woods dirt cheap.

BRATTSBERG: I wouldn't take them at any price, Mr Monsen.

MONSEN: Well, one good offer deserves another, Chamber- lain. Will you help me?

BRATTSBERG: What do you mean?

MONSEN: I'll give you security, of course. I've got plenty of property. Look here at these papers – will you let me show you how I stand?

BRATTSBERG [*waving the papers aside*]: Is it a loan you –

MONSEN: Not ready money – not by a long chalk. Just your support, Chamberlain. Mind you, you won't lose by it – and there's security, and –

BRATTSBERG: And you come to me with a proposal like this?

MONSEN: Yes, I do. I know how often, when a man's been in a tight spot, you've let bygones be bygones.

BRATTSBERG: In a way, I suppose I ought to thank you for your good opinion – especially at a time like this – but all the same . . .

MONSEN: Will you tell me what you've got against me, Chamberlain?

BRATTSBERG: Oh, what would be the good?

MONSEN: It might clear the air. I've never done you any harm, so far as I know.

BRATTSBERG: No? Then let me quote you one occasion when you've stood in my way. I founded a savings bank at my works for the benefit of my employees and others. And then you start a banking concern – people take their savings to you –

MONSEN: Of course they do, Chamberlain – I give higher interest.

BRATTSBERG: You also charge more on loans.

MONSEN: But I'm not so particular about security and the like.

BRATTSBERG: A pity; because now we find people concluding deals of ten or twenty thousand dollars, when neither party possesses more than a couple of Danish ha'pennies.[21] There, Mr Monsen; that's what I have against you. And there's another – more personal – reason. Do you think I like having my son mixed up in all these gimcrack undertakings?

MONSEN: But how can I help that?

BRATTSBERG: It was your example that corrupted him – just as it has done all the others. Why couldn't you stick to your last?

MONSEN: A lumberman, like my father?

BRATTSBERG: Was there any disgrace in being in my service? Your father earned an honest living, and was respected in his own circle.

MONSEN: Yes – working till his health gave out, and in the end going over the Falls on his raft. What do you know about life in that circle, Chamberlain? Have you ever for a moment thought what men go through, slaving for you deep in the forests and along the rivers, while you're sitting in your comfortable room enjoying the proceeds? Can you blame a man like that if he wants to work his way out of it? I had a little more schooling than my father – perhaps I had a little more brains, too.

BRATTSBERG: Possibly. But *how* did you work your way out? You began by selling brandy. Then you bought up bad debts and extorted them mercilessly – and so you went on and on. How many men have you ruined on your way?

MONSEN: That's how it goes in business – one goes up, another goes down.

BRATTSBERG: Yes, but there are methods and methods. There are respectable families here who've been brought to the workhouse by you.

MONSEN: Daniel Hejre isn't very far from the workhouse.

BRATTSBERG: I know what you mean; but I can justify my actions before God and man. After the secession from Denmark, the country was in distress and, to help it, my father went beyond his means, so that a part of our estate passed to the Hejre family. What was the result? The tenants on the estate suffered under Daniel Hejre's incompetent management. He cut down the forests till they were a disgrace – I might even say a tragedy – to the district. Wasn't it my plain duty to put a stop to that if I could? And I could. The law was on my side, and I was within my rights in taking over my property again.

MONSEN: I've never gone against the law, either.

BRATTSBERG: Only against your better feelings, and the conscience which it is to be hoped you possess. Look how you've trampled on good order here – how you've undermined the respect that wealth should bring. People no longer ask how a fortune was made or how long it has been in a family, they only ask: 'What is so-and-so worth?' and they judge him by that. I suffer by this; you and I have tended to become associated together – our names are linked, because we are the two biggest landowners here. And that I will not endure. Let me tell you, once and for all, that *that* is why I oppose you.

MONSEN: I'll stop all that, Chamberlain – I'll close my works, and give in to you in every way. I only ask you – I beg you – to help me.

BRATTSBERG: I will not.

MONSEN: I'll pay whatever you ask.

BRATTSBERG: Pay! How dare you?

MONSEN: If not for my sake, then for your son's.

BRATTSBERG: My son's?

MONSEN: Yes, he's in this with me – I reckon his share would come to twenty thousand.

BRATTSBERG: He stands to win that?

MONSEN: Yes.

BRATTSBERG: But, good God, who stands to lose all that?

MONSEN: What do you mean?

BRATTSBERG: If my son wins it, there must be someone who loses it.

MONSEN: It's a profitable deal – I'm not free to say more than that. But I need a reputable name. . . . You'd only have to endorse –

BRATTSBERG: To endorse? On a document?

MONSEN: Only for ten to fifteen thousand dollars.

BRATTSBERG: Do you really suppose for a single moment that *I* . . .? My name . . . in an affair like that? My name? As surety, presumably?

MONSEN: It's just a matter of form.

BRATTSBERG: My name – to a swindle? Not on any account. I've never put my name to another man's bill.

MONSEN: Never? You're exaggerating, Chamberlain.

BRATTSBERG: I assure you, it's the literal truth.

MONSEN: Not literal – I've seen it myself.

BRATTSBERG: What have you seen?

MONSEN: Your name, Chamberlain, on one bill at least.

BRATTSBERG: That's a lie. I tell you you've never seen it.

MONSEN: Oh yes – think again. On a bill for two thousand dollars.

BRATTSBERG: Not for two thousand or ten thousand. I give you my word of honour.

MONSEN: Then it's a forgery.

BRATTSBERG: A forgery?

MONSEN: Yes, a forgery – a copy of your signature. Because I *have* seen it.

BRATTSBERG: A forgery! Where did you see it? Who had it?

MONSEN: I'm not saying.

BRATTSBERG: Ha, we'll soon find out.

MONSEN: Listen to me –

BRATTSBERG: Be quiet! So it has come to this? Forgery! And *I'm* involved in the filthy business! No wonder that I'm bracketed with the rest! But now I shall take a hand!

MONSEN: Chamberlain, for your own sake – and for others' sakes, too –

BRATTSBERG: Out of my sight! Get out! You're at the bottom of all this. Yes, indeed. 'Woe unto him by whom offence cometh!' It's a sinful life that you lead at Storli. Look at the company you keep – people from Kristiania and such places, who don't mind whom they're with so long as they can eat and drink ... Hold your tongue! I've seen your fine guests at Christmas, tearing along the country roads like a pack of howling wolves. What's worse, there have been scandals about you and your own maidservants. It was your debauchery and cruelty that drove your wife out of her mind.

MONSEN: You've gone too far. You'll be sorry for this.

BRATTSBERG: Devil take your threats. What can you do to me? To *me*? You asked what I have against you – now I've told you. Now you know why I've had you barred from decent society.

MONSEN: Yes, and now I'll drag your decent society down –

BRATTSBERG: There is the way out!

MONSEN: I know my way, Chamberlain. [*He goes out at the back.*]

BRATTSBERG [*opening the door on the right, and calling*]: Ringdal! Ringdal, come in here.

RINGDAL: Sir?

BRATTSBERG [*calling into the drawing-room*]: Doctor – would you mind ...? Well, Ringdal, my prophecies are being fulfilled.

FJELDBO: Did you want something, Chamberlain?

RINGDAL: Have you been prophesying, sir?

BRATTSBERG: Doctor, you've always said that I was exaggerating when I maintained that Monsen was corrupting the people here. .... Well, what do you say to this?

FJELDBO: What's happened?

BRATTSBERG: Fine goings on, I can tell you. Just imagine – there are forged bills circulating here!

RINGDAL: Forged ...?

BRATTSBERG: Forged bills, yes. And whose name do you think is on them? Mine!

90

FJELDBO: But who's done this, for God's sake?

BRATTSBERG: How can I say – do I know all the scoundrels here? It will all come out in good time. Doctor, I want you to do something for me – these bills must have gone through either the Savings Bank or the Works Cashier. Drive over to Lundestad's – he's the most intelligent of the Bank directors – and find out if any such bills exist.

FJELDBO: Yes, at once.

RINGDAL: Lundestad is here at the Works today – there's a meeting of the school committee.

BRATTSBERG: All the better. Find him and bring him here.

FJELDBO: I'll see to it at once. [*He goes out at the back.*]

BRATTSBERG: And, Ringdal, you must make inquiries at the Cashier's. As soon as we get to the bottom of this, we'll inform the Police. I'll have no mercy on the scoundrels!

RINGDAL: Very good, sir. Good heavens, I'd never have believed such a thing.

[*He goes out to the right. The* CHAMBERLAIN *takes a few paces up and down the room, then, just as he is about to go to his study,* ERIK *comes in from the back.*]

ERIK: Father dear –

BRATTSBERG: Ah, Erik –

ERIK: I particularly want to talk to you.

BRATTSBERG: Hm, I'm not really in the mood to talk to anyone, but what is it?

ERIK: Well, Father, you know that up to now I've never involved you in any business dealings. . . .

BRATTSBERG: No – and I should certainly have declined.

ERIK: But today I'm forced –

BRATTSBERG: What are you forced to do?

ERIK: Father, you must help me.

BRATTSBERG: Money! Well, you can be quite sure that I shall not.

ERIK: Just this once. I swear to you that after this, I'll never

. . . The fact is that, to a certain extent, I'm involved with Monsen of Storli.

BRATTSBERG: I know, you have a very promising speculation on hand.

ERIK: A speculation – us? No. Who told you that?

BRATTSBERG: Monsen himself.

ERIK: Has Monsen been here?

BRATTSBERG: Just now. I showed him the door.

ERIK: Father, if you don't help me I'm ruined.

BRATTSBERG: You?

ERIK: Yes. Monsen had advanced me money. I had to pay a terrible rate on it, and, what's more, the bill is due now.

BRATTSBERG: So that's it. What did I tell you?

ERIK: Oh, I know. But now it's too late to talk –

BRATTSBERG: Ruined. In two years! Well, what else could you expect? What were *you* doing among charlatans who dazzle men's eyes with money that doesn't exist? They were no fit company for you. With these people, you must be cunning yourself or you get the worst of it – as you realize now.

ERIK: Father, will you help me, or not?

BRATTSBERG: No. For the last time, I will not.

ERIK: It's my honour that's at stake.

BRATTSBERG: Oh, spare me the high-sounding phrases. There's no honour in successful business – rather the reverse, I should think. Go home and make up your accounts – pay what you owe, and have done with it. And the sooner the better.

ERIK: Ah, you don't know . . .!

[SELMA *and* THORA *come from the drawing-room.*]

SELMA: Do I hear Erik? Good heavens, what's the matter?

BRATTSBERG: Nothing. Go back to the drawing-room.

SELMA: No, I'm not going: I want to know. Erik, what's the matter?

ERIK: It's just that I'm ruined.

THORA: Ruined?

BRATTSBERG: You see!

SELMA: How are you ruined?

ERIK: In every way.

SELMA: Do you mean your money?

ERIK: Money, home, inheritance – everything.

SELMA: Yes – that is everything for you.

ERIK: Let's go, Selma. You're all that I have left now. We must face this blow together.

SELMA: Face the blow together? [*With a cry*] Do you think I'm good enough for that now?

BRATTSBERG: In God's name –

ERIK: What do you mean?

THORA: Oh, Selma, mind what you're saying?

SELMA: No, I won't. I can't lie and pretend and hold my tongue any longer. Now you're going to hear. I won't face anything.

ERIK: Selma!

BRATTSBERG: What are you saying, child?

SELMA: How you've wronged me . . . shamefully, all of you! I must always be the one to take, I've never been allowed to give. I've been like a pauper among you. You've never come and asked any sacrifice from me; I've never been thought fit to face anything. I hate you – I loathe you!

ERIK: What do you mean?

BRATTSBERG: She isn't herself – she's ill.

SELMA: How I've longed to share your troubles! But if ever I asked about anything I was sent about my business with a clever joke. You dressed me like a doll, and played with me as they play with a child. Oh, it would have been so wonderful to suffer with you. I'm a serious person, with a longing for all the higher, more inspiring things in life. And it's only now – when Erik has nothing else – that I'm good enough. But I don't mean to be anyone's last hope. I'll have nothing to do with your troubles. . . . I'm leaving you. I'd rather dance and sing in the streets! Leave me alone – leave me alone! [*She rushes out at the back.*]

BRATTSBERG: Thora, did she really mean that, or . . .?

THORA: Oh yes, she meant it – I see it now. [*She follows.*]

ERIK: No! I'd lose everything else, but not *her*! Selma! [*He goes after them.*]

RINGDAL [*coming from the right*]: Sir –

BRATTSBERG: What is it?

RINGDAL: I've just come from the Cashier's –

BRATTSBERG: The Cashier? Well – the bill?

RINGDAL: Everything's in order: there never was a bill with your name on it.

[FJELDBO *and* LUNDESTAD *enter from the back.*]

FJELDBO: False alarm, Chamberlain.

BRATTSBERG: Ah! And at the Savings Bank, too?

LUNDESTAD: Not a thing. In all the years that I've been a director at the Bank I've never once seen your name. That's to say, except on your son's bill.

BRATTSBERG: My son's bill?

LUNDESTAD: Yes, the bill you backed for him earlier this year.

BRATTSBERG: My son? My son! How dare you . . .?

LUNDESTAD: But good heavens, don't you remember? Your son's bill for two thousand dollars –

BRATTSBERG [*feeling for a chair*]: Merciful God . . .

FJELDBO: For heaven's sake –

RINGDAL: It's impossible!

BRATTSBERG [*having sunk down on a chair*]: Wait a minute – wait a minute . . . my son's bill? Endorsed by me? For two thousand dollars?

FJELDBO [*to* LUNDESTAD]: This bill – is it in the Bank?

LUNDESTAD: Not now. It was redeemed last week by Monsen.

BRATTSBERG: By Monsen?

RINGDAL: Monsen may still be at the Works, I'll go and –

BRATTSBERG: Stay where you are.

HEJRE [*coming in at the back*]: Good morning, gentlemen. Good morning, my most honoured Chamberlain. I'm really most grateful for a delightful evening yesterday. And now I have a story for you. . . .

RINGDAL: I'm afraid we're busy.

HEJRE: Someone else has been busy, too – the Squire of Storli, for instance!

BRATTSBERG: Monsen?

HEJRE: Tee-hee, it's an odd story! The Election campaign's in full swing, and what d'you think is the latest? They want to bribe you, Chamberlain!

LUNDESTAD: You say . . . *bribe*?

BRATTSBERG: The tree is judged by its fruit.

HEJRE: Yes, upon my soul, it's the clumsiest thing I've ever heard. I looked in at Madam Rundholmen's for a glass of bitters, and there were Monsen and Stensgård drinking port . . . filthy stuff, I'm damned if I'd touch it – not that they offered me any, I'm sorry to say. And Monsen said: 'What'll you bet me the Chamberlain votes on our side at the Preliminaries tomorrow?' 'Well,' I said, 'how will you manage that?' 'Ah,' he said, 'with the help of this bill.'

FJELDBO AND RINGDAL: A bill?

LUNDESTAD: At the Preliminaries?

BRATTSBERG: What else?

HEJRE: Well, that's all I know. I heard it was a bill for two thousand dollars. So that's the price they put on people of standing! Oh, it's disgraceful!

BRATTSBERG: A bill for two thousand dollars?

RINGDAL: And Monsen has it?

HEJRE: No, he made it over to Stensgård.

LUNDESTAD: Ah –

FJELDBO: To Stensgård?

BRATTSBERG: You're sure of that?

HEJRE: Oh Lord, yes, I'm quite sure. 'You must make the best use of it you can,' he said. But I don't see –

LUNDESTAD: Come here, Mr Hejre – and you too, Ringdal. ... [*The three talk quietly together at the back.*]

FJELDBO: Chamberlain –

BRATTSBERG: Well?

FJELDBO: Your son's bill will be honoured, of course?

BRATTSBERG: Surely that's obvious.

FJELDBO: Of course. But suppose the forged bill were to turn up one day?

BRATTSBERG: I will lay no information with the authorities.

FJELDBO: Obviously. But you must do more than that.

BRATTSBERG [*rising*]: I can do nothing more.

FJELDBO: Yes – for God's sake – you not only can, you must! You must save the unfortunate boy.

BRATTSBERG: But how?

FJELDBO: Quite easily. By acknowledging the signature.

BRATTSBERG: Are you suggesting, Doctor, that a Brattsberg would do such a thing?

FJELDBO: I'm making the best suggestion that I can, Chamberlain.

BRATTSBERG: And do you suppose for a single instant that I would countenance a lie – be as underhand as the forgers themselves?

FJELDBO: You know the consequences if you don't?

BRATTSBERG: That is between the criminal and the Law. [*He goes out to the left.*]

The curtain falls

ACT FOUR

A sitting-room at Madam Rundholmen's hotel.
There is an entrance at the back, and smaller doors at either side.
To the right is a window, and in front of it a table with writing
materials; farther back, in the middle of the room, is another table.

MADAM [*off to the left, shouting*]: Yes, I've had enough of it!
You can tell them they've come here to vote, not to drink.
If they don't want to wait, they can please themselves.

STENSGÅRD [*entering at the back*]: Good morning. Ahem!
Madam Rundholmen! [*He goes and knocks at the door on the
left.*] Good morning, Madam Rundholmen!

MADAM [*off*]: Ugh, who's that?

STENSGÅRD: It's me – Stensgård, May I come in?

MADAM: No, you can't. I should think not, indeed! I'm not
dressed.

STENSGÅRD: Well! What's made you so late today?

MADAM: Oh, I was up before the devil got his shoes on – but
I must make myself look respectable. [*She peeps out, with a
scarf over her head.*] Well, what is it? No, Mr Stensgård,
you're not to look at me. Oh, here comes someone else!
[*She slams the door.*]

ASLAKSEN [*coming from the back with a bundle of newspapers*]:
Good morning, Mr Stensgård.

STENSGÅRD: Well, is it in?

ASLAKSEN: Yes, here it is – look. 'Independence Day Celebrations. From our Special Correspondent.' And here on
the opposite page is the founding of the League; and here's
your speech – up here. I've put all the abusive bits in heavy
type.

STENSGÅRD: It looks to me as if it's all in heavy type.

ASLAKSEN: Well, it is, pretty nearly.

STENSGÅRD: You got your Extra Edition distributed yesterday?

ASLAKSEN: Of course – all over the district. To subscribers and everyone else. D'you want to see it [*handing him a copy*]?

STENSGÅRD [*running his eye over it*]: '... Our worthy Member, Anders Lundestad, proposes to resign from the Storthing ... long and faithful service ... as the poet says,[22] "Now Labourer, to your well-earned rest."' Hm. '... The League of Youth, the organization founded on Independence Day ... Mr Stensgård, the leading spirit of the League ... timely reforms ... easier credit. ...' Yes, a good bit of writing. Has polling started?

ASLAKSEN: It's in full swing. The League – voters and others – is very much to the fore.

STENSGÅRD: Oh, devil take the others ... between ourselves, of course. Well, go out and talk to the ones you think are wavering –

ASLAKSEN: All right.

STENSGÅRD: You can tell them that Lundestad and I are in agreement.

ASLAKSEN: Leave it to me – I know the local conditions.

STENSGÅRD: One thing more ... be a good chap, Aslaksen, and don't drink today.

ASLAKSEN: Now, look here –

STENSGÅRD: We'll make a night of it later on. Meanwhile, remember how much this means to you, too – *and* your paper. So, my dear chap, just show me how you can –

ASLAKSEN: All right, that's enough. I can take care of myself. [*He goes out to the right.*]

MADAM [*coming in from the left, flashily dressed*]: Now, Mr Stensgård, here I am! Was it something important?

STENSGÅRD: No, just to ask – would you mind letting me know as soon as Mr Monsen arrives?

MADAM: Oh, he won't be here today.

STENSGÅRD: No?

MADAM: No, he was driving out this way at four o'clock this morning – he's always on the road these days. He came in and found me more or less in bed. Wanted to borrow money, if you please!

STENSGÅRD: Monsen did?

MADAM: Yes, he's a great one for getting through the money. Let's hope he's lucky today. And that goes for you, too – they do say you're going to stand for the Storthing.

STENSGÅRD: I? Nonsense – who says so?

MADAM: Oh, it was some of Anders Lundestad's people.

HEJRE [*entering from the back*]: Well, well – good morning. I'm not interrupting you?

MADAM: Lord, no.

HEJRE: Bless my soul, how magnificent! Is all this finery on my account?

MADAM: Well, of course. We always dress up to please the bachelors, don't we?

HEJRE: For wooers, Madam Rundholmen, for wooers! Alas, my lawsuits take up all my time.

MADAM: Rubbish! There's always time to get married.

HEJRE: No, by Jove, there isn't. Marriage is a thing that takes all your attention. Well, how shall I put it? Since you can't have me, you must make the best of someone else. Yes, you ought to get married.

MADAM: You know, I do sometimes think about it.

HEJRE: Naturally. Once one has tasted the joys of marriage ... Of course, the late Mr Rundholmen was a prize specimen ...

MADAM: Oh, I wouldn't say that – he was rough and he drank. . . . Still, a husband's a husband!

HEJRE: Very true, Madam Rundholmen; a husband's a husband, and a widow's a widow.

MADAM: And business is business. Oh, when I think of how much I have to see to, it's enough to drive me crazy. They all want to buy, but when settling-day comes round, then I have to use summonses and Court orders to get it out of them! I'll soon have to get a private lawyer all to myself!

HEJRE: You know what, Madam Rundholmen – upon my word you ought to get Mr Stensgård. He's unemployed – and a bachelor.

MADAM: Ugh! You've got a wicked tongue! I won't listen to you any more! [She goes off to the right.]

HEJRE: A substantial woman, sir! Smart and sprightly. No children to date, and money well invested. Educated, too, and very well read, my boy.

STENSGÅRD: Well read, is she?

HEJRE: Tee-hee, she ought to be – she had two years in the Lending Library here. .... Still, I expect you have other things on your mind today.

STENSGÅRD: Not at all – I may not even vote. But who are you voting for, Mr Hejre?

HEJRE: I'm not a voter, my dear sir. There was only *one* dog kennel for sale on the books, and you've got that.

STENSGÅRD: If you're ever homeless, I'll give it up to you.

HEJRE: Tee-hee! You're full of jokes. Ah, Youth – with its wonderful sense of humour! Well, I'll go out now and have a look at the menagerie. Your whole League's turned out, I hear. [Seeing DR FJELDBO, who enters from the back] And here's the Doctor, too! You must be here in the cause of Science?

FJELDBO: Of Science?

HEJRE: Yes, to study the epidemic! There's a virulent out-break of *Rabies Agitatoria* here! God be with you, my dear young friends. [He goes out to the right.]

STENSGÅRD: Tell me quickly, have you seen the Chamber-lain today?

FJELDBO: Yes.

STENSGÅRD: What did he say?

FJELDBO: Say?

STENSGÅRD: Yes, of course – I've written to him.

FJELDBO: You have? What did you write?

STENSGÅRD: I told him that I'm still hoping to marry his daughter, that I want to talk to him about it, and that I'll call on him about it tomorrow.

FJELDBO: Well, at any rate, you'd better put off your visit – it's his birthday tomorrow, there'll be a big crowd there –

STENSGÅRD: Exactly – the bigger the better. Let me tell you, I've got good cards in my hand.

FJELDBO: And perhaps you've already dropped a hint as to what those cards are?

STENSGÅRD: How do you mean?

FJELDBO: I mean, perhaps you've garnished your declaration of love with a few little threats and so on?

STENSGÅRD: Fjeldbo, you've seen my letter!

FJELDBO: No, I assure you.

STENSGÅRD: Well, yes, to tell the truth, I have threatened him, in a way.

FJELBDO: Ah, then, in a way, I have an answer for you.

STENSGÅRD: An answer? Out with it, man!

FJELDBO [showing him a sealed paper]: Look. The Chamberlain's voting paper.

STENSGÅRD: And who is he voting for?

FJELDBO: Not for you, at any rate.

STENSGÅRD: Who, then? Tell me who.

FJELDBO: For the Sheriff and the Dean.

STENSGÅRD: What? Not even for Lundestad?

FJELDBO: No. And do you know why? Because Lundestad means to propose you as his successor.

STENSGÅRD: And he dares to go as far as that?

FJELDBO: He does. What's more, he said: 'If you meet Stensgård, tell him how I'm voting – that'll show him how things stand between us.'

STENSGÅRD: Good – if that's how he wants it.

FJELDBO: Be careful. It's dangerous work pulling down an old tower – you may get caught in the debris.

STENSGÅRD: Ah, I've got a bit wiser these last few days.

FJELDBO: Oh? You haven't got too clever to let old Lundestad do what he likes with you?

STENSGÅRD: Do you suppose I haven't seen through Lundestad? Do you think I don't know that he came to me because he thought I'd won the Chamberlain over, and because he wanted to break up our League and keep Monsen out?

FJELDBO: But now that he knows that you haven't won over the Chamberlain –

STENSGÅRD: He's gone too far to be able to draw back. Besides, I've made good use of the time, distributing my leaflets. Most of his supporters won't turn out; mine are all here.

FJELDBO: A lot can happen between the Preliminaries and the Storthing!

STENSGÅRD: Lundestad knows quite well that if he lets me down over the Preliminaries, I'll raise an agitation that will unseat him from the Town Council.

FJELDBO: So you've thought it all out! But you realize that, if you're going to succeed, you'll need to be more firmly rooted here than you are?

STENSGÅRD: Yes, the people always want material guarantees – interests in common –

FJELDBO: Exactly. So Miss Brattsberg is to be sacrificed.

STENSGÅRD: Sacrificed? That would make me nothing but a scoundrel. No. I feel sure it'll be for her happiness. What is it, Fjeldbo? Look here, have you got something up your sleeve?

FJELDBO: I?

STENSGÅRD: You have! You've been quietly working behind my back. Why? Won't you be open about it?

FJELDBO: Frankly, no. You're too dangerous – too unscrupulous . . . all right, let's say too reckless – for anyone to risk being open with you. Anything you knew, you wouldn't hesitate to use. But I'll tell you this as a friend: put Miss Brattsberg out of your head.

STENSGÅRD: I can't. I must get away from these sordid surroundings – I can't live in squalor any longer. Here I have to rub shoulders with every Peer Olsen and Ole Peersen, whisper in corners with them, drink with them, laugh at their tap-room jokes, let board-school boys and half-educated louts be familiar with me. In these conditions, how can I really love the People? All the sparkle would go out of my speeches. I need elbow-room, and fresh air to breathe. I keep longing for the company of exquisite women. . . . I want a life with beauty in it. I lie here in a muddy backwater, while out there the clear, blue water streams past me. . . . Oh, you wouldn't understand!

LUNDESTAD [*coming in from the back*]: Ah, there's always good company here! Good morning.

STENSGÅRD: I've some news for you, Mr Lundestad. Do you know how the Chamberlain's voting?

FJELDBO: Shut up! That's a shabby trick!

STENSGÅRD: I can't help that. He's voting for the Sheriff and the Dean.

LUNDESTAD: Well, we might have known it. You ruined everything with him – and I particularly told you to play your cards carefully.

STENSGÅRD: I'm playing carefully from now on.

FJELDBO: Mind the others don't outplay you! [*He goes out to the right.*]

STENSGÅRD: That fellow's got something up his sleeve, do you know what it is?

LUNDESTAD: No, I don't. But that reminds me – I see you're featuring in the paper today.

STENSGÅRD: I am?

LUNDESTAD: Yes, with a charming funeral oration over me.

STENSGÅRD: That's that wretch Aslaksen.

LUNDESTAD: Your attack on the Chamberlain's in it, too.

STENSGÅRD: I don't mind about that. If I want to get at the Chamberlain, I have better weapons than that.

LUNDESTAD: Oh?

STENSGÅRD: Do you know about this bill? Look at it – is it genuine?

LUNDESTAD: Genuine – that bill?

STENSGÅRD: Yes. Take a good look at it.

HEJRE [coming in from the right]: What the devil ...? Well well! No, gentlemen, please don't move. D'you know what you remind me of? A summer night in the far north ...

LUNDESTAD: That's an odd simile.

HEJRE: A very obvious one – the setting sun and the rising sun in conjunction! Charming! By the way, what the deuce is going on outside? The inhabitants are running round like frightened hens – cackling and squawking as if they don't know which perch they want to settle on.

STENSGÅRD: Well, this is an important day.

HEJRE: You and your 'important day'! No, my dear chap, this is something quite different. There are whispers of a great failure – a bankruptcy. ... Oh, not a political one, Mr Lundestad – heaven forbid.

STENSGÅRD: Bankruptcy?

HEJRE: Tee-hee! That makes our lawyer sit up. Yes, bankruptcy. Someone's tottering – the axe is laid to the root of the tree ... enough said! Two strange gentlemen have driven past. ... But where to? Who is it they want? Do you know anything, Mr Lundestad?

LUNDESTAD: I know how to keep my mouth shut, Mr Hejre.

HEJRE: Of course you do, you're a political figure – a statesman. ... Tee-hee! My goodness, I must be off to throw some light on the situation. It's really most amusing to watch these bill-jobbers; they're like beads on a string – when one slips off, all the rest follow. [He goes out at the back.]

STENSGÅRD: Is there anything in all this gossip?

LUNDESTAD: You showed me a bill; I think I saw Erik Brattsberg's name on it.

STENSGÅRD: And the Chamberlain's.

LUNDESTAD: And then you asked me if it was genuine.

STENSGÅRD: Yes – look at it.

LUNDESTAD: Perhaps it's not altogether genuine.

STENSGÅRD: You see it too, then?

LUNDESTAD: What?

STENSGÅRD: That it's forged.

LUNDESTAD: Forged? Well, forged bills are really the safest – they get redeemed first!

STENSGÅRD: But what do you think? Isn't it forged?

LUNDESTAD: This is a bad business. . . .

STENSGÅRD: In what way?

LUNDESTAD: I'm afraid, Mr Stensgård, there are too many of these things about. . . .

STENSGÅRD: What? Surely it isn't possible that –

LUNDESTAD: If Erik Brattsberg slips off the string, then those nearest to him will follow.

STENSGÅRD [*clutching his arm*]: What do you mean by 'those nearest'?

LUNDESTAD: What's nearer than father and son?

STENSGÅRD: But, good God . . .!

LUNDESTAD: I've said nothing. Remember it was Daniel Hejre who was talking about bankruptcy and ruin. . . .

STENSGÅRD: This has come as a thunderbolt to me!

LUNDESTAD: Ah, many a substantial man comes to grief. Probably he's too good-natured – going backing bills like that. . . . Ready money isn't always easy to find – property has to be sold, and it goes for a song. . . .

STENSGÅRD: And of course all this affects – it affects the children, too.

LUNDESTAD: Yes, I'm really very sorry for Miss Brattsberg. What she got from her mother wasn't a great deal, and goodness only knows if what little she has is properly tied up. . . .

STENSGÅRD: Ah, now I understand Fjeldbo's advice – he's a real friend!

LUNDESTAD: What did Dr Fjeldbo say?

STENSGÅRD: He's too loyal to say anything, but I understand him, all the same. And I understand you too, now, Mr Lundestad.

LUNDESTAD: Didn't you understand me before?

STENSGÅRD: Not entirely; I forgot the proverb about the rats and the sinking ship.

LUNDESTAD: That wasn't a very nice thing to say. But what's the matter? You don't look at all well. Good gracious, I hope I haven't said anything to upset you.

STENSGÅRD: Upset me?

LUNDESTAD: Ah, yes, I see. What an old fool I am! My dear Mr Stensgård, if you really love the girl, what does it matter whether she's rich or poor?

STENSGÅRD: Matter? Oh, not at all. . . .

LUNDESTAD: Good gracious, a happy marriage isn't a matter of money, is it?

STENSGÅRD: No, of course not.

LUNDESTAD: And if you put your back into it and work hard you could soon be on your feet again. Don't let poverty frighten you. I know what love is; I used to read a lot about it in my young days . . . a happy home – a faithful wife. . . . Oh, my dear, dear fellow, don't do anything that you'll regret all the rest of your life!

STENSGÅRD: How is this going to affect you?

LUNDESTAD: Oh, that must look after itself. Do you think I would ask you to sacrifice your heart's desire for my sake?

STENSGÅRD: But I'll make the sacrifice! Yes, I'll show you that I'm strong enough for that. Out there stands the expectant throng, beseeching my help in a wordless plea! How could I have the heart to refuse them?

LUNDESTAD: Yes, but the Property Qualification?

STENSGÅRD: I shall manage to satisfy the demands of my fellow-citizens in that respect, Mr Lundestad. I see the way – a new way – that I will take. I renounce the joy of working in poverty for the woman I love. I say to the People: 'Here I am – take me!'

LUNDESTAD [*looking at him in silent admiration as he presses his hand*]: You are a man of great gifts, Mr Stensgård! [*He goes out to the right.*]

[STENSGÅRD *paces up and down the room for a while, now stopping at the window, now running his fingers through his hair. After a little,* BASTIAN MONSEN *comes in from the back.*]

BASTIAN: Here I am, old man![23]

STENSGÅRD: Where have you come from?

BASTIAN: From the Nation!

STENSGÅRD: The Nation? What do you mean by that?

BASTIAN: Don't you know what the Nation means? It means the People – the Common People – the People who have nothing and who *are* nothing, but who lie in chains –

STENSGÅRD: What monkey-tricks have you been up to?

BASTIAN: What do you mean?

STENSGÅRD: I've noticed lately that you've taken to imitating me; you're even copying my clothes and my style of writing. Stop it.

BASTIAN: Why? Don't we belong to the same Party?

STENSGÅRD: Yes, but I won't have this – you're making yourself ridiculous.

BASTIAN: What, by being like you?

STENSGÅRD: By aping me. Kindly stop it, Monsen, it's a disgusting sight! Now tell me – when does your father come back?

BASTIAN: I've no idea. I think he's gone over to Kristiania, he may not be back for a week.

STENSGÅRD: Oh? That'll be awkward. But they say he has a big business deal in hand?

BASTIAN: I've got business, too – look, Stensgård, you must do me a favour.

STENSGÅRD: Of course – what is it?

BASTIAN: I feel so energetic, thanks to you; you've woken me up. I must do something, you know – I want to get married.

STENSGÅRD: Married? Who to?

BASTIAN: Sh! Someone in this house.

STENSGÅRD: Madam Rundholmen?

BASTIAN: Sh! Yes, she's the one. Put in a good word for me, will you? It'd be the making of me. She's got a good business here, and she's been in with the Brattsbergs ever since her sister was housekeeper there. If I could get her, perhaps I'd be able to get jobs from the Council. Yes, on the whole, I love her – damned if I don't.

STENSGÅRD: Love! Love! Drop that nauseating hypocrisy!

BASTIAN: Hypocrisy?

STENSGÅRD: Yes, you're even lying to yourself. Here you are, talking about love and jobs from the Council in the same breath. Do at least call things by their real names. It's all rather sordid, and I won't have anything to do with it.

BASTIAN: But listen –

STENSGÅRD: Leave me out of it, I tell you. [*To* FJELDBO, *as he comes in from the right*] Well, how's the voting going?

FJELDBO: It's going splendidly for you. I was talking to Lundestad just now, and he said you were getting most of the votes.

STENSGÅRD: Am I really?

FJELDBO: But what the devil's the good of that? You haven't got the Property Qualification, so –

STENSGÅRD [*quietly*]: Isn't that damnable?

FJELDBO: Well, you can't do two things at once. What you win on one, you lose on the other. Good-bye. [*He goes out at the back.*]

BASTIAN: What did he mean about winning and losing?

STENSGÅRD: I'll tell you later. Now listen, my dear Monsen, to get back to what we were talking about – I promised to put in a good word for you –

BASTIAN: Did you? I thought you flatly refused.

STENSGÅRD: Nonsense, you wouldn't let me finish. I was going to say that there's something sordid about mixing love and business – something that offends all a man's finer feelings. And so, my dear friend, if you really love the girl –

BASTIAN: Widow . . .

STENSGÅRD: Well, it's the same thing. I believe that when one really loves a woman, that in itself should be enough to –

BASTIAN: That's what I think, too. So you'll put in a word for me?

STENSGÅRD: With the greatest of pleasure. On one condition.

BASTIAN: Well?

STENSGÅRD: Fair's fair, my dear Bastian; you must put in a good word for me in return.

BASTIAN: Me? Who with?

STENSGÅRD: Haven't you really noticed? And it's right under your nose, too.

BASTIAN: You can't possibly mean –

STENSGÅRD: Your sister Ragna, my dear fellow. Yes, that's who it is. Oh, you don't know how attractive I found the way she goes so quietly and unobtrusively about her household duties. . . .

BASTIAN: Well, is it possible!

STENSGÅRD: Surely *your* sharp eyes had noticed it?

BASTIAN: Well, there was a time when I thought – But now everyone says you're starting to go to the Chamberlain's –

STENSGÅRD: Oh, the Chamberlain's! Well, to be frank with you, Monsen, there *was* a time when perhaps I wavered a little, but that's all over now, thank heaven – now I'm quite sure of myself and what I must do.

BASTIAN: Shake on it! I'll put in a word for you, trust me. As for Ragna, she'd never dare do anything but what Father and I want.

STENSGÅRD: Ah yes, your father . . . that's what I wanted to talk about –

BASTIAN: Sh! Oh, damn – I can hear Madam Rundholmen. Speak up for me! Not if she's busy, though – she's a bit irritable then. Well, do the best you can for me, my dear chap, and leave the rest to me. Have you seen Aslaksen?

STENSGÅRD: He's at the Polling Booth.

[BASTIAN *goes out at the back, as* MADAM RUNDHOLMEN *comes in from the right.*]

MADAM: Everything's going swimmingly, Mr Stensgård; they're all voting for you.

STENSGÅRD: That's surprising.

MADAM: Yes, Lord knows what Monsen'll say.

STENSGÅRD: Look, I want a word with you, Madam Rundholmen.

MADAM: What about?

STENSGÅRD: Will you listen to me?

MADAM: Oh, my goodness yes, I'd like to.

STENSGÅRD: Well . . . you were saying just now how lonely you were . . .

MADAM: Oh, that was that nasty old man Hejre.

STENSGÅRD: You were complaining how hard it was being a widow . . .

MADAM: You should just try it, Mr Stensgård.

STENSGÅRD: But if a nice young man were to come along –

MADAM: A nice young man?

STENSGÅRD: – who's always been secretly in love with you –

MADAM: Now, look here, that's quite enough of that!

STENSGÅRD: No, you *must* listen. A young man who also finds it hard to live alone –

MADAM: What about him? I don't know what you're driving at.

STENSGÅRD: And if you could make two people happy, Madam Rundholmen – yourself and –

MADAM: And the nice young man?

STENSGÅRD: Yes. What would you say?

MADAM: Now, Mr Stensgård, you can't be serious!

STENSGÅRD: You don't think I'd fool you? Would you be ready . . .?

MADAM: God knows I would! You dear, sweet –

STENSGÅRD [a step back]: What!

MADAM: Ah! Someone's coming.

[MISS MONSEN comes in hurriedly from the back; she is upset.]

RAGNA: Excuse me, but isn't my father here?

MADAM: Your father? Oh no . . . I don't know, I'm afraid.

RAGNA: Where is he?

MADAM: Your father? Well, he drove past –

STENSGÅRD: On his way to Kristiania.

RAGNA: But that's impossible.

MADAM: Well, he drove past, that I do know. Oh, Miss Monsen, you wouldn't believe how happy I am. Wait a bit while I run down to the cellar for a bottle of the real stuff! [She goes out to the left.]

STENSGÅRD: Tell me, Miss Monsen, are you really looking for your father?

RAGNA: Yes, you heard me say so.

STENSGÅRD: And you didn't know he'd gone away?

RAGNA: How should I? No one tells me anything. But to Kristiania? – that's impossible. They would have met him. Good-bye!

STENSGÅRD [intercepting her]: Ragna, listen! Why have you changed so towards me?

RAGNA: I? Please stand aside – let me go.

STENSGÅRD: No, you mustn't go. Your coming here at this

moment is a sign from heaven. Oh, don't be shy with me, you never used to be.

RAGNA: Oh, that's all over – thank heaven.

STENSGÅRD: Then why . . .?

RAGNA: I've come to know you better – it's as well I found out in time.

STENSGÅRD: Oh? Has someone been lying about me? Well, it's probably my own fault. I've been in rather a muddle, but that's all over now. When I look at you I feel a different man. It's really and truly you that I care for – it's you I love, Ragna . . . you and no one else.

RAGNA: Let me go – you frighten me!

STENSGÅRD: But tomorrow, Ragna – may I come and talk to you?

RAGNA: Yes, yes – only for heaven's sake, not today.

STENSGÅRD: Only not today? Hurray! I've won! Oh, I'm so happy!

MADAM [*bringing wine and cake from the left*]: There! Now we'll have a glass together for luck.

STENSGÅRD: For luck in love. Here's to love and happiness! To tomorrow! [*Drinks.*]

HELLE [*coming from the right, to* RAGNA]: Have you found him?

RAGNA: No, he isn't here. Come on.

MADAM: But what's up, for heaven's sake?

HELLE: Nothing, only some strangers have come to Storli, and –

RAGNA: Thank you for all your kindness, Madam Rundholmen.

MADAM: Oh, have you got visitors on your hands again?

RAGNA: Yes, – I'm afraid I must go home. Good-bye.

STENSGÅRD: Good-bye – till tomorrow.

[HELLE *and* MISS MONSEN *go out at the back.*]

HEJRE [*coming in from the right*]: Aha! It's going like a house on fire! They're all cackling 'Stensgård – Stensgård –

Stensgård!' and they're all voting for him. You should have voted for him, Madam Rundholmen.

MADAM: Ah, now you're talking! But are they *all* for him?

HEJRE: They certainly are! Mr Stensgård 'enjoys the confidence of the People' as they put it. Old Lundestad's going round with a face like a pickled gherkin – it's a wonderful sight!

MADAM: They shan't vote for him for nothing. Even if I can't vote, I can stand treat! [*She goes out to the left.*]

HEJRE: You really have quite a way with the widows, you know, Mr Stensgård. I tell you what – you should clinch it with her, then you'd be all right, my boy.

STENSGÅRD: With Madam Rundholmen?

HEJRE: Of course. She's a substantial woman – in every way. She'll be the biggest hen in the coop as soon as that card-castle at Storli comes tumbling down!

STENSGÅRD: There's nothing wrong at Storli, is there?

HEJRE: You have a short memory, my dear sir – hasn't there been talk about ruin and bankruptcy?

STENSGÅRD: Yes, but what of that?

HEJRE: What of it? Well, you tell *me*! People looking for Monsen here – two men going to Storli. . . .

STENSGÅRD: Yes, I know, two guests.

HEJRE: Uninvited guests, my dear young friend. There's a whisper about police and irate creditors – something wrong with the accounts, you'll see! And by the way, what was that paper you got from Monsen yesterday?

STENSGÅRD: Oh, just a paper. Something wrong with the accounts, you say? Look, do you know Chamberlain Brattsberg's signature?

HEJRE: Tee-hee – I should think I do!

STENSGÅRD [*taking out the bill*]: Well, look at this.

HEJRE: Let us look – I'm rather short-sighted. [*Having examined it*] This, my dear sir? This was never the Chamberlain's signature!

STENSGÅRD: Not ...? Then ...?

HEJRE: Was this drawn by Monsen?

STENSGÅRD: No, by Erik Brattsberg.

HEJRE: Rubbish! Let me look. ... [*Looking at the paper and then handing it back*] You can use that to light your cigar!

STENSGÅRD: What? The drawer's name, too?

HEJRE: Forged, young fellow, forged – as sure as my name's Daniel. You've only to cast the sharp eye of suspicion over it –

STENSGÅRD: But how is that possible? Monsen can't have known –

HEJRE: Monsen? No, he's a man who knows nothing about papers – his own or anyone else's. What a good thing it's all over, Mr Stensgård. So gratifying to one's sense of fitness. Ah, I've sometimes found myself burning with righteous indignation – I don't mind admitting it – at having to stand by and look on, while ... enough said. But the really amusing thing about it is that when Monsen topples, the first person he'll bring down with him will be Erik Brattsberg; then Erik'll bring down the Chamberlain –

STENSGÅRD: Yes, that's what Lundestad said.

HEJRE: But of course there are ways and means, even in bankruptcy. Wait and see. I'm a prophet of some standing: Monsen'll go to the lock-up; Erik'll come to an arrangement with his creditors; and the Chamberlain'll be put under trustees, which'll mean that his creditors'll allow him a pension of a couple of thousand dollars a year to live on. That's how it'll be, Mr Stensgård, I know – I know! What do the classics say? '*Fiat justitia, pereat mundus*', which means 'Fie on the justice of this wicked world', my boy!

STENSGÅRD [*pacing the room*]: First one, then the other! Both ways blocked!

HEJRE: What the deuce ...?

STENSGÅRD: And just now, of all times! Just now!

ASLAKSEN [*coming in from the right*]: Congratulations, Mr Deputy, congratulations!

STENSGÅRD: I'm elected?

ASLAKSEN: By a hundred and seventeen votes. Lundestad got fifty-three; the rest are nowhere.

HEJRE: So this is your first step to fame, Mr Stensgård.

ASLAKSEN: And it'll cost you a bowl of punch!

HEJRE: Yes, it's the first step that counts, they say.

ASLAKSEN [*going out to the left and calling*]: Punch all round, Madam Rundholmen! Our new deputy is standing treat!
[LUNDESTAD *enters from the right, followed by a crowd of voters.*]

HEJRE: [*consolingly to* LUNDESTAD]: Fifty-three! What a reward for your grey hairs!

LUNDESTAD [*whispering to* STENSGÅRD]: You'll stand by what we –

STENSGÅRD: What's the good of standing by it when everything's crumbling?

LUNDESTAD: Do you think the game is lost?

ASLAKSEN [*returning from the left*]: Madam Rundholmen's treating us to the punch herself. She says it's up to her.

STENSGÅRD [*struck by a thought*]: Up to Madam Rundholmen?

LUNDESTAD: What?

STENSGÅRD: The game isn't lost, Mr Lundestad. [*He sits at the table to the right and writes.*]

LUNDESTAD [*quietly*]: Listen, Aslaksen – can I get something into the paper for the day after tomorrow?

ASLAKSEN: Of course you can. Is it strong meat?

LUNDESTAD: No, it isn't.

ASLAKSEN: Oh well, I'll take it all the same.

LUNDESTAD: It's my political testament – I'll write it tonight. [*He goes across the room.*]

A MAID [*coming from the left*]: Madam's sent this punch.

ASLAKSEN: Hurrah – now we're getting some life into local conditions!

[*He puts the bowl on the middle table and deals out the punch. During the following he drinks freely. Meanwhile,* BASTIAN MONSEN *has come in from the right.*]

BASTIAN [*low*]. Well? You'll remember my letter?

ASLAKSEN: Don't worry [*tapping his breast-pocket*] I've got it here.

BASTIAN: Give it to her as soon as you can – only make sure she isn't busy, you know.

ASLAKSEN: All right, I know! [*Calling*] Come along, I've filled the glasses!

BASTIAN: You won't lose by it, I'm damned if you will.

ASLAKSEN: Good – good. [*To the* MAID] A lemon, Karen – run like the wind!

[BASTIAN *leaves him.*]

STENSGÅRD: Listen a minute, Aslaksen – will you be out this way tomorrow evening?

ASLAKSEN: Tomorrow evening? Yes, I could be.

STENSGÅRD: Well then, will you look in and give Madam Rundholmen this letter?

ASLAKSEN: From you?

STENSGÅRD: Yes. Put it in your pocket – that's right. To-morrow evening, then.

ASLAKSEN: All right – don't worry.

[*The* MAID *brings the lemon.* STENSGÅRD *goes over to the window.*]

BASTIAN: Well, my dear chap, have you spoken to Madam Rundholmen?

STENSGÅRD: Spoken . . .? Oh yes, I said a word or two.

BASTIAN: And what do you think?

STENSGÅRD: Well . . . we were interrupted. I can't tell you anything definite.

BASTIAN: I'll risk it all the same. She's always complaining about being a widow. An hour from now, it'll all be settled.

STENSGÅRD: An hour from now?

BASTIAN [*seeing* MADAM RUNDHOLMEN *come in from the left*]: Sh! Don't let anyone notice! [*He goes across the room.*]

STENSGÅRD [*going to* ASLAKSEN, *quietly*]: Give me back my letter.

ASLAKSEN: You want it back?

STENSGÅRD: Yes, quickly – I'll deliver it myself.

ASLAKSEN: All right, here you are.

[STENSGÅRD *sticks the letter in his pocket, and mixes with the others during the following.*]

MADAM [*to* BASTIAN]: What do you think of the Election, Mr Monsen?

BASTIAN: Excellent. Stensgård and I are great friends, you know. I shouldn't be surprised if he gets into the House.

MADAM: Your father mightn't like that.

BASTIAN: Oh, Father has so many irons in the fire. Besides, if Stensgård gets in, I fancy the honour will stay in the family!

MADAM: How's that?

BASTIAN: He's going courting –

MADAM: Good heavens, has he said anything?

BASTIAN: Yes, and I've promised to speak for him, too. I'm quite sure it'll be all right – Ragna likes the look of him.

MADAM: Ragna?

LUNDESTAD [*approaching*]: Now then, what are you talking about so earnestly, Madam Rundholmen?

MADAM: Just imagine! He says Stensgård's going courting –

LUNDESTAD: Yes, but the Chamberlain won't be easy to win over.

BASTIAN: The Chamberlain?

LUNDESTAD: He's sure to think her too good for a mere lawyer.

MADAM: Who? Who?

LUNDESTAD: Miss Brattsberg – his daughter, of course.

BASTIAN: He's never after Miss Brattsberg, is he?

LUNDESTAD: He certainly is.

MADAM: Will you swear to that?

BASTIAN: But he told *me* ... Here, let me have a word with you.

[LUNDESTAD *and* BASTIAN *go to the back of the room.*]

MADAM [*going to* STENSGÅRD]: You must be on your guard, Mr Stensgård.

STENSGÅRD: Against whom?

MADAM: Wicked men – they're going round slandering you.

STENSGÅRD: Let them – as long as it doesn't influence one particular person.

MADAM: Who is that?

STENSGÅRD [*surreptitiously passing her the letter*]: Here – read this when you're alone.

MADAM: Ah, I knew it! [*She goes out to the left.*]

RINGDAL [*coming from the right*]: Well, I hear you've come off with flying colours, Mr Stensgård.

STENSGÅRD: Yes, Mr Ringdal, I have – in spite of all your esteemed master's efforts.

RINGDAL: What efforts?

STENSGÅRD: To keep me out.

RINGDAL: He has the right to vote as he pleases – just like everyone else.

STENSGÅRD: It's a pity he won't be having that right for much longer.

RINGDAL: What do you mean by that?

STENSGÅRD: I mean that there's a little matter of certain papers –

RINGDAL: Papers? What papers? What have you got into your head?

STENSGÅRD: Don't pretend you don't know! Isn't there a storm brewing? A crash on a grand scale?

RINGDAL: So everyone's saying.

STENSGÅRD: And I suppose the Chamberlain and Erik aren't involved in it?

RINGDAL: Excuse me, but have you gone mad?

STENSGÅRD: Oh, of course you'd try to hush it up.

RINGDAL: What would be the good? How could a thing like that be hushed up?

STENSGÅRD: Isn't it true, then?

RINGDAL: Not a word of it, as far as the Chamberlain's concerned. How could you believe such a thing? Who gave you the idea?

STENSGÅRD: For the moment I'm not saying.

RINGDAL: Please yourself. But whoever it was must have had a motive.

STENSGÅRD: A motive?

RINGDAL: Yes . . . Try to think – is there anyone here who might see some advantage in keeping you and the Chamberlain apart?

STENSGÅRD: Yes. My goodness, yes there is!

RINGDAL: Actually, the Chamberlain thinks a lot of you.

STENSGÅRD: Does he?

RINGDAL: Yes, and that's what they want to undermine. They're counting on your not knowing the situation here – on your being impulsive and trustful –

STENSGÅRD: Oh, the vipers! And Madam Rundholmen has my letter!

RINGDAL: What letter?

STENSGÅRD: Oh, nothing. But it's not too late. Shall you be seeing the Chamberlain tonight, my dear Mr Ringdal?

RINGDAL: I'm sure to.

STENSGÅRD: Then will you tell him that certain threats that he knows of don't mean anything. Tell him I'll come and see him tomorrow and explain it all.

RINGDAL: You'll come?

STENSGÅRD: Yes, to prove to him . . . Ah yes, proof! Look, Mr Ringdal, give him this bill from me.

RINGDAL: The bill!

STENSGÅRD: Yes, yes; it's something that you wouldn't know about, but just give it to him.

RINGDAL: But really, Mr Stensgård –

STENSGÅRD: And you can add just one word from me: 'This is how I deal with people who try to keep me out at an Election!'

RINGDAL: You can be sure I will. [*He goes out at the back.*]

STENSGÅRD: Look here, Mr Hejre, how could you try to take me in with that story about the Chamberlain?

HEJRE: Take you in?

STENSGÅRD: Precisely. It's a downright lie.

HEJRE: Eh? Well well, I *am* delighted! What do you think, Mr Lundestad? It's a lie – all that about the Chamberlain.

LUNDESTAD: Sh! We're on a false scent. It's someone nearer here.

STENSGÅRD: Nearer? How?

HEJRE: I don't *know* . . . but they *are* talking about Madam Rundholmen. . . .

STENSGÅRD: What!

HEJRE: Well, didn't I foretell it? Hand in glove with that fellow from Storli. . . .

LUNDESTAD: He drove away this morning before it was light –

HEJRE: And the family is out hunting for him –

LUNDESTAD: And the son has been struggling to see that his sister is properly provided for –

STENSGÅRD: Provided for? She was so upset about her father. . . . 'Tomorrow' she said.

HEJRE: Tee-hee – you'll see! Her father's gone and hanged himself, my boy.

ASLAKSEN: Has someone hanged himself?

LUNDESTAD: Mr Hejre says that Monsen of Storli –

MONSEN [*appearing at the back*]: Champagne all round!

ASLAKSEN AND OTHERS: Monsen!

MONSEN: Yes, Monsen! Champagne Monsen! Money Monsen! Wine, damn it!

HEJRE: But, my dear sir –

STENSGÅRD: You! Where have *you* come from?

MONSEN: From a business deal. Cleared a hundred thousand! Hey! Tomorrow I'm giving a thundering big lunch-party at Storli – you're all invited. Where's that champagne? Congratulations on your election, Stensgård.

STENSGÅRD: Yes, let me explain –

MONSEN: Tcha! What do I care? Wine! Where's Madam Rundholmen? [*Starts to go out to the left.*]

MAID [*coming through the door*]: Nobody can go in – Madam's reading a letter.

BASTIAN: Oh, damn! [*Goes out at the back.*]

STENSGÅRD: She's reading a letter?

MAID: Yes, it's upsetting her terribly.

STENSGÅRD: Good-bye, Mr Monsen. Lunch tomorrow at Storli . . .

MONSEN: Good-bye till then.

STENSGÅRD [*quietly*]: Mr Hejre, will you do something for me?

HEJRE: Why, of course, of course!

STENSGÅRD: Blacken my character a bit with Madam Rundholmen – make some insinuation against me – you're so good at that sort of thing.

HEJRE: What the deuce is all this?

STENSGÅRD: I have my reasons. Let's call it a joke – a bet with – with someone you've got a grudge against.

HEJRE: I understand. . . . Enough said.

STENSGÅRD: Don't overdo it, you know – just enough to make her mistrust her opinion of me; make her a little uncertain about me – just for the present, you know.

HEJRE: Trust me. It'll give me the greatest pleasure.

STENSGÅRD: Thank you, thank you. Good-bye for the moment. [*Going to the table*] Mr Lundestad, we'll have a word together at the Chamberlain's tomorrow morning.

LUNDESTAD: You're still hopeful?

STENSGÅRD: Trebly hopeful!

LUNDESTAD: Trebly? I don't understand.

STENSGÅRD: There's no need to. From now on, I'll look after myself. [*He goes out at the back.*]

MONSEN [*with the bowl of punch*]: Another glass, Aslaksen? Where's Bastian?

ASLAKSEN: He's gone out – but he's left me a letter to deliver for him.

MONSEN: Oh?

ASLAKSEN: To Madam Rundholmen.

MONSEN: Well, at last?

ASLAKSEN: But not till tomorrow evening, he said – no sooner and no later – on the dot! Your health!

HEJRE [*to* LUNDESTAD]: What the deuce is going on between Stensgård and Madam Rundholmen, eh?

LUNDESTAD [*quietly*]: He's courting her!

HEJRE: That's what *I* thought. But he's asked me to blacken his character – sow doubts about him. . . . enough said.

LUNDESTAD: And you agreed?

HEJRE: Naturally.

LUNDESTAD: He must have felt that what you promise in the East, you perform in the West!

HEJRE: Tee-hee! The dear boy – he'll find he's wrong this time.

MADAM [*at the left-hand door, with an open letter*]: Where's Mr Stensgård?

HEJRE: He's just kissed your maid and gone, Madam Rundholmen.

The curtain falls

ACT FIVE

A large reception room at the Chamberlain's.
There is an entrance at the back, and doors right and left.

> [RINGDAL *is standing at a table looking through some papers.*
> *There is a knock on the door.*]

RINGDAL: Come in.

FJELDBO [*coming from the back*]: Good morning.

RINGDAL: Good morning, Doctor.

FJELDBO: Well, is everything all right?

RINGDAL: Yes, thank you, it's all right here. But . . .

FJELDBO: But?

RINGDAL: Well, I suppose you've heard the news.

FJELDBO: No, what is it?

RINGDAL: What? You haven't heard what's happened at Storli?

FJELDBO: No.

RINGDAL: Monsen decamped last night.

FJELDBO: Decamped? Monsen?

RINGDAL: Decamped.

FJELDBO: But good heavens –

RINGDAL: There were some odd rumours flying about yesterday, but then Monsen came back, knowing that would put everyone off the scent.

FJELDBO: But why? Why?

RINGDAL: Huge losses in timber, they say. Several firms in Kristiania have stopped payment, and so . . .

FJELDBO: And so he's decamped!

RINGDAL: Over to Sweden, probably. The authorities were at Storli this morning, making inventories and fixing seals.

FJELDBO: And the unfortunate family . . .?

RINGDAL: The son's always kept clear of the business; anyway, I hear he's putting a good face on it.

FJELDBO: Yes, but the daughter?

RINGDAL: Sh! the daughter's here.

FJELDBO: Here?

RINGDAL: The tutor brought her and the children over here this morning, and Miss Brattsberg is looking after them on the quiet.

FJELDBO: But how is she taking it?

RINGDAL: Pretty well, I think. Well, you'll agree that after the way they treated her at home ... Besides, I can tell you, she – Sh, here's the Chamberlain.

BRATTSBERG [coming in from the left]: Ah, my dear Doctor ...

FJELBDO: I'm out here rather early today. Let me wish you many happy returns of the day, Chamberlain.

BRATTSBERG: Heaven preserve us from the sort of happiness that today has brought! But thank you – I know you meant it well.

FJELDBO: Might I ask you, Chamberlain –

BRATTSBERG: Just a minute: You must drop the title from now on.

FJELDBO: What do you mean?

BRATTSBERG: I'm an ironmaster, pure and simple.

FJELDBO: What an extraordinary idea!

BRATTSBERG: I'm resigning my title and my office. I'm sending in my letter of resignation today.

FJELDBO: Surely you ought to sleep on it first?

BRATTSBERG: When the King did me the honour to appoint me to a post at Court, he did so because of the honourable reputation that my family has borne for so many generations.

FJELDBO: Well?

BRATTSBERG: My family has been disgraced just as much as Monsen's. I suppose you've heard about Monsen?

FJELDBO: Yes.

BRATTSBERG [*to* RINGDAL]: Is there any more news?

RINGDAL: No – except that he's dragged down a lot of the younger farmers with him.

BRATTSBERG: And my son?

RINGDAL: Your son has sent me a balance sheet. He can pay in full, but there'll be nothing over.

BRATTSBERG: Hm. Then will you send in my resignation.

RINGDAL: As you say. [*He goes out by the farthest door on the right.*]

FJELDBO: But have you thought it over? Everything can be put right without anyone knowing.

BRATTSBERG: Indeed? Can I wipe out my knowledge of what has happened?

FJELDBO: Ah, but what really *has* happened? He's written to you, admitting his foolishness and asking your forgiveness. This is the first time he's ever committed such a fault. I ask you – what harm has been done?

BRATTSBERG: Would you behave as my son has done?

FJELDBO: The important thing is that he won't do it again.

BRATTSBERG: How do you know he won't do it again?

FJELDBO: If only because of what you've told me yourself – about your daughter-in-law. Whatever else comes of this, that will bring him to his senses.

BRATTSBERG [*pacing the floor*]: My poor Selma! All our happiness and quiet contentment – gone.

FJELDBO: But there is something better than that. Your happiness has only been on the surface. Let me tell you something: in this, as in so many other things, you've built on sand. You've been proud and short-sighted, Chamberlain.

BRATTSBERG [*stopping*]: *I* have?

FJELDBO: Yes, you. You've prided yourself on your family honour, but when has that honour ever been put to the test? How do you know that it would have withstood temptation?

BRATTSBERG: You may spare me your sermons, Doctor. The events of these last few days have not passed without leaving their mark on me.

FJELDBO: I'm sure they haven't; so let it show itself in a greater tolerance and a clearer understanding. You reproach your son, but what have you ever done for him? You've been careful to develop his faculties, but not to mould his character. You've lectured him on what he owes to the honour of his family, but you've never guided and trained him so that it was second nature to him to act honourably.

BRATTSBERG: Do you believe that?

FJELDBO: I not only believe it, I know it. But that's the usual way here; people set more store by what a man knows than by what he *is*. Now we see where that leads. Look at the hundreds of really talented men who go about only half-finished – one thing in their thoughts and feelings, and something quite different in their acts and dealings. Just look at Stensgård.

BRATTSBERG: Stensgård? What about Stensgård?

FJELDBO: A patchwork! I've known him all his life. His father was a little wizened idler – a scarecrow, a nobody. He ran a little general shop, with some pawnbroking on the side – or, more accurately, it was his wife who ran it. She was coarse and gross – the most unwomanly woman I've ever known. She had her husband declared unfit to manage his affairs. She hadn't a kindly thought in her. . . . That was the home where Stensgård grew up. He went to the grammar school. 'He must be educated,' said the mother, 'he'll make a fine debt-collector.' An ugly life at home – high ideals at school; his mind, his character, his will, his talents, all pulling different ways . . . what else could it lead to but a split in his personality?[24]

BRATTSBERG: I don't know anything about that; but I wish I knew what would satisfy you. We're to expect nothing of Stensgård, or of my son either. But of *you*, of course – of you –

FJELDBO: Yes, exactly – of me. Oh, you needn't laugh, I'm not boasting. It's just that I've been lucky enough to have everything that helps to form character and stability. I grew up in an atmosphere of harmony and peace in a quiet middle-class family; my mother was every inch a woman; our wants were never allowed to outrun our means – we had no longings that foundered on the rocks of circumstance; and the hand of death didn't visit our circle to bring emptiness and loss. We loved beauty, and it wasn't just a side-issue, it coloured our whole way of life. There were no excesses, either of thought or emotion –

BRATTSBERG: Well, well – so that is what has made you so utterly perfect!

FJELDBO: I'm very far from claiming *that*. I've had a very fortunate life, and I feel that I have certain obligations.

BRATTSBERG: Possibly. But if Stensgård has no such obligations it's all the more to his credit that he –

FJELDBO: Why? What has he done?

BRATTSBERG: You've misjudged him, my good Doctor. Look. What do you say to this?

FJELDBO: Your son's bill!

BRATTSBERG: Yes, he's sent it back to me.

FJELDBO: Of his own free will?

BRATTSBERG: Of his own free will, and with no conditions. That was fine and noble, and so, from now on, my house is open to him.

FJELDBO: No, stop and think – for your own sake and for your daughter's.

BRATTSBERG: That's enough of that! He's a far better man than you – at least he's straightforward, but you – you're underhand!

FJELDBO: I am?

BRATTSBERG: Yes, you. You've become the guiding spirit

in this house, you come and go freely, I take your advice in everything – and yet . . .

FJELDBO: Well? And yet?

BRATTSBERG: And yet with you, there's something behind it all – something damnably superior that I cannot stand!

FJELDBO: Would you mind explaining?

BRATTSBERG: I? No, it's you who should explain – you certainly should! And now's your chance.

FJELDBO: We're at cross-purposes, Chamberlain. I haven't any bill to send back to you, but it could very well be that I'm making an even greater sacrifice for you.

BRATTSBERG: Oh? How?

FJELDBO: By knowing how to hold my tongue.

BRATTSBERG: To hold your tongue? Shall I tell you what I wish? I wish I could become coarse and foul-mouthed as they are in the League of Youth: you're an egregious prig – and that won't do in our free society. But Stensgård – he's not like that at all, and that's why he's welcome in my house – oh yes, he is. Upon my soul, I wish . . . But it serves you right – you've made your bed, you must lie on it!

LUNDESTAD [*coming from the back*]: Many happy returns, Chamberlain. And may I wish you all the greatest honour –

BRATTSBERG: Oh, to the . . . I almost said 'To the devil with that!' It's all humbug, my dear Lundestad; there's nothing in this world that stands up to the test.

LUNDESTAD: That's what Monsen's creditors are saying.

BRATTSBERG: Yes, this Monsen affair . . . like a thunderbolt, was it not?

LUNDESTAD: Well, Chamberlain, you've been foretelling it for a long time.

BRATTSBERG: Hm – well, I suppose I have. And it's not so long ago either – the day before yesterday, in fact – that he came here to beg me –

FJELDBO: To save him, perhaps.

LUNDESTAD: That wouldn't have been possible, he was too deeply involved. Things are better as they are.

BRATTSBERG: Do you think so? Is it for the better that you were beaten at yesterday's election?

LUNDESTAD: I wasn't beaten; in fact, everything went just as I wanted. Stensgård isn't a man to cross – he has something that the rest of us would give our ears for.

BRATTSBERG: I don't quite see what –

LUNDESTAD: He has the gift of swaying the crowd. And he's lucky enough not to be hampered by scruples or convictions or social position, so that it's very easy for him to be liberal minded.

BRATTSBERG: Really, I should have thought that we're liberal, too.

LUNDESTAD: Oh lord yes, we're Liberals, Chamberlain, there's no doubt about that. But the point is that we're only Liberals for our own sakes. Now, along comes Stensgård, who's Liberal for other people's sake, too. That's what's new about it.

BRATTSBERG: And do you mean to support all these revolutionary ideas?

LUNDESTAD: I've read in the old story-books that once upon a time there were people who could call up spirits, but couldn't lay them again.

BRATTSBERG: My dear Lundestad, how can you, as an intelligent man . . .?

LUNDESTAD: I know it sounds like Papist superstition, Chamberlain, but new ideas are like spirits – you can't lay them again, so the only thing is to make the best one can of them.

BRATTSBERG: Yes; but now that Monsen's come to grief and probably brought down the whole crew of agitators with him –

LUNDESTAD: If Monsen had failed two or three days earlier, things would have been very different.

BRATTSBERG: Yes, unfortunately. You've been too hasty.

LUNDESTAD: I was thinking of you, too, Chamberlain.

BRATTSBERG: Of me?

LUNDESTAD: Our party must keep its reputation in the people's eyes. We represent the old solid Norwegian tradition of honesty. Do you know that, if I had failed Stensgård, he has a paper –

BRATTSBERG: Not any longer.

LUNDESTAD: What?

BRATTSBERG: Here it is.

LUNDESTAD. He's sent it back to you?

BRATTSBERG: Yes, in personal matters, he's a man of honour, I must say that for him.

LUNDESTAD [*thoughtfully*]: Mr Stensgård has great gifts.

STENSGÅRD [*appearing at the back, but remaining in the doorway*]: May I come in?

BRATTSBERG [*going to him*]: Of course you may.

STENSGÅRD: And will you accept my best wishes?

BRATTSBERG: Gladly.

STENSGÅRD: Then let me give you them, warmly and sincerely. And I hope you'll overlook all the stupid things that I've written –

BRATTSBERG: I judge a man by his actions, Mr Stensgård.

STENSGÅRD: Ah, thank you.

BRATTSBERG: And from now on – if that's what you want – you may consider yourself at home here.

STENSGÅRD: May I? May I really?

[*There is a knock on the door.*]

BRATTSBERG: Come in.

[*Several local worthies, townspeople, foremen, and so on, enter. The* CHAMBERLAIN *goes to receive their birthday wishes and to talk with them.*]

THORA [*who has meanwhile come in through the farthest door to the left*]: Mr Stensgård, I should like to thank you.

STENSGÅRD: You, Miss Brattsberg?

THORA: Father has told me how wonderfully you've behaved.

STENSGÅRD: But ...?

THORA: How we've misjudged you.

STENSGÅRD: Have you?

THORA: Still, it was your own fault. .... No, no, it was ours. Oh, I do most sincerely wish I could make amends.

STENSGÅRD: Do you? You personally? Would you really...?

THORA: All of us – if only we could.

BRATTSBERG: Some refreshments for these gentlemen, my dear.

THORA: I'm coming.

[*She goes back to the door, through which, soon after, the* MAID *comes with wine and cakes, which are handed round during the following.*]

STENSGÅRD: My dear Lundestad, I feel like a victorious god!

LUNDESTAD: You must have felt like that yesterday, too.

STENSGÅRD: Tcha! Today's quite different – the best thing of all, that crowns everything. Life has become a splendid, wonderful thing!

LUNDESTAD: Aha! Thoughts of love?

STENSGÅRD: Not thoughts! Achievement – glorious achievement!

LUNDESTAD: So Bastian, your brother-in-law to be, has brought you the answer.

STENSGÅRD: Bastian?

LUNDESTAD: Yes, he dropped a hint yesterday ... hasn't he promised to speak for you to a certain little girl?

STENSGÅRD: What nonsense!

LUNDESTAD: Don't be shy with me. If you don't know already, I can tell you. You've won, Mr Stensgård! I have it from Ringdal.

STENSGÅRD: What have you from Ringdal?

LUNDESTAD: Miss Monsen has given her consent.

STENSGÅRD: *What* did you say?

LUNDESTAD: Her consent, I said.

STENSGÅRD: Consent? Her consent? When her father has bolted?

LUNDESTAD: But not his daughter.

STENSGÅRD: Her consent – in the middle of a family scandal like this! How immodest! It's enough to put off any man with decent feelings! But it's all a mistake; I never asked Bastian ... How could the fool ...? Still, it's nothing to do with me – he must answer for his own acts.

HEJRE [coming in at the back]: Tee-hee – what a gathering! Ah, of course – paying their respects – getting their stockings green, as the saying goes. May I, too, perhaps, be allowed ...?

BRATTSBERG: Thank you, old friend, thank you.

HEJRE: Good gracious, my dear sir – you're too kind!

[New guests arrive.]

Look, here come the minions of Justice – the power of life and death. ... Enough said. [Going to STENSGÅRD] Ah, you lucky young man, are you here? Give me your hand. Accept this assurance of an old man's sincere pleasure. ...

STENSGÅRD: What about?

HEJRE: You asked me yesterday to tell her something a little equivocal about you, you know. ...

STENSGÅRD: Yes. Well, what happened?

HEJRE: I had the greatest pleasure in carrying out your mission –

STENSGÅRD: Well, what happened? I'm asking you what happened. How did she take it?

HEJRE: Like a woman in love, of course. Burst into tears – locked herself in, wouldn't either answer or show herself.

STENSGÅRD: Thank heaven!

HEJRE: It's barbarous of you to inflict such a cruel test on a widow's heart – to go gloating over the pangs of jealousy. But love has sharp eyes. ... Enough said. Because today when I drove past, there was Madam Rundholmen, bright and cheerful at her open window, combing her hair and looking, if you'll pardon the simile, like a mermaid! Ah, she's a fine woman!

STENSGÅRD: Well, what then?

HEJRE: Ah, she laughed like one possessed, my boy, then she waved a letter in the air and called out: 'A love letter, Mr Hejre. I got engaged yesterday!'

STENSGÅRD: What? Engaged?

HEJRE: My heartiest congratulations, young fellow. I can't tell you how pleased I am to be the first to break it to you –

STENSGÅRD: This is absurd! It's nonsense!

HEJRE: What's nonsense?

STENSGÅRD: You misunderstood her. Or else she misunderstood. . . . Engaged? Are you mad? Now that Monsen's gone, she'll probably go, too.

HEJRE: Not she, upon my word. Madam Rundholmen's as firm as a rock.

STENSGÅRD: It doesn't matter to me. My thoughts are running in quite a different direction. All that business with the letter was only a joke – a bet, as I told you. Dear Mr Hejre, do me a favour and don't breathe a word of this absurd story to anyone.

HEJRE: I understand, I understand – it's to be a secret. How romantic! Ah, youth – that's the time for poetry!

STENSGÅRD: Yes, yes – but just keep quiet. I'll make it worth your while – I'll help with your lawsuits – Sh! I rely on you. [*He gets away.*]

BRATTSBERG [*who has been talking with* LUNDESTAD]: But Lundestad, I really can't believe that.

LUNDESTAD: I assure you, Chamberlain, I have it from Daniel Hejre's own mouth.

HEJRE: What have you from my mouth, may I ask?

BRATTSBERG: Tell me, did Mr Stensgård show you a bill yesterday?

HEJRE: Yes, damn it, he did. What does it all mean?

BRATTSBERG: I'll explain later. But you told him . . .?

LUNDESTAD: You persuaded him it was a forgery?

HEJRE: Pooh – a harmless joke. Just to add a little to the intoxication of victory.

LUNDESTAD: But you said that both signatures were forgeries.

HEJRE: Well, why the devil shouldn't both have been? *One* was.

BRATTSBERG: So that was it!

LUNDESTAD [*to* BRATTSBERG]: And when he heard *that* . . .

BRATTSBERG: – he gave the bill to Ringdal!

LUNDESTAD: When it was no longer any use as a threat!

BRATTSBERG: To play the benefactor! To make a fool of me a second time! To gain admission to my house – to extort my thanks! Oh the – the –! And this is the fellow who –

HEJRE: But my dear sir, what are you so upset about?

BRATTSBERG: Later, later, my dear chap. [*Drawing* LUNDESTAD *aside*] And this is the fellow you've been sponsoring – pushing forward – encouraging!

LUNDESTAD: And so have you.

BRATTSBERG: Oh, I should like to . . .!

LUNDESTAD [*pointing to* STENSGÅRD, *who is talking to* THORA]: Look there! What must people be thinking?

BRATTSBERG: Whatever they think, I'll soon put a stop to it!

LUNDESTAD: It's too late, Chamberlain; he'll push himself forward with plausible tricks and promises –

BRATTSBERG: I know a trick or two myself, Mr Lundestad.

LUNDESTAD: What will you do?

BRATTSBERG: Wait and see. [*Going over to* FJELDBO] Dr Fjeldbo, will you do me a favour?

FJELDBO: I'd be glad to.

BRATTSBERG: Then throw that fellow out of my house.

FJELDBO: Stensgård?

BRATTSBERG: Yes, the fortune-hunter; I can't even bear to hear his name. Throw him out!

FJELDBO: But how can I ...?

BRATTSBERG: That's your affair. I give you a free hand.

FJELDBO: A free hand? Do you? In every way?

BRATTSBERG: Yes, damn it, yes!

FJELDBO: Shake hands on that, Chamberlain.

BRATTSBERG: Here.

FJELDBO: Then by God, it's now or never! [*Loudly*] May I ask for your attention for a moment?

BRATTSBERG: Silence for Dr Fjeldbo.

FJELDBO: I have the pleasure, with Chamberlain Brattsberg's consent, of announcing my engagement to his daughter.

[*An outburst of amazement.* THORA *gives a little scream.* BRATTSBERG *is about to speak, but checks himself. A hubbub of congratulations.*]

STENSGÅRD: Engagement? *Your* engagement?

HEJRE: To Miss ... To your ... To – to ...

LUNDESTAD: Are you mad, Doctor?

STENSGÅRD: But, Chamberlain ...?

BRATTSBERG: What can I do? I'm a Liberal – I shall join the League of Youth!

FJELDBO: Thank you – thank you. And forgive me.

BRATTSBERG: New alliances are in the air, Mr Stensgård; here's to free competition.

THORA: Oh, Father dear ...!

LUNDESTAD: Engagements are in the air, too; I can tell you of another. ...

STENSGÅRD: A fabrication!

LUNDESTAD: No, indeed it isn't. Miss Monsen is engaged to –

STENSGÅRD: It's a lie, it's a lie, I tell you!

THORA: No, it's true; they're both here, Father.

BRATTSBERG: Who? Where?

THORA: Ragna and Mr Helle. They're in there. [*Going to the farthest door on the right.*]

LUNDESTAD: Mr Helle? So it's he who –

BRATTSBERG: Here? In my house? [*Going to the door*] Come out here, my dear child.

RAGNA [*hanging back shyly*]: Oh no – there are too many people. . . .

BRATTSBERG: Don't be shy. You're not to blame for what has happened.

HELLE: She's homeless now, Chamberlain.

RAGNA: Please help us.

BRATTSBERG: I will. I'm very glad that you came to me.

HEJRE: Well, upon my word, engagements *are* in the air – I can add another to the list.

BRATTSBERG: What, you? At your age? Ridiculous!

HEJRE: Well – enough said.

LUNDESTAD: The game's up, Mr Stensgård.

STENSGÅRD: *Is* it? [*Aloud*] No, Mr Daniel Hejre. *I'm* going to add to the list! An announcement, Gentlemen! I, too, have come safely to harbour.

BRATTSBERG: How?

STENSGÅRD: When it's necessary one must play a double game, and hide one's true intentions. If it's for the general good, I feel that's permissible. My life's work is clearly mapped out before me, and it means everything to me. All my energies are devoted to this district. New ideas are at work here that need clarifying. But that is not the task for an adventurer. The People here need a leader who is one of themselves. That is why I have decided to link my interests firmly and irrevocably with yours – and to link them with my heart-strings! If I have given rise to any misunderstanding anywhere, I ask your forgiveness. I, too, am engaged.

BRATTSBERG: You?

FJELDBO: Engaged?

HEJRE: I can bear witness.

BRATTSBERG: But how . . .?

FJELDBO: To whom?

LUNDESTAD: It can't be . . .?

STENSGÅRD: I have consulted both my heart and my head, and this is the outcome. Yes, Fellow-townsmen,[25] I'm engaged to Madam Rundholmen!

FJELDBO: To Madam Rundholmen?

BRATTSBERG: The publican's widow?

LUNDESTAD: Aha, so *that's* it!

BRATTSBERG: I'm all at sea in this. How could you . . .?

STENSGÅRD: A stratagem, Mr Ironmaster!

LUNDESTAD: He's a talented man!

ASLAKSEN [*looking in from the door at the back*]: A thousand pardons, but –

BRATTSBERG: Ah, come in, Aslaksen. Have you brought me your good wishes, too?

ASLAKSEN: Oh, my goodness, I wouldn't presume! But I must speak urgently to Mr Stensgård.

STENSGÅRD: Later. You can wait outside.

ASLAKSEN: No, damn it, I *must* tell you –

STENSGÅRD: Hold your tongue! How dare you intrude like this? Yes, Gentlemen, the workings of Destiny are wonderful. There was a need for a close and lasting bond between this District and myself, and I have found a woman of riper years who will make a home for me. Now I have cast off the skin of the fortune-hunter, and here I stand in your midst, a sedate man of the People. Take me! I am ready to stand or fall in whatever post you may entrust to me.

LUNDESTAD: He's won!

BRATTSBERG: Really, I must say – [*To the* MAID, *who has come up to him from the door at the back*] Well, well, what is it? What are you giggling about?

MAID: Madam Rundholmen –

SEVERAL BYSTANDERS: Madam Rundholmen?

BRATTSBERG: What about her?

MAID: Madam Rundholmen's waiting outside with her young man. . . .

THE GUESTS [*to one another*]: Her young man? Madam Rundholmen? But who . . .?

STENSGÅRD: What nonsense!

ASLAKSEN: Well, I told you –

BRATTSBERG [*at the door*]: Come in – come in!

[BASTIAN MONSEN, *with* MADAM RUNDHOLMEN *on his arm, comes in from the back. General sensation.*]

MADAM: I do hope you don't mind, sir –

BRATTSBERG: Not at all, not at all.

MADAM: But I really had to come up and show my fiancé to you and Miss Thora.

BRATTSBERG: Well, well, so you're engaged. But –

THORA: But we didn't know –

STENSGÅRD [*to* ASLAKSEN]: But how on earth . . .?

ASLAKSEN: So much went to my head yesterday – I mean, I had so much to think about –

STENSGÅRD: But she had my letter? And –

ASLAKSEN: No, she had Bastian Monsen's. Here's yours.

STENSGÅRD: Bastian's? And here's – [*Glancing at the envelope, he screws it up and stuffs it in his pocket.*] Oh, damn you for a clumsy coot!

MADAM: Yes, of course I accept him. A girl's got to be careful of philanderers, but when you've got it in black and white that a certain person's intentions are honourable, why then . . . Oh look, here's Mr Stensgård too! Well, Mr Stensgård, aren't you going to congratulate me?

HEJRE [*to* LUNDESTAD]: If looks could kill . . .!

BRATTSBERG: I'm sure he is, Madam Rundholmen, but won't you congratulate your future sister-in-law?

MADAM: Who's that?

THORA: Ragna – she's engaged, too.

BASTIAN: Are you, Ragna?

MADAM: Really? Well, my fiancé told me that a certain person was going courting. Best wishes to both of you – and welcome to the family, Mr Stensgård.

FJELDBO: No, no, not Mr Stensgård.

BRATTSBERG: No, it's Mr Helle – an excellent choice. And you must really congratulate my daughter, too.

MADAM: Miss Thora! Well, so Mr Lundestad was right after all. Congratulations, Miss Thora – congratulations, Mr Stensgård.

FJELDBO: Fjeldbo, you mean![26]

MADAM: What?

FJELDBO: I'm the lucky man.

MADAM: Well! I don't know if I'm on my head or my heels.

BRATTSBERG: But now at last *I* do!

STENSGÅRD: Excuse me ... urgent business ...

BRATTSBERG [*quietly*]: Lundestad, what *was* the other thing?

LUNDESTAD: What other thing?

BRATTSBERG: Not 'fortune-hunter', but the other word?

LUNDESTAD: 'Charlatan'.

STENSGÅRD: I must be going.

BRATTSBERG: A word with you, Mr Stensgård, if you don't mind. Just one word – a word that's been on the tip of my tongue for some time –

STENSGÅRD [*making for the door*]: Excuse me, I'm in a hurry.

BRATTSBERG [*following him*]: Charlatan!

STENSGÅRD: Good-bye! [*He goes out at the back.*]

BRATTSBERG: Well, friends, that's cleared the air!

BASTIAN: I do hope, sir, you don't blame me for what's happened at home.

BRATTSBERG: We must all sweep our own doorsteps.

BASTIAN: I really had no part in it.

SELMA [*who has heard the last few lines from the farthest door on the right*]: Father, now that you're in a good mood – may he come in?

BRATTSBERG: Selma – you? Are you pleading for him? Why, only two days ago, you –

SELMA: Ah, two days is a long time. Everything's all right. Now I know that he can behave foolishly. . . .

BRATTSBERG: And does that please you?

SELMA: Yes – to know that he *can* . . . but I'm not going to let him!

BRATTSBERG: Bring him in. [SELMA *goes out again to the right.*]

RINGDAL [*coming in by the nearest door on the right*]: Here is your letter of resignation.

BRATTSBERG: Thank you, you can tear it up.

RINGDAL: Tear it up?

BRATTSBERG: Yes, Ringdal – that wouldn't be the right way. I can atone in other ways – by working in earnest to –

ERIK [*coming from the right, with* SELMA]: Can you forgive me?

BRATTSBERG [*handing him the bill*]: I dare not be less merciful than fate.

ERIK: Father! From today I'm giving up this business of mine that you dislike so much.

BRATTSBERG: Thank you – but no, you must stick at it. No cowardice, no running away from temptation. But I shall stand by you. [*Aloud*] Gentlemen, have you heard the news? I'm going into business with my son!

GUESTS: What? *You*, Chamberlain?

HEJRE: You, my dear sir?

BRATTSBERG: Yes, it's an honourable occupation, and a profitable one – or at least it can be made so. And now there's no longer any reason why I should keep out of it.

LUNDESTAD: Well, you know, Chamberlain, if you're going to work for the benefit of the district, it'd be a downright shame if an old toiler like me were to shirk my duty!

BRATTSBERG: You! Really?

LUNDESTAD: I couldn't, in any case. After the way Mr Stensgård has been crossed in love today, heaven forbid that we should force the poor man into politics. He needs time to recover; he ought to travel – and I mean to see that he does! So, if my fellow townsmen need me, here I am.

TOWNSMEN [*grasping his hand with feeling*]: Thank you, Lundestad. Good old chap. You won't desert us!

BRATTSBERG: Ah, this is as it should be – everything's falling back into place again. But who was really to blame for it all?

FJELDBO: Aslaksen, you must know something about it.

ASLAKSEN [*alarmed*]: I, Doctor? I'm as innocent as a babe unborn.

FJELDBO: But that letter that –

ASLAKSEN: It wasn't me, I tell you. It was the Election, and Bastian Monsen, and Fate, and Madam Rundholmen's punch – there wasn't any lemon in it. . . . And there was I, the Representative of the Press –

BRATTSBERG [*drawing nearer*]: How? What?

ASLAKSEN: The Press, Chamberlain.

BRATTSBERG: The Press. There we have it! Isn't that what I've always said? That the Press has extraordinary power these days.

ASLAKSEN: Oh, but, Chamberlain –

BRATTSBERG: No false modesty, Mr Aslaksen. So far, I've not read your paper, but I mean to from now on. I should like to order ten copies.

ASLAKSEN: You could have twenty, Chamberlain.

BRATTSBERG: All right, thank you, let me have twenty. And if you're short of money, come to me. I mean to support the Press; but I tell you one thing – I won't write for it.

RINGDAL: What's this I hear? Your daughter engaged?

BRATTSBERG: Yes, what do you think of that?

RINGDAL: Splendid. When did it happen?

FJELDBO [*hastily*]: Oh, I'll tell you later.

BRATTSBERG: It was settled on Independence Day.

FJELDBO: But how did you . . .?

BRATTSBERG: The same day that little Ragna –

THORA: Father! Did you *know*, Father?

BRATTSBERG: Yes, my dear, I've known all the time.

FJELDBO: Oh, Chamberlain!

THORA: But how?

BRATTSBERG: Another time little girls should lower their voices a bit when I'm sitting dozing on the balcony.

THORA: Oh, my goodness, were you out there behind that curtain?[27]

FJELDBO: Now I see why you were so –

BRATTSBERG: Yes, when you kept coming here and never saying a word –

FJELDBO: Would it have been any good if I'd spoken before today?

BRATTSBERG: No, you're right. What's happened in the meantime has made all the difference.

THORA [*quietly to* FJELDBO]: Well, you know how to hold your tongue! All this business with Stensgård – why wasn't I told about it?

FJELDBO: When there's a hawk hovering over your dovecote, you protect your little dove, you don't frighten her.

[*They are interrupted by* MADAM RUNDHOLMEN.]

HEJRE [*to* BRATTSBERG]: Look, you'll really have to excuse me, but we'll have to postpone our lawsuit indefinitely.

BRATTSBERG: Shall we? Well, well!

HEJRE: Let me tell you that I've taken a job as a reporter on Aslaksen's paper.

BRATTSBERG: I'm delighted to hear it.

HEJRE: And as you'll realize, that'll keep me busy.

BRATTSBERG: Well, well, old friend, I can wait.

MADAM [*to* THORA]: Oh, the tears I've wept over that dreadful man! But now, thank heaven for Bastian! That other one was as treacherous as the scum on a pond! And you know, Miss, he never stopped smoking, and always wanting the best of everything – Oh, he was a proper glutton!

MAID [*from the left*]: Lunch is served.

BRATTSBERG: Now, you must all join me. Mr Lundestad, will you sit by me – and you, too, Mr Aslaksen?

RINGDAL: We'll certainly have plenty of healths to drink.

HEJRE: And I hope it won't be out of place for an old man to propose the toast to 'Absent Friends'.

LUNDESTAD: One absent friend will be coming back, Mr Hejre.

HEJRE: Stensgård?

LUNDESTAD: Yes, mark my words, gentlemen; in ten or fifteen years, Stensgård'll have a seat in the Storthing – or on the Privy Council – perhaps both at once.[28]

FJELDBO: Ten or fifteen years? Well, he won't be at the head of the League of Youth!

HEJRE: Why not?

FJELDBO: Well, by that time he'll be of a somewhat uncertain age.

HEJRE: Then, my dear chap, he can stand at the head of a League of Uncertainty. That's what Lundestad means. He agrees with Napoleon: 'Uncertain men,' he said, 'are the stuff from which politicians are made.' Tee-hee!

FJELDBO: Well, be that as it may, *our* League will endure through both young *and* uncertain times, and it'll still be the League of Youth. When Stensgård founded it, and was carried shoulder-high in all the noise and enthusiasm of Independence Day, he said: 'Providence is on the side of the League of Youth!' I think even our theologian here would let us apply those words to ourselves.[29]

BRATTSBERG: I think you're right, my friend, because while we've been stumbling and groping in the dark, our good angels have certainly looked after us.

LUNDESTAD: Oh, heaven help us, the angels were only moderately good ones!

ASLAKSEN: Ah, Mr Lundestad, that's the fault of our local conditions!

The curtain falls

A DOLL'S HOUSE

A Play in Three Acts

CHARACTERS

TORVALD HELMER, a lawyer
NORA, his wife
DR RANK
NILS KROGSTAD, a barrister
MRS LINDE
Helmer's three small children
ANNA-MARIA, the nurse
A housemaid
A porter

The action takes place in Helmer's flat

ACT ONE

A comfortable room, furnished inexpensively, but with taste. In the back wall there are two doors; that to the right leads out to a hall, the other, to the left, leads to Helmer's study. Between them stands a piano.

In the middle of the left-hand wall is a door, with a window on its nearer side. Near the window is a round table with armchairs and a small sofa.

In the wall on the right-hand side, rather to the back, is a door, and farther forward on this wall there is a tiled stove with a couple of easy chairs and a rocking-chair in front of it. Between the door and the stove stands a little table.

There are etchings on the walls, and there is a cabinet with china ornaments and other bric-à-brac, and a small bookcase with handsomely bound books. There is a carpet on the floor, and the stove is lit. It is a winter day.

[*A bell rings in the hall outside, and a moment later the door is heard to open.* NORA *comes into the room, humming happily. She is in outdoor clothes, and is carrying an armful of parcels which she puts down on the table to the right. Through the hall door, which she has left open, can be seen a* PORTER; *he is holding a Christmas tree and a hamper, and he gives them to the* MAID *who has opened the front door.*]

NORA: Hide the Christmas tree properly, Helena. The children mustn't see it till this evening, when it's been decorated. [*To the* PORTER, *taking out her purse*] How much is that?

PORTER: Fifty øre.[1]

NORA: There's a krone. No, keep the change.

[*The* PORTER *thanks her and goes.* NORA *shuts the door, and takes off her outdoor clothes, laughing quietly and happily to herself. Taking a bag of macaroons from her pocket, she eats one or two, then goes cautiously to her husband's door and listens.*]

Yes, he's in. [*She starts humming again as she goes over to the table on the right.*]

HELMER [*from his study*]: Is that my little skylark twittering out there?

NORA [*busy opening the parcels*]: It is.

HELMER: Scampering about like a little squirrel?

NORA: Yes.

HELMER: When did the squirrel get home?

NORA: Just this minute. [*She slips the bag of macaroons in her pocket and wipes her mouth.*] Come in here, Torvald,[2] and you can see what I've bought.

HELMER: I'm busy! [*A moment later he opens the door and looks out, pen in hand.*] Did you say 'bought'? What, all that? Has my little featherbrain been out wasting money again?

NORA: But, Torvald, surely this year we can let ourselves go just a little bit? It's the first Christmas that we haven't had to economize.

HELMER: Still, we mustn't waste money, you know.

NORA: Oh, Torvald, surely we can waste a little now – just the teeniest bit? Now that you're going to earn a big salary, you'll have lots and lots of money.

HELMER: After New Year's Day, yes – but there'll be a whole quarter before I get paid.

NORA: Pooh, we can always borrow till then.

HELMER: Nora! [*He goes to her and takes her playfully by the ear.*] The same little scatterbrain. Just suppose I borrowed a thousand kroner today and you went and spent it all by Christmas, and then on New Year's Eve a tile fell on my head, and there I lay –

NORA [*putting a hand over his mouth*]: Sh! Don't say such horrid things!

HELMER: But suppose something of the sort were to happen. . . .

NORA: If anything as horrid as that were to happen, I don't expect I should care whether I owed money or not.

HELMER: But what about the people I'd borrowed from?

NORA: Them? Who bothers about them? They're just strangers.

HELMER: Nora, Nora! Just like a woman! But seriously, Nora, you know what I think about that sort of thing. No debts, no borrowing. There's something constrained, something ugly even, about a home that's founded on borrowing and debt. You and I have managed to keep clear up till now, and we shall still do so for the little time that is left.

NORA [*going over to the stove*]: Very well, Torvald, if you say so.

HELMER [*following her*]: Now, now, my little song-bird mustn't be so crestfallen. Well? Is the squirrel sulking? [*Taking out his wallet*] Nora . . . guess what I have here!

NORA [*turning quickly*]: Money!

HELMER: There! [*He hands her some notes.*] Good heavens, I know what a lot has to go on housekeeping at Christmas time.

NORA [*counting*]: Ten – twenty – thirty – forty! Oh, thank you, Torvald, thank you! This'll keep me going for a long time!

HELMER: Well, you must see that it does.

NORA: Oh yes, of course I will. But now come and see all the things I've bought – so cheaply, too. Look, here's a new suit for Ivar, and a sword too. Here's a horse and a trumpet for Bob; and here's a doll and a doll's bed for Emmy. They're rather plain, but she'll soon smash them to bits anyway. And these are dress-lengths and handkerchiefs for the maids. . . . Old Nanny really ought to have something more. . . .

HELMER: And what's in *that* parcel?

NORA [*squealing*]: No, Torvald! You're not to see that till this evening!

HELMER: Aha! And now, little prodigal, what do you think you want for yourself?

NORA: Oh, me? I don't want anything at all.

HELMER: Ah, but you must. Now tell me anything – within reason – that you feel you'd like.

NORA: No ... I really can't think of anything. Unless ... Torvald ...

HELMER: Well?

NORA [*not looking at him – playing with his waistcoat buttons*]: If you *really* want to give me something, you could – well, you could ...

HELMER: Come along – out with it!

NORA [*in a rush*]: You could give me money, Torvald. Only what you think you could spare – and then one of these days I'll buy something with it.

HELMER: But, Nora –

NORA: Oh, *do*, Torvald ... please, please do! Then I'll wrap it in pretty gold paper and hang it on the Christmas tree. Wouldn't that be fun?

HELMER: What do they call little birds who are always making money fly?

NORA: Yes, I know – ducks-and-drakes! But let's do what I said, Torvald, and then I'll have time to think of something that I really want. Now, that's very sensible, isn't it?

HELMER [*smiling*]: Oh, very. That is, it would be if you really kept the money I give you, and actually bought something for yourself with it. But if it goes in with the housekeeping, and gets spent on all sorts of useless things, then I only have to pay out again.

NORA: Oh, but, Torvald –

HELMER: You can't deny it, little Nora, now can you? [*Putting an arm round her waist*] It's a sweet little bird, but it gets through a terrible amount of money. You wouldn't believe how much it costs a man when he's got a little song bird like you!

NORA: Oh, how *can* you say that? I really do save all I can.

HELMER [*laughing*]: Yes, that's very true – 'all you can'. But the thing is, you *can't*!

NORA [*nodding and smiling happily*]: Ah, if you only knew what expenses we skylarks and squirrels have, Torvald.

HELMER: What a funny little one you are! Just like your father – always on the look-out for all the money you can get, but the moment you have it, it seems to slip through your fingers and you never know what becomes of it. Well, I must take you as you are – it's in your blood. Oh yes, Nora, these things are hereditary.

NORA: I wish I'd inherited more of papa's good qualities.

HELMER: And I wouldn't want you to be any different from what you are – just my sweet little song bird. But now I come to think of it, you look rather – rather – how shall I put it? – rather as if you've been up to mischief today.

NORA: Do I?

HELMER: Yes, you certainly do. Look me straight in the face.

NORA [*looking at him*]: Well?

HELMER [*wagging a finger at her*]: Surely your sweet tooth didn't get the better of you in town today?

NORA: No ... how could you think that?

HELMER: Didn't Little Sweet-Tooth just look in at the confectioner's?

NORA: No, honestly, Torvald.

HELMER: Not to taste one little sweet?

NORA: No, of course not.

HELMER: Not even to nibble a macaroon or two?

NORA: No, Torvald, really; I promise you.

HELMER: There, there, of course I was only joking.

NORA [*going to the table on the right*]: I wouldn't do anything that you don't like.

HELMER: No, I know you wouldn't – besides, you've given me your word. [*Going over to her*] Well, you keep your little Christmas secrets to yourself, Nora darling; I daresay I shall know them all this evening when the Christmas tree's lighted up.

NORA: Did you remember to invite Dr Rank?

HELMER: No, but there's no need to – it's an understood thing that he dines with us. Still, I'll ask him when he looks in before lunch. I've ordered an excellent wine. . . . Oh, Nora, you can't imagine how much I'm looking forward to this evening.

NORA: So am I, Torvald – and how the children will love it.

HELMER: Oh, it's certainly wonderful to think that one has a good safe post and ample means. It's a very comforting thought, isn't it?

NORA: Oh, it's wonderful!

HELMER: Do you remember last Christmas? For three whole weeks beforehand you shut yourself up every evening till long after midnight, making flowers for the Christmas tree, and all the other wonderful surprises for us. Ugh, those were the most boring three weeks I've ever had to live through.

NORA: It wasn't the least bit boring for me.

HELMER [*smiling*]: But there was so little to show for it, Nora!

NORA: Now, you mustn't tease me about that again. How could I help it if the cat got in and tore everything to bits?

HELMER: Poor little Nora – of course you couldn't. You did your best to please us – that's the main thing. But it's certainly good that the hard times are over.

NORA: Oh, it's really wonderful!

HELMER: Now I needn't sit here by myself and be bored, and you needn't tire your pretty eyes or your sweet little fingers –

NORA [*clapping her hands*]: No, I needn't, need I? Not any

more. Oh, it's really wonderful to know that. [*Taking his arm*] Now I'll tell you how I've been thinking we ought to arrange things, Torvald. As soon as Christmas is over –
[*A bell rings in the hall.*]
Oh, that's the door! [*She tidies the room a little.*] It must be someone to see us – oh, that *is* tiresome!

HELMER: I'm not at home to callers, remember.

MAID [*at the door*]: There's a lady to see you, madam.

NORA: Well, show her in.

MAID [*to* HELMER]: And the Doctor's here as well, sir.

HELMER: Has he gone straight to my study?

MAID: Yes, sir.

[HELMER *goes to his study. The* MAID *shows in* MRS LINDE, *who is in travelling clothes, and shuts the door after her.*]

MRS LINDE [*subdued and rather hesitant*]: How do you do, Nora?

NORA [*doubtfully*]: How do you do . . .

MRS LINDE: You don't remember me.

NORA: No, I'm afraid I – Wait a minute . . . surely it's –
[*Impulsively*] Kristina! Is it really you?

MRS LINDE: Yes, it really is.

NORA: Kristina! And to think I didn't know you! But how could *I*? [*More gently*] You *have* changed, Kristina.

MRS LINDE: Yes, I have . . . nine years – nearly ten – it's a long time.

NORA: Is it really as long as that since we saw each other? Yes, I suppose it is. But you know, I've been so happy these last eight years! And now you've come to town too? How brave of you to travel all that way in the middle of winter.

MRS LINDE: I arrived by steamer this morning.

NORA: In time to have a lovely Christmas. Oh, this is wonderful! We'll have a splendid time. But do take your things off – aren't you absolutely frozen? [*Helping her*] There! Now come and sit by the stove where it's cosy. No, you have the armchair, I'll sit in the rocking-chair. [*Taking her hands*] Yes, now you look like your old self again – it was just the first moment. . . . But you're paler, Kristina, and a little thinner, perhaps. . . .

MRS LINDE: And a lot older, Nora.

NORA: A little older, perhaps – just a teeny bit – but certainly not a lot. [*Suddenly checking herself and speaking seriously*] Oh, how thoughtless of me! Here I am, chattering away . . . dear sweet Kristina, can you ever forgive me?

MRS LINDE: What do you mean, Nora?

NORA: Poor Kristina, you're a widow now.

MRS LINDE: Yes . . . three years ago.

NORA: Yes, I know; I saw it in the papers. Oh, Kristina, I kept meaning to write to you, honestly I did, but something always cropped up and I put it off . . .

MRS LINDE: Dear Nora, I do understand.

NORA: No, it was horrid of me. Oh, poor Kristina, what you must have gone through! And he didn't leave you anything to live on?

MRS LINDE: No.

NORA: And no children?

MRS LINDE: No.

NORA: Nothing at all?

MRS LINDE: Not even any regrets to break my heart over.

NORA [*looking at her incredulously*]: Oh, but Kristina, that can't be true.

MRS LINDE [*stroking* NORA'S *hair with a sad smile*]: It happens like that sometimes, Nora.

NORA: But to be so completely alone – that must be terribly sad for you. *I* have three lovely children; you can't see them just now, they're out with their Nanny. . . . But now you must tell me all about it.

MRS LINDE: No, no, I want to hear about you.

NORA: No, you first – I mustn't be selfish today – I'm not going to think about anything but your troubles. I must just tell you one thing, though. Do you know, we've just had the most wonderful stroke of luck – only the other day.

MRS LINDE: Oh? What was it?

NORA: Just think – my husband's been made Manager of the Savings Bank.

MRS LINDE: Your husband? But that's wonderful.

NORA: Yes, it's magnificent! A barrister's life is such an uncertain one – especially when he won't touch any case that isn't absolutely respectable. Of course Torvald never would – and I quite agree with him. Well, you can imagine how delighted we are. He's to start at the Bank on New Year's Day, and he'll have a big salary and lots of commission. Oh, we shall be able to live quite differently from now on – to live as we'd like to. Oh, Kristina, I'm so happy! It'll be really wonderful to have lots of money, and never need to worry, won't it?

MRS LINDE: Yes, it must be pleasant to have everything you need.

NORA: Oh, not just what we need! Heaps and heaps of money!

MRS LINDE [with a smile]: Nora, Nora! Haven't you learned sense yet? Even at school you were a terrible spendthrift.

NORA [laughing quietly]: Yes, Torvald says I still am. [Wagging her finger] But 'Nora, Nora' isn't as silly as you think. We simply hadn't the money for me to waste; we both had to work.

MRS LINDE: You as well?

NORA: Yes, with odds and ends of needlework – crochet and embroidery and so on. [Casually] And in other ways too. You see, when we married, Torvald gave up his government post – there wasn't any hope of promotion in his department, and of course he had to earn more money than before. But he overworked dreadfully that first year; you see, he had to take on all sorts of extra jobs, and he worked from morning till night. He couldn't stand it; he was dreadfully ill, and the doctors said he'd simply *have* to go to the south.

MRS LINDE: Oh yes, you went to Italy for a whole year, didn't you?

NORA: Yes, we did. It wasn't easy to manage, I can tell you. It was just after Ivar was born, but of course we had to go. Oh, it was a wonderful trip – beautiful! And it saved Torvald's life. But it cost a terrible lot of money, Kristina!

MRS LINDE: I'm sure it did.

NORA: Twelve hundred dollars – four thousand eight hundred kroner.[3] That's a lot of money.

MRS LINDE: Yes, at times like that, it's very lucky to have money.

NORA: Well, you see, we got it from Papa.

MRS LINDE: Oh? Yes, I remember, your father died just about then.

NORA: Yes, just then. And just think, Kristina, I couldn't go and nurse him. I was expecting Ivar to arrive any day, and there was my poor Torvald, dreadfully ill, to look after. Dear, kind Papa – I never saw him again – that was the hardest thing I've had to bear in all my married life, Kristina.

MRS LINDE: I know how fond of him you were. . . . And so you went to Italy?

NORA: Yes, we left a month later. We had the money then, and the doctors said there was no time to lose.

MRS LINDE: And when you came back your husband was cured?

NORA: Fit as a fiddle!

MRS LINDE: But the doctor . . .?

NORA: What doctor?

MRS LINDE: That man who arrived at the same time as I did –I thought your maid said he was the doctor?

NORA: Ah, that was Dr Rank – but he doesn't come here professionally, he's our best friend, he always looks in at least once a day. No, Torvald's never had a day's illness since. And the children are well and strong, and so am I. [*Jumping up and clapping her hands*] Oh Lord, Kristina, it's wonderful to be alive and happy! Oh, but how awful of me, I've just gone on talking about myself! [*She sits on a footstool beside* KRISTINA *and puts her arms on her knees.*] Now, you mustn't be angry with me. Tell me, is it really true that you didn't love your husband? Why did you marry him, then?

MRS LINDE: My mother was still alive; she was bedridden and helpless, and I had my two younger brothers to look after – I didn't feel I *could* refuse his offer.

NORA: No, no, I suppose you couldn't. And he was rich in those days?

MRS LINDE: I believe he was quite well off; but his business wasn't sound, and when he died it went to pieces and there wasn't anything left.

NORA: And you . . .?

MRS LINDE: Well, I just had to struggle along – I ran a little shop, then a small school, and anything else I could turn my hand to. These last three years I never seem to have stopped working. Still, that's all over now, Nora – poor Mother's gone, she doesn't need me any longer. Nor do the boys – they're working, and they can look after themselves.

NORA: How relieved you must feel.

MRS LINDE: No . . . just unspeakably empty – I've no one to live for any more. [*She gets up restlessly.*] That's why I couldn't bear to stay in that little backwater any longer. It must be easier to find some sort of work here that'll keep me busy and take my mind off things. If only I could be lucky enough to find some office work . . .

NORA: But, Kristina, that's terribly tiring, and you look worn out already. It'd be much better for you to go for a holiday.

MRS LINDE [*going over to the window*]: I haven't a father to pay my fare, Nora.

NORA [*rising*]: Oh, don't be angry with me.

MRS LINDE [*going to her*]: No, Nora, it's you who mustn't be angry with me. That's the worst of my sort of life – it makes you so bitter. There's no one to work for, yet you can never relax. You must live, so you become self-centred. Why, do you know, when you told me the news of your good fortune, I wasn't nearly so glad for your sake as for my own!

NORA: But . . . Oh, I see what you mean – you think perhaps Torvald might be able to do something for you.

MRS LINDE: Yes, I thought he might.

NORA: Oh, he will, Kristina; just leave it to me. I'll bring the subject up very cleverly. . . . I'll think of some wonderful way to put him in a good mood. . . . Oh, I should so like to help you.

MRS LINDE: It *is* kind of you, Nora, to want to do this for me . . . especially when *you* know so little about the troubles and hardships of life.

NORA: I? So little?

MRS LINDE [*smiling*]: Well, good heavens, a little bit of sewing and that sort of thing! You're only a baby, Nora!

NORA [*crossing the room with a toss of her head*]: Don't be so superior.

MRS LINDE: No?

NORA: You're like all the others – you none of you think I could do anything worth while. . . .

MRS LINDE: Well?

NORA: And you think I've had an easy life, with nothing to contend with.

MRS LINDE: But, Nora dear, you've just told me all your troubles.

NORAH: Pooh, they were nothing. [*Dropping her voice*] I haven't told you the really important thing.

MRS LINDE: The important thing? What was that?

NORA: I expect you look down on me, Kristina, but you've

no right to. You're proud because you worked so hard for your mother all those years.

MRS LINDE: I don't look down on anyone; but of course I'm proud – and glad – to know that I was able to make Mother's last days a little easier.

NORA: And you're proud of what you did for your brothers.

MRS LINDE: I think I have every right to be.

NORA: I quite agree. But now let me tell you something, Kristina; I've got something to be proud of, too.

MRS LINDE: I'm sure you have; what is it?

NORA: Not so loud – suppose Torvald were to hear! I wouldn't have him find out for the world. No one must know about it – no one but you, Kristina.

MRS LINDE: But what is it?

NORA: Come over here. [*Pulling her down on the sofa beside her*] Oh yes, I've something to be proud of. It was I who saved Torvald's life.

MRS LINDE: Saved his life? But how?

NORA: I told you about our trip to Italy. Torvald would never have got better if we hadn't gone there.

MRS LINDE: Yes, but your father gave you the money you needed.

NORA [*smiling*]: That's what Torvald thinks – and so does everyone else – but . . .

MRS LINDE: Well?

NORA: Papa never gave us a penny. It was I who raised the money.

MRS LINDE: You? All that money?

NORA: Twelve hundred dollars – four thousand eight hundred kroner. What do you think of that?

MRS LINDE: But how could you, Nora? Did you win it in a lottery?

NORA [*contemptuously*]: A lottery! [*With a snort*] Pooh – where would be the glory in *that*?

MRS LINDE: Where did you get it then?

NORA [*with an enigmatic smile*]: Aha! [*Humming*] Tra-la-la!

MRS LINDE: Because you certainly couldn't have borrowed it.

NORA: Oh? Why not?

MRS LINDE: Because a wife can't borrow without her husband's consent.

NORA [*with a toss of her head*]: Ah, yes she can – when it's a wife with a little flair for business – a wife who knows how to set about it . . .

MRS LINDE: But, Nora, I don't see how –

NORA: There's no reason why you should. Besides, I never said anything about *borrowing* the money. There are all sorts of ways I might have got it. [*Lying back on the sofa*] I might have got it from some admirer or other – after all, I'm quite attractive . . .

MRS LINDE: Don't be so silly!

NORA: You know, you're simply dying of curiosity, Kristina!

MRS LINDE: Now, Nora dear, listen to me – you haven't done anything rash, have you?

NORA [*sitting up*]: Is it rash to save your husband's life?

MRS LINDE: I think it's rash to do something without his knowing . . .

NORA: But I couldn't possibly let him know. Good heavens, don't you see? – it would never have done for him to realize how ill he was. It was to *me* that the doctors came; they said that his life was in danger and that the only way to save him was to take him to the south. Do you think I didn't try to wheedle him into it first? I told him how nice it would be for me to have a holiday abroad like all the other young wives. I tried tears and entreaties – I told him that he really ought to think about my condition – that he must be a dear and do what I asked. I hinted that he could easily borrow the money. But then, Kristina, he nearly lost his temper, he told me I was frivolous, and that it was his duty as a husband not to give in to what I believe he called my 'whims and fancies'. 'All right,' I thought, 'but your life must be saved somehow.' And then I thought of a way . . .

MRS LINDE: But surely your father must have told him that the money didn't come from *him*?

NORA: No – it was just then that Papa died. I'd always meant to tell him about it and ask him not to give me away, but he was so ill . . . and I'm afraid in the end there was no need.

MRS LINDE: And *you've* never told your husband?

NORA: Good heavens no, how could I? When he's so strict about that sort of thing. . . . Besides, Torvald has his pride – most men have – he'd be terribly hurt and humiliated if he thought he owed anything to me. It'd spoil everything between us, and our lovely happy home would never be the same again.

MRS LINDE: Aren't you ever going to tell him?

NORA [*thoughtfully, with a little smile*]: Well – one day, perhaps. But not for a long time. When I'm not pretty any more. No, you mustn't laugh. What I mean, of course, is when Torvald isn't as fond of me as he is now – when my dancing and dressing up and reciting don't amuse him any longer. It might be a good thing, then, to have something up my sleeve . . . [*breaking off*]. But that's nonsense – that time'll never come. Well, Kristina, what do you think of my great secret? Am I still no use? What's more, you can take my word for it that it's all been a great worry to me – it hasn't been at all easy to meet all my obligations punctually. In business, you know, there are things called 'quarterly payments' and 'instalments', and they're always dreadfully hard to meet, so you see, I've had to scrape together a little bit here and a little bit there, whenever I could. I couldn't save much out of the housekeeping money, because Torvald has to live properly, and I couldn't have the children looking shabby. I didn't feel I could touch the money that I had for my little darlings.

MRS LINDE: So it all had to come out of your own pocket-money? Poor Nora.

NORA: Of course. After all, it was my own doing. So whenever Torvald gave me money for new dresses and things, I never spent more than half of it – I always bought the simplest, cheapest things. Thank goodness anything looks well on me, so Torvald never noticed. But, oh Kristina, it hasn't been at all easy, because it's so nice to be beautifully dressed, isn't it?

MRS LINDE: It certainly is.

NORA: Then I've found other ways of earning money too. Last winter I was lucky enough to get a lot of copying to do, so I locked myself in and sat writing – often till after midnight. Oh, I was so tired sometimes . . . so tired. Still, it was really tremendous fun sitting there working and earning money. It was almost like being a man.

MRS LINDE: But how much have you been able to pay off?

NORA: Well, I don't really know exactly. You see, with a thing like that, it's very difficult to keep accounts. All I know is that I've paid out every penny that I've been able to scrape together. Often I've been at my wits' end. . . . [Smiling] Then I use to sit here and imagine that a rich old gentleman had fallen in love with me –

MRS LINDE: Oh? Who was it?

NORA: Wait a minute – and that he died, and when they read his will, there it was, as large as life: 'All my money is to go to the lovely Mrs Nora Helmer – cash down.'

MRS LINDE: But, Nora dear, who was he?

NORA: Oh, good heavens, don't you see? There wasn't really any old gentleman, it was just something that I used to sit here and imagine – often and often – when I simply didn't know which way to turn for the money. But that's all over now; the silly old gentleman can stay where he is for all I care – I've finished with him and his will, my troubles are all over! [*Jumping up*] Oh, goodness, Kristina, just think of it! No more worries! To be able to have no more worries at all! To be able to romp with the children, and to have all the lovely up-to-date things about the house that Torvald likes so much. . . . And then it'll soon be spring, and the sky'll be so blue, and perhaps we'll be able to go away for a bit. Perhaps I shall see the sea again. Oh, isn't it wonderful to be alive and happy?

[*The doorbell is heard from the hall.*]

MRS LINDE [*getting up*]: There's someone at the door – perhaps I'd better go.

NORA: No, stay. It'll be someone for Torvald, they won't come in here.

MAID [*at the hall door*]: Excuse me, Madam, there's a gentleman to see the Lawyer –

NORA: The Bank Manager, you mean.

MAID: Yes, the Bank Manager. But I didn't know – seeing the Doctor's with him –

NORA: Who is it?

KROGSTAD [*in the doorway*]: It's me, Mrs Helmer.

[MRS LINDE *gives a start, then, collecting herself, turns away to the window.*]

NORA [*tensely and in a low voice, taking a step towards him*]: You? What is it? Why do you want to see my husband?

KROGSTAD: Bank business – in a way. I have a small post at the Savings Bank, and I hear your husband is to be our new Manager –

NORA: So it's only –

KROGSTAD: Only dull official business, Mrs Helmer; nothing else whatever.

NORA: Well, you'll find him in his study. [*She bows perfunctorily and shuts the hall door. Then she goes over and attends to the stove.*]

MRS LINDE: Nora . . . who was that man?

NORA: He's a lawyer named Krogstad.

MRS LINDE: So it was really he. . . .

NORA: Do you know him?

MRS LINDE: I used to know him – years ago. He was once in a lawyer's office back at home.

NORA: Yes, so he was.

MRS LINDE: How he's changed!

NORA: He's had a very unhappy married life.

MRS LINDE: And now he's a widower?

NORA: With lots of children. There, that should burn up now. [*She shuts the door of the stove and pushes the rocking-chair a little to one side.*]

MRS LINDE: He has a finger in all sorts of business, they say.

NORA: Really? Well, they may be right, I don't know anything about. . . . But don't let's talk about business – it's so boring.

[*DR RANK comes out of HELMER'S room.*]

RANK [*in the doorway*]: No no, my dear fellow, I don't want to be in the way. Besides, I'd like to see your wife for a bit. [*As he shuts the door he notices MRS LINDE.*] Oh, I'm sorry – I'm in the way here, too.

NORA: Not in the least. [*Introducing them*] This is Dr Rank – Mrs Linde.

RANK: Ah, now that's a name that I'm constantly hearing in this house. I think I passed you on the stairs as I came up.

MRS LINDE: Yes, I don't like stairs – I have to take them very slowly.

RANK: Ah, some little internal weakness?

MRS LINDE: Only overwork, I think.

RANK: Is that all? So you've come to town for a rest – at all the parties?

MRS LINDE: I've come here to look for work.

RANK: Is that a wise remedy for overwork?

MRS LINDE: One must live, Doctor.

RANK: Yes, there seems to be a general impression that it's necessary.

NORA: Now, Dr Rank, you know you want to live, too.

RANK: Yes, indeed I do. However wretched I may be, I always want to prolong the agony as long as possible. All my patients have the same idea. And it's the same with people whose sickness is moral, too. At this very moment there's a moral invalid in there with Helmer, and –

MRS LINDE [*softly*]: Ah.

NORA: Whom do you mean?

RANK: Oh, you wouldn't know him – it's a lawyer named Krogstad. He's rotten to the core, but the first thing he said – as if it were something really important – was that he must live.

NORA: Oh. What did he want to see Torvald about?

RANK: I don't really know; all I heard was that it was something to do with the Bank.

NORA: I didn't know that Krog—that this lawyer had anything to do with the Bank.

RANK: Yes, he has some sort of post there. [*To* MRS LINDE] I don't know if it's the same where you live, but here there are people who grub around sniffing out moral corruption, and when they've found it they put it in a good job somewhere where they can keep an eye on it. The honest man probably finds himself left out in the cold.

MRS LINDE: Well, I suppose the sick need looking after.

RANK [*shrugging his shoulders*]: There you are! That's the sort of theory that's turning the community into a regular hospital!

[NORA, *deep in her own thoughts, suddenly gives a quiet laugh and claps her hands.*]

RANK: Why do you laugh at that? Do you really know what the community is?

NORA: What do I care for your dreary old community? I was

laughing at something quite different – something frightfully funny. Tell me, Dr Rank, do all the people who work at the Bank depend on Torvald now?

RANK: Is that what you found so 'frightfully funny'?

NORA [*smiling and humming*]: Ah, that's my business – that's my business! [*Pacing round the room*] Yes, it really is frightfully funny to think that we – that Torvald has all that power over so many people. [*Taking a bag from her pocket*] Won't you have a macaroon, Dr Rank?

RANK: Macaroons? Now, now! I thought they were forbidden here!

NORA: Yes, but these are some that Kristina gave me.

MRS LINDE: What? But I . . .?

NORA: No, no, don't be frightened; you weren't to know that Torvald had forbidden them. The thing is, he's afraid I shall spoil my teeth with them. But pooh – just this once! That's right, isn't it, Dr Rank? Here! [*She pops a macaroon into his mouth.*] And now you, Kristina. And I'll have one as well – just a little one. Or two at the most. [*Pacing about again*] Oh, I'm really terribly happy! Now there's just one thing in the world that I want terribly badly.

RANK: Oh? What is it?

NORA: It's something that I've been wanting terribly to say in front of Torvald.

RANK: Then why can't you say it?

NORA: Oh, I daren't – it's very bad.

MRS LINDE: Bad?

RANK: Then you'd better not say it. Though surely to *us* . . . What is it that you want so much to say in front of Torvald?

NORA: I terribly want to say – 'Well I'm damned!'[4]

RANK: You must be mad!

MRS LINDE: But, good gracious, Nora –

RANK: Well, here he comes. Say it.

NORA [*hiding the macaroons*]: Sh! Sh!

[HELMER *comes out of his room with a coat over his arm and a hat in his hand.*]

NORA [*going to him*]: Well, so you got rid of him, Torvald dear?

HELMER: Yes, he's just gone.

NORA: Let me introduce you: this is Kristina – she's come to town.

HELMER: Kristina . . .? I'm sorry, I'm afraid I don't –

NORA: Mrs Linde, Torvald dear! Kristina Linde.

HELMER: Oh yes – surely you and my wife were girls together?

MRS LINDE: Yes, we knew each other in the old days.

NORA: And just think, she's come all this way to see you!

HELMER: To see *me*?

NORA: Kristina's frightfully clever at office work, and she wants terribly to work under a really able man so that she can learn more still. . . .

HELMER: That's very wise of you, Mrs Linde.

NORA: So when she heard that you'd been made a Bank Manager – they had a telegram about it – she came down here as quickly as she could. You'll be able to do something for her, Torvald, won't you? Just to please me?

HELMER: Well, it's not impossible. . . . I take it that you're a widow, Mrs Linde?

MRS LINDE: Yes.

HELMER: And you've had commercial experience?

MRS LINDE: A certain amount, yes.

HELMER: Ah, then it's highly probable that I shall be able to find a post for you.

NORA [*clapping her hands*]: There you are! You see!

HELMER: You've come at just the right moment, Mrs Linde . . .

MRS LINDE: I can't tell you how grateful I am.

HELMER: Oh, there's no need . . . [*Putting on his overcoat*] But now you must excuse me. . . .

RANK: Wait, I'll come with you. [*He gets his fur coat from the hall and warms it at the stove.*]

NORA: Don't be long, Torvald dear.

HELMER: I shan't be more than about an hour.

NORA: Are you going too, Kristina?

MRS LINDE [*putting on her outdoor things*]: Yes, I must go and look for a room.

HELMER: Then perhaps we can all go down the street together.

NORA [*helping her*]: How tiresome that we're so short of room here – we couldn't possibly –

MRS LINDE: Oh no, you mustn't think of it. Good-bye, Nora dear – and thank you.

NORA: Good-bye for the present – you'll come back this evening, won't you? And you, too, Dr Rank. What? 'If you feel up to it'? Of course you will. Wrap up well, now!

[*They go out into the hall still talking: the children's voices are heard on the stairs.*]

NORA: Here they are! Here they are!

[*She runs out and opens the door; the nurse, ANNA-MARIA, comes in with the CHILDREN.*]

Come in, come in! [*She stoops down and kisses them.*] Oh, my little darlings! Look at them, Kristina, aren't they sweet?

RANK: Don't stand there chattering in the draught!

HELMER: Come along, Mrs Linde, this is no place for anyone but a mother!

[*He and DR RANK and MRS LINDE go down the stairs. The NURSE comes into the room with the CHILDREN, and NORA follows, shutting the hall door.*]

NORA: How nice and healthy you look! Oh, what pink cheeks – like apples and roses!

[*The CHILDREN keep chattering to her during the following:*] Did you enjoy yourselves? That's good. And so you gave Emmy and Bob a ride on your sledge? Both together? Well, fancy that! What a big boy you are, Ivar. Oh, let me take her for a minute, Nanny – my little baby dolly! [*She takes the youngest from the* NURSE *and dances with her.*] Yes, yes, Mummy'll dance with Bob too! What? You've been snowballing? Oh, I wish I'd been there. No, leave them, Nanny, I'll take their things off. Yes, let me do it, it's such fun. You look frozen – there's some hot coffee for you on the stove in the next room.

[*The* NURSE *goes into the room on the left.* NORA *takes off the* CHILDREN'S *outdoor things, throwing them down anywhere, while the* CHILDREN *all talk at once.*]

NORA: Well! So a great big dog ran after you? But he didn't bite you? No, dogs don't bite dear little baby dollies! No, don't look inside those parcels, Ivar. What's in them? Ah, wouldn't you like to know? No, no, it isn't anything nice at all! What, you want a game? What shall we play? Hide and seek? Yes, let's play hide and seek. Bob, you hide first. Me? All right, I'll hide first.

[*She and the* CHILDREN *play, laughing and shouting, both in this room and the room on the right. At last,* NORA *hides under the table. The* CHILDREN *come rushing in to look for her but they can't find her. Then, hearing her smothered laughter, they run to the table, lift the cloth, and see her. Loud shouts. She comes out on all fours as if to frighten them. Fresh shouts. Meanwhile there has been knocking on the front door, but no one has noticed it. Now the door half opens, revealing* KROGSTAD. *He waits a little as the game continues.*]

KROGSTAD: Excuse me, Mrs Helmer . . .

NORA [*with a stifled cry she turns and half rises*]: Oh! What do you want?

KROGSTAD: I'm sorry; the front door was open. Somebody must have forgotten to shut it.

NORA [*getting up*]: My husband is out, Mr Krogstad.

KROGSTAD: Yes, I know.

NORA: Then . . . what do you want here?

KROGSTAD: A word with you.

NORA: With . . .? [*Quietly, to the* CHILDREN] Go to Nanny.
What? No, the strange man isn't going to hurt Mummy –
directly he's gone, we'll go on with our game. [*She takes
the* CHILDREN *out to the room on the left, shutting the door
after them. Then, tense and wary*] You want to see me?

KROGSTAD: Yes, I do.

NORA: Today? But it isn't the first of the month yet. . . .

KROGSTAD: No, it's Christmas Eve. It all depends on you
whether you have a happy Christmas or not.

NORA: What do you want? I can't manage any today –

KROGSTAD: We'll talk about that later; this is something
different. Can you spare a moment?

NORA: Well, yes . . . I can, but –

KROGSTAD: Good. I was sitting in Olsen's restaurant, and I
saw your husband go down the street –

NORA: Well?

KROGSTAD: – with a lady.

NORA: What of it?

KROGSTAD: May I be so bold as to ask if the lady was a Mrs
Linde?

NORA: She was.

KROGSTAD: She's just arrived in town?

NORA: Today, yes.

KROGSTAD: She's a great friend of yours?

NORA: Yes, she is. But I don't see –

KROGSTAD: I knew her once, too.

NORA: Yes, I know.

KROGSTAD: Oh? So you know about it? I thought so. All
right, then I can ask you straight out: is Mrs Linde to have
a post at the Bank?

NORA: How dare you question me, Mr Krogstad – one of my
husband's subordinates. But since you ask, I'll tell you. Yes,
Mrs Linde is to have a post, and it was I who recommended
her, Mr Krogstad. So now you know.

KROGSTAD: Yes, I guessed as much.

NORA [*walking up and down*]: So it looks as if one has a *little* influence – just because one's a woman, it doesn't necessarily mean that – and people in subordinate positions, Mr Krogstad, should be careful not to offend anyone who – well –

KROGSTAD: ... who has influence?

NORA: Exactly.

KROGSTAD [*changing his tone*]: Mrs Helmer ... would you please be good enough to use your influence on my behalf?

NORA: How? What do you mean?

KROGSTAD: Would you be so kind as to see that I keep my subordinate position at the Bank?

NORA: What do you mean? Who's trying to take it away?

KROGSTAD: Oh, you needn't pretend to *me* that you don't know. I can quite see that it wouldn't be pleasant for your friend to have to keep running into me. What's more, I know now whom I shall have to thank for getting me dismissed.

NORA: But I assure you –

KROGSTAD: Oh, of course, of course. But don't let's beat about the bush – I advise you, while there's still time, to use your influence to prevent it.

NORA: But, Mr Krogstad, I haven't any influence.

KROGSTAD: No? I thought you said just now –

NORA: I didn't mean it like that, of course. I? How do you think I could influence my husband in that sort of thing?

KROGSTAD: Well ... I've known your husband since his student days – I don't think our noble Bank Manager is more inflexible than any other husband.

NORA: If you speak disrespectfully of my husband I shall show you the door!

KROGSTAD: How brave of you!

NORA: I'm not afraid of you any more. After the New Year I shall very quickly be free of the whole thing.

KROGSTAD [*controlling himself*]: Listen to me, Mrs Helmer. If need be, I shall fight to keep my little post at the Bank as I'd fight for my life.

NORA: So it seems.

KROGSTAD: It not just for the money – that's the least important thing about it. No, there's something else . . . Well, I might as well tell you – it's this: of course you know – everyone does – that I got into trouble a few years ago.

NORA: I believe I heard something of the sort.

KROGSTAD: It never came to court, but since then it's been as if every way was closed to me – that's why I took to the business that you know about. I had to live somehow, and I think I can claim that I haven't been as bad as some. But now I want to give up all that sort of thing. My sons are growing up, and in fairness to them I must try to win back as much respect as I can in the town. This post at the Bank was the first step for me – and now your husband's going to kick me off the ladder again, back into the mud.

NORA: But honestly, Mr Krogstad, there's nothing that I can do to help you.

KROGSTAD: That's because you don't want to. But I have ways of making you.

NORA: You won't tell my husband that I owe you money?

KROGSTAD: Ah . . . suppose I did?

NORA: That would be a vile thing to do. [*With tears in her voice*] I've been so proud of my secret; I couldn't bear to have him hear it like that – brutally and clumsily – and from *you*. It would put me in a most unpleasant position.

KROGSTAD: Only unpleasant?

NORA [*impetuously*]: All right, then – tell him! But it'll be the worse for you, because my husband will see what a brute you are, and then you'll certainly lose your post.

KROGSTAD: I asked you if it was only domestic unpleasantness that you were afraid of?

NORA: If my husband finds out, naturally he'll pay you whatever I still owe, and then we'll have nothing more to do with you.

KROGSTAD [*taking a step towards her*]: Listen, Mrs Helmer; either my memory isn't very good, or you don't know much about business. I shall have to make things a little clearer to you.

NORA: How?

KROGSTAD: When your husband was ill you came to me to borrow twelve hundred dollars.

NORA: I didn't know where else to go.

KROGSTAD: I promised to find you the money –

NORA: And you did find it.

KROGSTAD: I promised to find you the money on certain conditions. At the time you were so worried about your husband's illness, and so anxious to get the money for your journey, that I don't think you paid much attention to the details – so it won't be out of place if I remind you of them. Well ... I promised to find you the money against a note of hand which I drew up.

NORA: Yes, and which I signed.

KROGSTAD: Exactly. But below that I'd added a few lines making your father surety for the money. Your father was to sign this clause.

NORA: Was to? But he did sign.

KROGSTAD: I'd left the date blank – that's to say, your father was to fill in the date when he signed the paper. Do you remember?

NORA: Yes, I think so ...

KROGSTAD: Then I gave you the document so that you could post it to your father. Is that correct?

NORA: Yes.

KROGSTAD: And of course you sent it at once, because only five or six days later you brought it back to me with your father's signature ... and I handed over the money.

NORA: Well? Haven't I paid it off regularly?

KROGSTAD: Yes, fairly regularly. But – to get back to the point – you were going through a trying time just then, Mrs Helmer?

NORA: I certainly was.

KROGSTAD: Your father was ill, I believe?

NORA: He was dying.

KROGSTAD: He died soon afterwards?

NORA: Yes.

KROGSTAD: Tell me, Mrs Helmer, do you happen to remember the day he died? The day of the month, I mean?

NORA: Papa died on the twenty-ninth of September.

KROGSTAD: That is correct – I've confirmed that for myself. And that brings us to a curious thing [*producing a paper*] which I'm quite unable to explain.

NORA: What curious thing? I don't know of any –

KROGSTAD: The curious thing, Mrs Helmer, is that your father signed this note of hand three days after his death.

NORA: How? I don't understand.

KROGSTAD: Your father died on the twenty-ninth of September. But look at this – your father has dated his signature the second of October. Isn't that a curious thing, Mrs Helmer?

[NORA *is silent.*]

Can you explain it?

[NORA *is still silent.*]

It's odd, too, that the words October the second and the year aren't in your father's handwriting, but in a writing that I think I know. Well, of course, that could be explained – your father might have forgotten to date his signature, and someone else might have guessed at the date before they knew of his death. There's nothing wrong in that. It's the signature that really matters. That *is* genuine, isn't it, Mrs Helmer? It really was your father himself who wrote his name there?

NORA [*after a moment's pause, throwing her head back and looking defiantly at him*]: No, it was not. *I* wrote Papa's name.

KROGSTAD: Look, Mrs Helmer, you know that that's a very dangerous admission?

NORA: Why? You'll soon get your money.

KROGSTAD: May I ask you something? Why didn't you send the paper to your father?

NORA: I couldn't; he was far too ill. If I'd asked him for his signature, I should have had to tell him what the money was for – and when he was so ill himself, I couldn't tell him that my husband's life was in danger – I couldn't possibly.

KROGSTAD: Then it would have been better for you if you'd given up your trip abroad.

NORA: I couldn't do that. The journey was to save my husband's life – how could I give it up?

KROGSTAD: But didn't it occur to you that you were tricking me?

NORA: I couldn't worry about that – I wasn't thinking about you at all. I couldn't bear the way you were so cold-blooded – the way you made difficulties although you knew how desperately ill my husband was.

KROGSTAD: Mrs Helmer, you obviously don't realize what you've been guilty of; but let me tell you that the thing that I once did that ruined my reputation was nothing more – and nothing worse – than that.

NORA: You? Are you trying to tell me that you would have done a brave deed to save your wife's life?

KROGSTAD: The law is not concerned with motives.

NORA: Then it must be a very stupid law.

KROGSTAD: Stupid or not, it's the law that you'll be judged by if I produce this paper in court.

NORA: I simply don't believe that. Hasn't a daughter the right to protect her dying father from worry and anxiety? Hasn't a wife the right to save her husband's life? I don't know much about the law, but I'm quite certain that it must say somewhere that things like that are allowed. Don't you, a lawyer, know that? You must be a very stupid lawyer, Mr Krogstad.

KROGSTAD: Possibly. But you'll admit that I do understand business – the sort of business that you and I have been engaged in? Very well, you do as you please. But I tell you this – if I'm to be flung out for the second time, you'll keep me company! [*He bows and goes out through the hall.*]

NORA [*after a moment's thought, with a toss of her head*]: What nonsense! Trying to frighten me like that! I'm not as silly as all that. [*She starts to busy herself by tidying the children's clothes, but soon stops.*] But . . . No, it isn't possible . . . I did it for love!

CHILDREN [*at the door to the left*]. Mamma, the strange man's just gone out of the front door.

NORA: Yes . . . yes, I know. Now, you're not to tell anyone about the strange man, do you hear? Not even Papa.

CHILDREN: No, Mamma. Will you come and play with us again now?

NORA: No – not just now.

CHILDREN: But, Mamma, you promised!

NORA: Yes, but now I can't. Run along. I'm busy – run along, there's good children. [*She pushes them gently into the other room and shuts the door after them. She sits on the sofa and, picking up her needlework, she does a stitch or two but soon stops.*] No! [*She throws down the work and, rising, goes to the hall door and calls*] Helena – bring me the tree, please. [*Going to the table on the left, she opens the drawer, then pauses again.*] No! It's simply not possible!

MAID [*with the Christmas tree*]: Where shall I put it, Madam?

NORA: Here, in the middle of the room.

MAID: Is there anything else you want?

NORA: No, thank you, I've got all I want.

[*The MAID, having put the tree down, goes out.*]

NORA [*busily decorating the tree*]: A candle here . . . and flowers here. . . . That horrible man! It's all nonsense . . . nonsense, there's nothing in it! We shall have a lovely tree – I'll do all the things you like, Torvald, I'll sing and dance –

[HELMER *comes in with a bundle of papers under his arm.*]

NORA: Oh, are you back already?

HELMER: Yes. Has there been anyone here?

NORA: Here? No.

HELMER: That's odd; I saw Krogstad coming out of the gate.

NORA: Did you? Oh yes, that's right; Krogstad *was* here for a moment.

HELMER: Nora, I can see by your face that he's been here begging you to put in a good word for him.

NORA: Yes.

HELMER: And you were to make it look as if it was your own idea. You weren't to let me know that he'd been here. That was what he asked, wasn't it?

NORA: Yes, Torvald, but –

HELMER: Nora, Nora, would you lend yourself to that sort of thing? Talking to a man like that – making him promises? And, worst of all, telling me a lie!

NORA: A lie?

HELMER: Didn't you say that no one had been here? [*Shaking a finger at her*] My little songbird mustn't ever do that again. A songbird must have a clear voice to sing with – no false notes. [*Putting his arm round her*] That's true, isn't it? Yes, I knew it was. [*Letting her go*] Now we won't say any more about it. [*Sitting by the stove*] Ah, this is nice and comfortable! [*He glances through his papers.*]

NORA [*after working at the Christmas tree for a little*]: Torvald?

HELMER: Yes?

NORA: I'm terribly looking forward to the day after tomorrow – the fancy-dress party at the Stenborgs.

HELMER: And I'm 'terribly' curious to see what surprise you're planning for me.

NORA: Oh, it's so silly . . .

HELMER: What is?

NORA: I can't think of anything that'll do. Everything seems so stupid and pointless.

HELMER: So little Nora's realized that?

NORA [*behind his chair, with her arms on the chair-back*]: Are you very busy, Torvald?

HELMER: Well . . .

NORA: What are all those papers?

HELMER: Bank business.

NORA: Already?

HELMER: I've asked the retiring Manager to give me full authority to make some necessary changes in the staff, and the working arrangements – that'll take me all Christmas week. I want to have everything ready by New Year's Day.

NORA: So that was why poor Krogstad –

HELMER: Hm!

NORA [*still leaning over the chair-back, and gently stroking his hair*]: If you hadn't been so busy, Torvald, I'd have asked you a terribly great favour. . . .

HELMER: Well, what is it? Tell me.

NORA: No one has such good taste as you have, and I do so want to look nice at the fancy-dress party. Torvald, couldn't you take me in hand and decide what I'm to go as – what my costume's to be?

HELMER: Aha! So my little obstinate one's out of her depth, and wants someone to rescue her?

NORA: Yes, Torvald, I can't do anything without you to help me.

HELMER: Well, well . . . I'll think about it. We'll find something.

NORA: Oh, that *is* nice of you! [*She goes to the Christmas tree again. Pause.*] How pretty these red flowers look. . . . Tell me about this Krogstad – was it really so bad, what he did?

HELMER: He forged a signature. Have you any idea what that means?

NORA: Mightn't he have done it from dire necessity?

HELMER: Possibly – or, like so many others, from sheer fool-hardiness. Oh, I'm not so hard-hearted that I'd condemn a man outright for just a single slip.

NORA: No, you wouldn't, would you, Torvald?

HELMER: Many a man can redeem his character if he freely confesses his guilt and takes his punishment.

NORA: Punishment . . .?

HELMER: But Krogstad did nothing of the sort – he tried to wriggle out of it with tricks and subterfuges. That's what has corrupted him.

NORA: Do you think that would . . .?

HELMER: Just think how a guilty man like that must have to lie and cheat and play the hypocrite with everyone. How he must wear a mask even with those nearest and dearest to him – yes, even with his own wife and children. Yes, even with his children – that's the most dreadful thing, Nora.

NORA: Why?

HELMER: Because an atmosphere of lies like that infects and poisons the whole life of a home. In a house like that, every breath that the children take is filled with the germs of evil.

NORA [closer behind him]: Are you certain of that?

HELMER: Oh, my dear, as a lawyer I've seen it so often; nearly all young men who go to the bad have had lying mothers.

NORA: Why only mothers?

HELMER: It's generally the fault of the mother, though of course a father can have the same effect – as every lawyer very well knows. And certainly for years this fellow Krog-stad has been going home and poisoning his own children with lies and deceit. That's why I call him a moral out-cast. [Holding out his hands to her] So my darling little Nora must promise me not to plead his cause. Let's shake hands

on that. Now then, what's this? Give me your hand. . . .
That's better; now it's a bargain. I tell you, it'd be quite
impossible for me to work with him; when I'm near people
like that, I actually feel physically ill.

NORA [*withdrawing her hand and going over to the far side of the
Christmas tree*]: How hot it is in here! And I have so much
to see to.

HELMER [*rising and collecting his papers*]: Yes, and I must try
to look through a few of these before dinner. And I'll
think about your fancy-dress, too. And perhaps I'll have
something in gold paper to hang on the Christmas tree.
[*Taking her head in his hands*] My darling little songbird!
[*He goes to his room, shutting the door behind him.*]

NORA [*in a hushed voice, after a moment*]: Oh no! It can't be
true . . . no, it's not possible. It *can't* be possible!

NURSE [*at the door on the left*]: The children want to come in
to Mamma – they're asking so prettily.

NORA: No! No! Don't let then come near me! Keep them
with you, Nanny.

NURSE: Yes Ma'am. [*She shuts the door.*]

NORA [*white with fear*]: Corrupt my little children – poison
my home? [*She pauses, then throws up her head.*] That's not
true! It could never, never be true.

ACT TWO

The same room. In the corner by the piano stands the Christmas tree; it is stripped[5] and dishevelled, with the stumps of burnt-out candles. Nora's outdoor clothes are on the sofa.

[NORA, *alone in the room, walks about restlessly. Eventually she stops by the sofa and picks up her cloak.*]

NORA [*letting the cloak fall again*]: Someone's coming! [*She goes to the door to listen.*] No – there's no one there. Of course no one would come today – not on Christmas Day. Nor tomorrow either. But perhaps ... [*She opens the door and looks out.*] No, there's nothing in the letter-box – it's quite empty. [*Coming back into the room*] What nonsense – he can't really have meant it. A thing like that *couldn't* happen. It isn't possible – I have three little children!

[*The* NURSE *comes in from the room on the left, with a huge cardboard box.*]

NURSE: I've found the box with the fancy-dress at last.

NORA: Thank you; put it on the table.

NURSE [*doing so*]: But it's in a terrible state.

NORA: I should like to tear it all to pieces.

NURSE: Heaven forbid! It can soon be put right – it only needs a little patience.

NORA: Yes, I'll go and get Mrs Linde to help me.

NURSE: You're never going out again – in this awful weather? You'll catch your death of cold, Miss Nora, Ma'am!

NORA: Well, there are worse things than that. How are the children?

NURSE: The poor little mites are playing with their presents, but –

NORA: Do they ask for me much?

NURSE: You see, they're so used to having their Mamma with them.

NORA: But, Nanny, I *can't* be with them like I used to.

NURSE: Oh well, young children'll get used to anything.

NORA: Do you think so? Do you think they'd forget their Mamma if she went away altogether?

NURSE: Went away altogether? But bless my soul . . .!

NORA: Tell me, Nanny . . . I've often wondered, how did you ever have the heart to hand over your child to strangers?

NURSE: But I had to, so that I could come and be Nanny to my little Nora.

NORA: Yes, but how could you *want* to?

NURSE: When I had the chance of such a good place? Any poor girl who'd got into trouble would be glad to. And that blackguard of a man never did a thing for me.

NORA: I suppose your daughter's quite forgotten you?

NURSE: No, indeed she hasn't. She wrote to me when she was confirmed, and again when she got married.

NORA [*putting her arms round her*]: Dear old Nanny, you were a wonderful mother to me when I was little.

NURSE: Poor little Nora – she hadn't any other mother but me.

NORA: And if *my* babies hadn't any other mother, I know you'd . . . Oh, I'm talking nonsense. [*Opening the box*] Go to them now; I must just – You'll see how fine I shall look tomorrow.

NURSE: I'm sure there won't be anyone in all the party as fine as you, Miss Nora, Ma'am. [*She goes out to the room on the left.*]

NORA [*starting to unpack the box, but soon pushing it away*]: Oh, if only I dared go out! If I could be sure that no one would come – that nothing would happen here in the meantime. . . . Don't be so silly – no one will come. I just mustn't think about it. I'll brush the muff. Pretty, pretty

gloves! Don't think about it – don't think! One . . . two . . .
three . . . four . . . five . . . six—[*She screams*] Ah, they're
coming!

[*She starts for the door, but stands irresolute.* MRS LINDE
comes in from the hall, where she has left her street clothes.]

NORA: Oh, it's you, Kristina! There isn't anyone else out
there? Oh, it was good of you to come!

MRS LINDE: They told me you'd been over to ask for me.

NORA: Yes, I was just passing. Actually, there's something
you could help me with. Come and sit on the sofa. Look,
the people upstairs, the Stenborgs, are having a fancy-dress
party tomorrow night, and Torvald wants me to go as a
Neopolitan fisher-girl and dance the tarantella that I learnt
in Capri.

MRS LINDE: I see, you're going to give a real performance?

NORA: Yes, Torvald says I ought to. Look, here's the costume
– Torvald had it made for me when we were out there, but
it's so torn now – I really don't know –

MRS LINDE: Oh, we can easily put that right – it's just that
some of the trimming's come undone in places. Have you
got a needle and cotton? There, that's all we want.

NORA: Oh, this *is* kind of you.

MRS LINDE [*as she sews*]: So tomorrow you'll be all dressed
up? I tell you what, Nora, I'll drop in for a moment and
see you in all your finery. But I'm quite forgetting to thank
you for a lovely evening yesterday.

NORA [*getting up and crossing the room*]: Oh, yesterday . . . I
didn't think it was as nice as usual. I wish you'd come up to
town earlier, Kristina. Yes, Torvald certainly knows how to
make a house attractive and comfortable.

MRS LINDE: And so do you, if you ask *me*, or you wouldn't
be your father's daughter. But tell me, is Dr Rank always as
depressed as he was last night?

NORA: No, it was worse than usual last night. But he's really
very ill, poor man, he has consumption of the spine. The

fact is, his father was a horrible man who had mistresses and that sort of thing, so, you see, the son's been delicate all his life.

MRS LINDE [*putting down her sewing*]: But, dearest Nora, how do you come to know about things like that?

NORA [*walking about*]: Pooh – when you've had three children, you get visits from – from women with a certain amount of medical knowledge – and they gossip about these things.

MRS LINDE [*after a short silence – sewing again*]: Does Dr Rank come here every day?

NORA: Oh yes, he and Torvald have been friends all their lives, and he's a great friend of mine too. Why, Dr Rank's almost one of the family.

MRS LINDE: But tell me, is he quite sincere? I mean doesn't he rather like saying things to please people?

NORA: Not in the least. Whatever makes you think that?

MRS LINDE: Well, when you introduced us yesterday, he said he'd often heard my name in this house, but I noticed later that your husband had no idea who I was. So how could Dr Rank . . .?

NORA: Yes, that's quite right, Kristina. You see, Torvald's so incredibly fond of me that he wants to keep me all to himself, as he says. In the early days he used to get quite jealous if I even mentioned people I'd liked back at home, so of course I gave it up. But I often talk to Dr Rank, because, you see, he likes to hear about them.

MRS LINDE: Look, Nora, in lots of things you're still a child. I'm older than you in many ways and I've had a little more experience. There's something I'd like to say to you: you ought to stop all this with Dr Rank.

NORA: What ought I to stop?

MRS LINDE: Well ... two things, I think. Yesterday you were talking about a rich admirer who was going to bring you money –

NORA: Yes, but he doesn't exist – unfortunately. But what about it?

MRS LINDE: Is Dr Rank rich?

NORA: Oh yes.

MRS LINDE: And has no one to provide for?

NORA: No one; but –

MRS LINDE: And he comes to the house every day?

NORA: Yes, I just said so.

MRS LINDE: How can a man of his breeding be so tactless?

NORA: I simply don't know what you mean.

MRS LINDE: Don't pretend, Nora. Do you think I don't know whom you borrowed that twelve hundred dollars from?

NORA: Have you gone completely mad? How could you think a thing like that? From a friend who comes here every single day? That would have been an absolutely impossible situation.

MRS LINDE: It really wasn't him?

NORA: No, I promise you. Why, it would never have entered my head for a moment. Besides, in those days he hadn't the money to lend – he came into it later.

MRS LINDE: Well, Nora dear, I think that was lucky for you.

NORA: No, it would never have entered my head to ask Dr Rank. Though I'm quite sure that if I *were* to ask him . . .

MRS LINDE: But of course you wouldn't.

NORA: Of course not. I can't imagine that there'd ever be any need. But I'm quite sure that if I told Dr Rank –

MRS LINDE: Behind your husband's back?

NORA: I must get clear of this other thing – that's behind his back too. I must get clear of that.

MRS LINDE: Yes, that's what I was saying yesterday, but –

NORA [*pacing up and down*]: A man can straighten out these things so much better than a woman . . .

MRS LINDE: Her husband, yes.

NORA: Nonsense. [*Coming to a halt*] When you've paid off everything you owe, you do get your bond back, don't you?

MRS LINDE: Of course.

NORA: And you can tear it into little pieces and burn it – the horrid filthy thing?

MRS LINDE [*giving her a penetrating look, she puts down her sewing and rises slowly*]: Nora, you're hiding something from me.

NORA: Is it as obvious as all that?

MRS LINDE: Something's happened to you since yesterday morning. Nora, what is it?

NORA [*going to her*]: Kristina – [*Listening*] Sh! Here's Torvald coming back. Look, go in and sit with the children for a bit – Torvald can't bear to see dressmaking. Let Nanny help you.

MRS LINDE [*picking up a pile of things*]: All right then; but I'm not going away till we've talked the whole thing over. [*She goes out to the left as* TORVALD *comes in from the hall.*]

NORA [*going to him*]: Oh, Torvald dear, I've been so longing for you to come back.

TORVALD: Was that the dressmaker?

NORA: No, it was Kristina – she's helping me to mend my costume. You know, I'm going to look so nice. . . .

TORVALD: Now wasn't that a good idea of mine?

NORA: Splendid. But wasn't it nice of me to do as you said?

TORVALD [*lifting her chin*]: Nice? To do what your husband says? All right, little scatterbrain, I know you didn't mean it like that. But don't let me interrupt you – I know you'll be wanting to try it on.

NORA: I suppose you've got work to do?

TORVALD: Yes; [*showing her a bundle of papers*] look, I've been down to the Bank. [*He starts to go to his study.*]

NORA: Torvald . . .

HELMER [*stopping*]: Yes?

NORA: If your little squirrel were to ask you very prettily for something . . .

HELMER: Well?

NORA: Would you do it?

HELMER: Well, naturally I should have to know what it is, first.

NORA: Your squirrel will scamper about and do all her tricks, if you'll be nice and do what she asks.

HELMER: Out with it, then.

NORA: Your skylark'll sing all over the house – up and down the scale . . .

HELMER: Oh well, my skylark does that anyhow!

NORA: I'll be a fairy and dance on a moonbeam for you, Torvald.

HELMER: Nora, you surely don't mean that matter you mentioned this morning?

NORA [*nearer*]: Yes, Torvald, I really do beg you –

HELMER: I'm surprised at your bringing that up again.

NORA: Oh, but you must do as I ask – you must let Krogstad keep his place at the Bank.

HELMER: My dear Nora, it's his place that I'm giving to Mrs Linde.

NORA: Yes, that's terribly nice of you. But you could dismiss some other clerk instead of Krogstad.

HELMER: Now, you're just being extremely obstinate. Because you're irresponsible enough to go and promise to put in a word for him, you expect me to –

NORA: No, it isn't that, Torvald – it's for your own sake. The man writes for the most scurrilous newspapers – you told me so yourself – there's no knowing what harm he could do you. I'm simply frightened to death of him. . . .

HELMER: Ah, now I understand; you remember what happened before, and that frightens you.

NORA: What do you mean?

HELMER: You're obviously thinking of your father.

NORA: Yes – yes, that's it. Just remember the wicked things they put in the papers about Papa – how cruelly they slandered him. I believe they'd have had him dismissed if the Ministry hadn't sent you to look into it, and if you hadn't been so kind and helpful to him.

HELMER: Dear little Nora, there's a considerable difference between your father and me. Your father's reputation as an official was not above suspicion – mine is, and I hope it will continue to be as long as I hold this position.

NORA: But you never know what harm people can do. We could live so happily and peacefully now, you and I and the children, Torvald, without a care in the world in our comfortable home. That's why I do implore you –

HELMER: But it's precisely by pleading for him that you make it impossible for me to keep him. They know already at the Bank that I mean to dismiss Krogstad; suppose it were to get about that the new Manager had let himself be influenced by his wife. . . .

NORA: Well, would that matter?

HELMER: No, of course not! So long as an obstinate little woman got her own way! So I'm to make a laughing-stock of myself before the whole staff – with everybody saying that I can be swayed by all sorts of outside influences? I should soon have to face the consequences, I can tell you. Besides, there's one thing which makes it quite impossible for Krogstad to stay at the Bank so long as I'm Manager.

NORA: What?

HELMER: Perhaps at a pinch I might have overlooked his moral failings –

NORA: Yes, Torvald, couldn't you?

HELMER: And I hear that he's quite a good worker, too. But he was at school with me – it was one of those unfortunate friendships that one so often comes to regret later in life. I may as well tell you frankly that we were on Christian-name terms,[6] and he's tactless enough to keep it up still – in

front of everyone! In fact, he seems to think he has a *righ*
to be familiar with me, and out he comes with 'Torvald
this' and 'Torvald that' all the time. I tell you, it's most
unpleasant for me – he'll make my position in the Bank
quite intolerable.

NORA: You surely can't mean that, Torvald!

HELMER: Oh? Why not?

NORA: Well – that's such a petty reason.

HELMER: What do you mean? Petty? Do you think I'm
petty?

NORA: No, Torvald dear – far from it; that's just why –

TORVALD: Never mind! You said my motives were petty,
so I must be petty too. Petty! Very well, we'll settle this
matter once and for all. [*He goes to the hall door and calls*]
Helena!

NORA: What are you going to do?

HELMER [*searching among his papers*]: Settle things.
    [*The* MAID *comes in.*]
Here, take this letter downstairs at once, find a messenger,
and get him to deliver it. Immediately, mind. The address
is on it. Wait – here's the money.

MAID: Yes, sir. [*She goes with the letter.*]

HELMER [*collecting his papers*]: There, little Miss Stubborn!

NORA [*breathless*]: Torvald . . . what was in that letter?

HELMER: Krogstad's notice.

NORA: Call it back, Torvald – there's still time. Oh Torvald,
call it back, for my sake – for your own sake – for the
children's sake. Listen, Torvald, you don't know what that
letter can do to us all.

TORVALD: It's too late.

NORA: Yes . . . it's too late.

HELMER: My dear Nora, I can forgive your anxiety – though
actually it's rather insulting to me. Oh yes, it is. Isn't it
insulting to believe that I could be afraid of some wretched
scribbler's revenge? Still, it's a very touching proof of your

love for me, so I forgive you. [*He takes her in his arms.*]
Now, my own darling Nora, that's all settled. Whatever
happens, when it comes to the point you can be quite sure
that I shall have the necessary courage and strength. You'll
see that I'm man enough to take it all on myself.

NORA [*horror-struck*]: What do you mean?

HELMER: Exactly what I say.

NORA [*recovering*]: You shall never never have to do that.

HELMER: Very well, Nora, then we shall share it as man and
wife; that's what we'll do. [*Caressing her*] Are you happy
now? There – there – there – don't look like a little frightened dove – the whole thing's just sheer imagination. Now
you must rehearse your tarantella – with the tambourine.
I'll go and sit in the inner room and shut the doors, so you
can make all the noise you like – I shan't hear a thing.
[*Turning in the doorway*] And when Dr Rank comes, tell
him where I am. [*Taking his papers, he gives her a nod and
goes into his room, shutting the door behind him.*]

NORA [*half crazy with fear, she stands as if rooted to the spot and
whispers*]: He'd really do it – he'd do it! He'd do it in spite
of everything. No – never in the world! Anything rather
than that! There must be some way out – some help.

   [*There is a ring at the door.*]

Dr Rank! Yes, anything rather than that – anything-
whatever it is.

   [*Passing her hands over her face, she pulls herself together and
goes and opens the hall door. DR RANK is standing there hanging up his fur coat. During the following scene it begins to
grow dark.*]

NORA: Good afternoon, Dr Rank – I recognized your ring.
But you mustn't go in to Torvald now, I think he's got
some work to finish.

RANK: What about you?

NORA [*shutting the door after him as he comes into the room*]:
Oh, I always have time for you – you know that.

RANK: Thank you. I shall take advantage of that for as long as I'm able.

NORA: What do you mean by that? As long as you're able?

RANK: Yes . . . does that alarm you?

NORA: It seemed such an odd way to put it. Is anything going to happen?

RANK: Yes . . . something that I've been expecting for a long time – though I never really thought it'd come quite so soon.

NORA [clutching his arm]: What have you just learned? Dr Rank, you must tell me!

RANK [sitting by the stove]: The sands are running out for me. . . . There's nothing to be done about it.

NORA [with a sigh of relief]: Then it's *you* . . .!

RANK: Who else? There's no point in deceiving myself – I'm the most wretched of all my patients, Mrs Helmer. These last few days I've been holding an audit of my internal economy. Bankrupt! In less than a month, perhaps, I shall lie rotting in the churchyard.

NORA: Oh no – that's a horrible thing to say.

RANK: The thing itself is damnably horrible. But worst of all is the horror that must be gone through first. There's still one more test to make, and when I've finished *that* I shall know pretty well when the final disintegration will begin. But there's something I want to say to you; Helmer's too sensitive to be able to face anything ugly – I won't have him in my sick-room.

NORA: But, Dr Rank –

RANK: I won't have him there – not on any account. I shall lock the door against him. As soon as I'm quite certain that the worst has come, I shall send you my card with a black cross on it and then you'll know that my disgusting end has begun.

NORA: No, you're really being absurd today – and just when I so wanted you to be in a particularly good mood.

RANK: What, with death just round the corner? And when it's to pay for someone else's sins! Where's the justice in that? Yet in one way or another there isn't a single family where some such inexorable retribution isn't being exacted.

NORA [*stopping her ears*]: Nonsense! Cheer up – cheer up!

RANK: Yes, indeed, the whole thing's nothing but a joke! My poor innocent spine must pay for my father's amusements as a gay young subaltern.

NORA [*by the table on the left*]: He was too fond of asparagus and *foie gras* – isn't that it?

RANK: Yes, and truffles.

NORA: Truffles, yes. And oysters, too, I suppose?

RANK: Oysters? Oh yes, certainly oysters.

NORA: And then all that port and champagne. What a shame that all those nice things should attack the bones.

RANK: Especially when the unfortunate bones that they attack never had the least enjoyment out of them.

NORA: Yes, that's the saddest part of all.

RANK [*with a searching look at her*]: Hm! . . .

NORA [*after a moment*]: Why did you smile?

RANK: No, it's you who were laughing.

NORA: No, you smiled, Dr Rank.

RANK [*getting up*]: You're more of a rascal than I thought.

NORA: I'm in a ridiculous mood today.

RANK: So it seems.

NORA [*putting both hands on his shoulders*]: Dear, dear Dr Rank, you mustn't die and leave Torvald and me.

RANK: Oh, you'd soon get over it – those who go away are quickly forgotten.

NORA [*looking at him anxiously*]: Do you believe that?

RANK: People make new friends, and then . . .

NORA: Who makes new friends?

RANK: You and Torvald will, when I'm gone. It looks to me as if *you're* starting already. What was that Mrs Linde doing here last night?

NORA: Oh, surely you're not jealous of poor Kristina.

RANK: Yes, I am. She'll take my place in this house. After I've gone, I expect that woman will –

NORA: Sh! Not so loud – she's in there!

RANK: There you are! She's here again today.

NORA: Only to mend my dress. Good gracious, you *are* being absurd. [*Sitting on the sofa*] Now be nice, Dr Rank, and tomorrow you'll see how beautifully I shall dance, and you can tell yourself that it's all for you – and for Torvald too, of course. [*Taking various things out of the box*] Come and sit here, Dr Rank, and I'll show you something.

RANK: What is it?

NORA: Look here. Look.

RANK: Silk stockings.

NORA: Flesh coloured – aren't they lovely? The light's bad in here now, but tomorrow ... No, no, no, you must only look at the feet. Oh well, you may see the rest, too.

RANK: Hm ...

NORA: Why are you looking so critical? Don't you think they'll fit?

RANK: I can't possibly give you an opinion on that.

NORA [*looking at him for a moment*]: You ought to be ashamed of yourself! [*She flips him lightly on the cheek with the stockings.*] Take that! [*She rolls them up again.*]

RANK: What other pretty things have you to show me?

NORA: You shan't see another thing – you've been very naughty. [*She hums a little as she rummages among her things.*]

RANK [*after a short pause*]: When I sit here like this talking to you so intimately, I can't imagine – no, I really can't – what would have become of me if I hadn't had this house to come to.

NORA [*smiling*]: I believe you really do feel at home with us.

RANK [*more quietly, looking straight in front of him*]: And to have to leave it all!

NORA: Nonsense, you're not going to leave us.

RANK [*as before*]: Not to be able to leave behind even the smallest token of gratitude – hardly even a passing regret. Nothing but an empty place that the next person to come along will fill just as well.

NORA: Suppose I were to ask you for a . . . No . . .

RANK: For a what?

NORA: For a great proof of your friendship.

RANK: Yes.

NORA: No, I mean a terribly great favour.

RANK: I should be very happy if – just for once – you'd give me the chance.

NORA: Ah, but you don't know what it is.

RANK: Tell me, then.

NORA: No, Dr Rank, I can't. It's something really enormous – not just advice or help, but a really great favour.

RANK: The greater the better. I can't think what it can be, so tell me. Don't you trust me?

NORA: There's no one else I'd trust more than you. I know you're my best, most faithful friend, so I'll tell you. . . . Well, Dr Rank – it's something you must help me to stave off. You know how much – how incredibly deeply – Torvald loves me. He wouldn't hesitate for a moment to give his life for me.

RANK [*leaning nearer to her*]: Nora . . . Do you think he's the only one?

NORA [*with a slight start*]: The only one . . .?

RANK: Who'd gladly give his life for you?

NORA [*sadly*]: Ah . . .

RANK: I promised myself that I'd tell you before I went away, and I could never have a better opportunity. Well, Nora, now you know. And you know, too, that you can trust me – more than anyone else.

NORA [*calmly and evenly; rising*]: I must go.

RANK [*making way for her, but still sitting*]: Nora . . .

NORA [*in the hall doorway*]: Helena, bring the lamp. [*Going to the stove*] Oh, dear Dr Rank, that was really horrid of you.

RANK [*rising*]: To have loved you as deeply as anyone else – was that horrid?

NORA: No . . . but to go and tell me so. There was really no need to do that.

RANK: What do you mean? Did you know?

[*The* MAID *brings in the lamp, puts it on the table, and goes again.*]

RANK: Nora – Mrs Helmer – I ask you: did you know?

NORA: Oh, how can I say if I knew or didn't know? I've really no idea. How could you be so clumsy, Dr Rank? When everything was going so well. . . .

RANK: Well, at any rate you know that I'm at your service – body and soul. So won't you say what it is?

NORA [*looking at him*]: After what's happened?

RANK: Please – please tell me what it is.

NORA: I can never tell you now.

RANK: Please. You mustn't punish me like this. If you'll let me, I promise to do anything for you that a man can.

NORA: There's nothing you can do for me now. Besides, I certainly don't need any help – it was all my imagination, really it was. Honestly. [*Smiling*] You're a fine one, Dr Rank! Aren't you ashamed of yourself, now that the lamp's come in?

RANK: No . . . not really. But perhaps I ought to go – for good.

NORA: No, you certainly mustn't do that – of course you must come here just as usual. You know Torvald couldn't get on without you.

RANK: But what about you?

NORA: Oh, I'm always tremendously glad to see you.

RANK: That's just what misled me. You're a mystery to me. . . . I've sometimes thought you'd as soon be with me as with Helmer.

NORA: You see, there are some people that one loves, and others that perhaps one would rather be with.

RANK: Yes, there's something in that.

NORA: When I lived at home, naturally I loved Papa best, but I always found it terribly amusing to slip into the servants' hall, because they always talked about such interesting things, and they never lectured me at all.

RANK: Ah, and now I've taken their place?

NORA [*jumping up and going over to him*]: Oh, dear kind Dr Rank, that isn't what I meant at all. But I'm sure you can see that being with Torvald is very like being with Papa.

[*The* MAID *comes in from the hall.*]

MAID: Excuse me, Madam. . . . [*She whispers to* NORA *as she hands her a card.*]

NORA [*glancing at the card*]: Oh! [*She puts it in her pocket.*]

RANK: Is there anything wrong?

NORA: No, no, not in the least. It's only something . . . it's my new dress.

RANK: But . . .? Surely your dress is out there?

NORA: Ah, that one, yes. But this is another one that I've ordered – I don't want Torvald to know. . . .

RANK: Aha! So *that's* your great secret?

NORA: Yes, of course. Go in to Torvald – he's in the inner room – keep him there till . . .

RANK: Don't worry, I shan't let him escape. [*He goes into* HELMER'S *room.*]

NORA [*to the* MAID]: Is he waiting in the kitchen?

MAID: Yes, Madam, he came up the back stairs.

NORA: But didn't you tell him there was someone here?

MAID: Yes, but it wasn't any good.

NORA: He wouldn't go away?

MAID: No, he won't go till he's seen you, Madam.

NORA: Oh, all right, let him come in. Quietly, though. Helena, you mustn't mention this to anyone – it's a surprise for my husband.

MAID: Yes, I understand. [*She goes.*]

NORA: Oh, this is dreadful – it's going to happen after all. No, no, no, it *can't* – I won't let it!

[*She goes and pushes the bolt home on* HELMER'S *door. The* MAID *opens the hall door to let* KROGSTAD *in, and shuts it after him. He is wearing travelling clothes, high boots, and a fur cap.*]

NORA [*going to him*]: Keep your voice down – my husband's at home.

KROGSTAD: What of it?

NORA: What do you want?

KROGSTAD: To find out something.

NORA: Be quick, then; what is it?

KROGSTAD: You know that I've been dismissed?

NORA: I couldn't stop it, Mr Krogstad. I did absolutely everything I could for you, but it was no good.

KROGSTAD: Your husband can't love you very much, can he? He knows that I can expose you, and yet he dares to –

NORA: You surely don't imagine that he knows about it?

KROGSTAD: Well, no – I didn't really think so; it wouldn't be at all like our worthy Torvald Helmer to have so much courage.

NORA: Kindly show some respect for my husband, Mr Krogstad.

KROGSTAD: But of course – all the respect he deserves. As you seem so anxious to keep things secret, I presume that you have a rather clearer idea than you had yesterday of what it is that you've actually done.

NORA: Clearer than you could ever make it.

KROGSTAD: Oh yes, I'm such a stupid lawyer!

NORA: What do you want?

KROGSTAD: Only to see how things stood with you, Mrs Helmer. I've been thinking about you all day. Even a mere cashier, a scribbler, a – well, a man like me, has a certain amount of what is called 'feeling', you know.

NORA: Then show it. Think of my little children.

KROGSTAD: Have you or your husband ever thought of mine? But never mind that; I only wanted to tell you that you needn't take all this too seriously – I shan't make any accusation for the present.

NORA: No, of course not – I didn't think you would.

KROGSTAD: It can all be settled quite amicably. Nothing need come out – it can just be arranged between us three.

NORA: My husband must never know anything about it.

KROGSTAD: How can you stop it? Unless, perhaps, you can pay off the rest of the debt.

NORA: Well, not at the moment.

KROGSTAD: Then perhaps you've found some way to raise the money within the next day or two.

NORA: No way that I'd use.

KROGSTAD: Well, it wouldn't have helped you, anyhow. Even if you were to stand there with a mint of money in your hand, you wouldn't get your bond back from me.

NORA: What are you going to do with it? Tell me.

KROGSTAD: Just keep it – have it in my possession. No one who isn't concerned need know anything about it. So if you have any desperate plan –

NORA: I have.

KROGSTAD: – if you've thought of running away from your home –

NORA: I have.

KROGSTAD: – or of anything worse –

NORA: How did you know?

KROGSTAD: – you'd better give up the idea.

NORA: How did you know that I'd thought of *that*?

KROGSTAD: Most of us think of that at first. I thought of it, too – only I hadn't the courage.

NORA [*dully*]: Nor had I.

KROGSTAD [*relieved*]: No, you haven't the courage either, have you?

NORA: No, I haven't – I haven't.

KROGSTAD: Besides, it would have been a very stupid thing to do. You've only got just one domestic storm to go through, then ... I have a letter to your husband in my pocket.

NORA: Telling him everything?

KROGSTAD: In the gentlest possible way.

NORA [*quickly*]: He must never see it. Tear it up. I'll get the money somehow.

KROGSTAD: Excuse me, Mrs Helmer, but I believe I told you just now –

NORA: Oh, I don't mean the money I owe you. Tell me how much you're asking from my husband, and I'll get it.

KROGSTAD: I'm not asking your husband for any money.

NORA: What are you asking, then?

KROGSTAD: I'll tell you. I want to get back my standing in the world, Mrs Helmer; I want to get on, and that's where your husband's going to help me. For the last eighteen months I haven't touched anything dishonest, and all that time I've been struggling against the most difficult conditions. I was prepared to work my way up step by step. Now I'm being thrown down again, and it's not going to be good enough for me to be taken back as a favour. I want to get on, I tell you; I want to get back into the Bank – and in a better job. Your husband must make one for me.

NORA: He'll never do that.

KROGSTAD: I know him – he'll do it! He daren't so much as murmur. And once I'm in there with him, then you'll see! Inside a year, I shall be the Manager's right-hand man. It'll be Nils Krogstad who runs the Bank, not Torvald Helmer.

NORA: That'll never happen as long as you live.

KROGSTAD: Do you mean that you'll –

NORA: Yes, I have the courage now.

KROGSTAD: Oh, you can't frighten me! A fine pampered lady like you –

NORA: You'll see – you'll see!

KROGSTAD: Under the ice, perhaps? Down into the cold black water? And then in the spring you'd float up to the top, ugly, hairless, unrecognizable –

NORA: You can't frighten me.

KROGSTAD: Nor can you frighten me. People don't do such things, Mrs Helmer. And what good would it be, anyhow? I'd still have the letter in my pocket!

NORA: Still? Even if I weren't . . .

KROGSTAD: You forget that *then* your reputation would be in my hands.

[NORA *stands speechless, looking at him.*]

KROGSTAD: Yes, now you've been warned, so don't do anything stupid. I shall expect to hear from Helmer as soon as he gets my letter. And remember, it's your husband who's forced me to do this sort of thing again. I shall never forgive him for that. Good-bye, Mrs Helmer. [*He goes out into the hall.*]

NORA [*going to the hall door and opening it a little to listen*]: He's going! He hasn't left the letter. No, no, it couldn't happen! [*She opens the door inch by inch.*] Listen – he's standing just outside – he's not going down the stairs. . . . Has he changed his mind? Is he . . .?

[*A letter falls into the box.* KROGSTAD'S *footsteps are heard fading away down the staircase.*]

NORA [*with a stifled cry, runs over to the sofa table. A short pause.*] It's in the letter-box! [*Creeping stealthily back to the hall door*] Yes, it's there. Oh, Torvald . . . Torvald – there's no hope for us now!

MRS LINDE [*coming in from the left with the dress*]: There – I don't think there's anything else that wants mending. Let's try it on.

NORA [*in a hoarse whisper*]: Kristina, come here.

MRS LINDE [*throwing the dress on the sofa*]: What's the matter? What's upset you so?

NORA: Come here. Do you see that letter? There, look – through the glass of the letter-box.

MRS LINDE: I can see it – Well?

NORA: That letter's from Krogstad.

MRS LINDE: Nora ... it was Krogstad who lent you the money!

NORA: Yes. And now Torvald'll find out everything.

MRS LINDE: But, Nora, believe me, that'll be best for both of you.

NORA: There's something that you don't know. I forged a signature.

MRS LINDE: Good heavens ...!

NORA: There's just one thing I want to say, Kristina, and you shall be my witness.

MRS LINDE: Witness? But what am I to –

NORA: If I were to go mad – as I easily might –

MRS LINDE: Nora!

NORA: Or if anything else were to happen to me, so that I shouldn't be here –

MRS LINDE: Nora, Nora, you must be out of your senses!

NORA: And in case there was someone else who tried to take it all on himself – all the blame, you understand –

MRS LINDE: Yes ... but how can you think ...?

NORA: – then, Kristina, you must bear witness that it isn't true. I'm perfectly sane, and I know exactly what I'm doing now, and I tell you this: no one else knew anything about it – I did it all by myself. Remember that.

MRS LINDE: Of course I will. But I don't understand.

NORA: How could you understand this? We're going to see – a miracle.

MRS LINDE: A miracle?

NORA: Yes, a miracle. But it's so dreadful. Kristina, it *mustn't* happen – not for anything in the world.

MRS LINDE: I'm going straight round to talk to Krogstad.

NORA: No, don't go to him, he might do you some harm.

MRS LINDE: There was a time when he would gladly have done anything for me.

NORA: Krogstad?

MRS LINDE: Where does he live?

NORA: How should I know? Wait – [*feeling in her pocket*] – here's his card. But the letter – the letter . . .!

HELMER [*from inside his room, knocking on the door*]: Nora!

NORA [*with a frightened cry*]: What is it? What do you want?

HELMER [*off*]: All right, there's nothing to be frightened of; we're not coming in. You've locked the door – are you trying on your dress?

NORA: Yes, I'm trying it on. I look so nice in it, Helmer.

MRS LINDE [*having read the card*]: He lives only just round the corner.

NORA: Yes, but it's no good; there's no hope for us now – the letter's in the box.

MRS LINDE: And your husband has the key!

NORA: He always keeps it.

MRS LINDE: Krogstad must ask for his letter back – unopened. He must find some excuse.

NORA: But this is just the time when Torvald always –

MRS LINDE: Put him off. I'll be back as soon as I can. Go in to him now. [*She hurries out through the hall.*]

NORA [*going to* HELMER'S *door, unlocking it, and peeping in*]: Torvald.

HELMER [*from the inner room*]: Well, am I allowed in my own room again? Come along, Rank, now we're going to see – [*At the door*] But what's all this?

NORA: What, Torvald dear?

HELMER: Rank led me to expect a great transformation scene.

RANK [*at the door*]: I certainly thought so – I must have been wrong.

NORA: No one's allowed to admire me in all my finery till tomorrow.

HELMER: But, Nora dear, you look tired out – have you been rehearsing too much?

NORA: No, I haven't rehearsed at all.

HELMER: Oh, but you should have.

NORA: Yes, I know I should have, but I can't do anything unless you help me, Torvald. I've forgotten absolutely everything.

HELMER: Oh, we'll soon polish it up again.

NORA: Yes, do take me in hand, Torvald – promise you will. I'm so nervous – all those people . . . You must give up the whole evening to me; you mustn't do a scrap of business – not even pick up a pen! You'll do that, won't you, dear Torvald?

TORVALD: I promise. This evening I'll be wholly and entirely at your service – you poor helpless little creature! Ah, but first, while I think of it, I must just – [going towards the hall door].

NORA: What do you want out there?

TORVALD: I'm just seeing if the post's come.

NORA: No, no, Torvald – don't do that.

HELMER: Why not?

NORA: Please don't Torvald – there's nothing there.

TORVALD: I'll just look [He starts to go.]

[NORA, at the piano, plays the opening bars of the tarantella.]

HELMER [stopping in the doorway]: Aha!

NORA: I shan't be able to dance tomorrow if I don't go over it with you.

HELMER [going to her]: Nora dear, are you really so worried about it?

NORA: Yes, terribly worried. Let me rehearse it now – there's still time before dinner. Sit down and play for me, Torvald dear; criticize me, and show me where I'm wrong, the way you always do.

HELMER: I'd like to, if that's what you want. [He sits at the piano.]

[NORA *pulls a tambourine out of the box, then a long parti-coloured shawl which she quickly drapes round herself. Then, with a bound, she takes up her position in the middle of the floor, and calls:*]

NORA: Now play for me, and I'll dance!

[HELMER *plays and* NORA *dances.* DR RANK *stands behind* HELMER *at the piano and looks on.*]

HELMER [*as he plays*]: Slower – slower!

NORA: I can only do it this way.

HELMER: Not so violently, Nora!

NORA: This is how it should go.

HELMER [*stops playing*]: No, no, that's all wrong.

NORA [*laughing and brandishing her tambourine*]: There! Didn't I tell you?

RANK: Let me play for her.

HELMER [*rising*]: Yes, do; then I can show her better.

[RANK *sits at the piano and plays.* NORA *dances more and more wildly.* HELMER, *taking up a position by the stove, gives her frequent directions as she dances. She seems not to hear them, her hair comes down and falls over her shoulders, but she goes on dancing without taking any notice.* MRS LINDE *comes in.*]

MRS LINDE [*stopping spellbound in the doorway*]: Ah!

NORA [*as she dances*]: Oh, this is fun, Kristina!

HELMER: But, Nora darling, you're dancing as if your life depended on it!

NORA: So it does.

HELMER: Stop, Rank. This is sheer madness – stop, I tell you!

[RANK *stops playing, and* NORA *comes to an abrupt halt.*]

HELMER [*going to her*]: I'd never have believed it – you've forgotten everything I taught you.

NORA [*throwing the tambourine aside*]: There! You see.

HELMER: Well, you'll certainly need a lot of coaching.

NORA: Yes, you see how much I need. You must coach me up to the last minute – promise me you will, Torvald?

HELMER: You can rely on me.

NORA: All today and all tomorrow, you mustn't think of anything else but me. You mustn't open any letters – you mustn't even open the letter-box.

HELMER: Ah, you're still afraid of that man.

NORA: Oh yes, that as well.

HELMER: Nora, I can see by your face that there's a letter from him already.

NORA: There may be – I don't know. But you mustn't read anything like that now; we won't let anything horrid come between us till this is all over.

RANK [*quietly to* HELMER]: You'd better not upset her.

HELMER [*putting his arm round her*]: My baby shall have her own way. But tomorrow night, after you've danced –

NORA: Then you'll be free.

MAID [*at the door on the right*]: Dinner is served, Madam.

NORA: We'll have champagne, Helena.

MAID: Very good, Madam. [*She goes.*]

HELMER: Well, well – so we're having a banquet!

NORA: A champagne supper – lasting till dawn. [*Calling*] And some macaroons, Helena – lots and lots, just for once.

HELMER [*taking her hands*]: Now, now, now! You mustn't be so wild and excitable. Be my own little skylark again.

NORA: Oh yes, I will. But go into the dining-room now – and you too, Dr Rank. Kristina, you must help me put my hair straight.

RANK [*quietly as they go*]: There isn't anything . . .? I mean, she's not expecting . . .?

HELMER: Oh no, my dear fellow. I've told you – she gets over-excited, like a child.

[*They go out to the right.*]

NORA: Well?

MRS LINDE: He's gone out of town.

NORA: I saw it in your face.

MRS LINDE: He'll be back tomorrow night; I left a note for him.

NORA: You should have let things alone – not tried to stop them. After all, it's a wonderful thing to be waiting for a miracle.

MRS LINDE: What is it you're expecting?

NORA: You wouldn't understand. Go in and join the others – I'll come in a minute.

[MRS LINDE *goes into the dining-room.*]

NORA [*standing for a moment as if to collect herself, then looking at her watch*]: Seven hours till midnight. Then twenty-four hours till midnight tomorrow. Then the tarantella will be over. Twenty-four and seven . . . thirty-one hours to live.

HELMER [*at the door on the right*]: But where's my little skylark?

NORA [*going to him with arms outstretched*]: Here she is!

ACT THREE

The same scene. The table and chairs round it have been moved to the middle of the room; a lamp is alight on the table. The hall door is open and music for dancing can be heard from the flat above.

> [MRS LINDE *is sitting at the table, idly turning the pages of a book. She tries to read, but seems unable to concentrate. Once or twice she listens anxiously for the outer door.*]

MRS LINDE [*looking at her watch*]: Not here yet! There's not much more time – I do hope he hasn't – [*Listening again*] Ah, here he is.

> [*She goes out to the hall and carefully opens the front door. Soft footsteps are heard on the stairs. She whispers:*]

Come in – there's no one here.

KROGSTAD [*in the doorway*]: I found a note from you at home. What's this about?

MRS LINDE: I had to have a talk with you.

KROGSTAD: Oh? And did you have to have it in this house?

MRS LINDE: I couldn't see you at the place where I'm staying – there's no separate entrance to my room. Come in, we're quite alone; the maid's asleep, and the Helmers are upstairs at the dance.

KROGSTAD [*coming into the room*]: What? The Helmers at a dance tonight? Really?

MRS LINDE: Yes. Why not?

KROGSTAD: True – why not?

MRS LINDE: Well, Nils,[8] let us have a talk.

KROGSTAD: Have you and I got anything more to talk about?

MRS LINDE: A great deal.

KROGSTAD: I shouldn't have thought so.

MRS LINDE: Well, you never really understood me.

KROGSTAD: Was there anything to understand – except what was so obvious to the whole world: a heartless woman throwing a man over when someone richer turns up?

MRS LINDE: Do you really think I'm as heartless as all that? And do you think it was easy to break with you?

KROGSTAD: Wasn't it?

MRS LINDE: Nils, did you really think that?

KROGSTAD: If it wasn't true, why did you write to me as you did at the time?

MRS LINDE: What else could I do? I had to break with you, so it was up to me to kill any feeling that you might have had for me.

KROGSTAD [*clenching his hands*]: So that was it? You did it – all of it – for the sake of the money?

MRS LINDE: You mustn't forget that my mother was quite helpless, and that I had two small brothers. We couldn't wait for you, Nils – especially as you had no prospects in those days.

KROGSTAD: Even so, you had no right to throw me over for someone else.

MRS LINDE: I've often asked myself if I had the right . . . I really don't know.

KROGSTAD [*softly*]: When I lost you, it was just as if the very ground had given way under my feet. Look at me now – a shipwrecked man clinging to a spar.

MRS LINDE: Help could be near.

KROGSTAD: It *was* near – until you came and got in the way.

MRS LINDE: Without knowing it, Nils. I only found out today that it's *your* place that I'm to have at the Bank.

KROGSTAD: I'll believe you if you say so. But now that you do know, aren't you going to give it up?

MRS LINDE: No. You see, that wouldn't benefit you in the least.

KROGSTAD: 'Benefit – benefit'! *I* would have done it.

MRS LINDE: I've learned to think before I act. Life and bitter necessity have taught me that.

KROGSTAD: Life has taught me not to believe in fine speeches.

MRS LINDE: Then life has taught you something valuable. But you must believe in deeds?

KROGSTAD: What do you mean by that?

MRS LINDE: You said you were like a shipwrecked man clinging to a spar.

KROGSTAD: I had good reason to say so.

MRS LINDE: I'm like a shipwrecked woman clinging to a spar – no one to cry over, and no one to care for.

KROGSTAD: It was your own choice.

MRS LINDE: There was no other choice at the time.

KROGSTAD: Well?

MRS LINDE: Nils ... suppose we two shipwrecked people could join forces?

KROGSTAD: What do you mean?

MRS LINDE: Two on one spar would be better off than each of us alone.

KROGSTAD: Kristina!

MRS LINDE: Why do you suppose I came to town?

KROGSTAD: Were you really thinking of me?

MRS LINDE: I must work or life isn't bearable. All my life, as long as I can remember, I've worked – that's been my one great joy. But now that I'm alone in the world I feel completely lost and empty. There's no joy in working for oneself. Nils ... let me have something – and someone – to work for.

KROGSTAD: I don't trust that. It's nothing but a woman's exaggerated sense of nobility prompting her to sacrifice herself.

MRS LINDE: Have you ever noticed anything exaggerated in me?

KROGSTAD: Could you really do it? Tell me, do you know all about my past?

MRS LINDE: Yes.

KROGSTAD: And do you know my reputation here?

MRS LINDE: You suggested just now that with me you might have been a different man.

KROGSTAD: I'm certain of it.

MRS LINDE: Couldn't that still happen?

KROGSTAD: Kristina – have you really thought about what you're saying? Yes, you have – I see it in your face. And you really have the courage?

MRS LINDE: I need someone to be a mother to, and your children need a mother. You and I need each other. I have faith in you – the real you – Nils, with you I could dare anything.

KROGSTAD [*grasping her hands*]: Thank you – thank you, Kristina. Now I shall be able to set myself right in the eyes of the world too. Oh, but I'm forgetting –

MRS LINDE [*listening*]: Sh! The tarantella! Go – quickly.

KROGSTAD: Why? What is it?

MRS LINDE: Don't you hear the dancing up there? As soon as this is over, they'll be coming back.

KROGSTAD: Yes – I'll go. But all this will come to nothing . . . you see, you don't know what I've done against the Helmers.

MRS LINDE: Yes, Nils, I know about it.

KROGSTAD: And you still have the courage . . .?

MRS LINDE: I know only too well how far despair can drive a man like you.

KROGSTAD: Oh, if only I could undo it!

MRS LINDE: You can – your letter's still in the box.

KROGSTAD: Are you sure?

MRS LINDE: Quite sure – but . . .

KROGSTAD [*with a searching look at her*]: You want to save your friend at any price – is that it? Tell me frankly – is it?

MRS LINDE: Nils, when you've sold yourself once for the sake of others, you don't do it a second time.

KROGSTAD: I shall ask for my letter back.

MRS LINDE: No, no!

KROGSTAD: But of course. I'll wait here till Helmer comes down, and I'll tell him that he must give me my letter back – that it's only about my dismissal, and that he's not to read it.

MRS LINDE: No, Nils, you mustn't ask for your letter back.

KROGSTAD: But surely that was the very reason why you asked me to come here?

MRS LINDE: Yes – in my first moment of panic. But now, a whole day's gone by and I've witnessed things in this house that I could hardly believe. Helmer must know the whole story. This wretched secret must be brought into the open so that there's complete understanding between them. That'd be impossible while there's so much concealment and subterfuge.

KROGSTAD: Very well – if you'll take the risk. . . . But there's one thing I can do – and it shall be done at once –

MRS LINDE [listening]: Go – quickly! The dance is over – we can't stay here a moment longer.

KROGSTAD: I'll wait for you downstairs.

MRS LINDE: Yes, do. You must see me home.

KROGSTAD: Kristina, this is the most marvellous thing that's ever happened to me.

[He goes out by the front door. The door between the room and the hall remains open.]

MRS LINDE [tidying the room a little, and putting her hat and cape ready]: What a difference – what a difference! Someone to work for – and live for. A home to look after – and oh, I'll make it so comfortable. Oh, if they'd only hurry up and come! [Listening] Ah, here they are – I'll put my things on. [She picks up her hat and cape. HELMER'S and NORA'S voices are heard outside. A key turns, and HELMER pulls NORA almost forcibly into the room. She is in Italian costume with a great black shawl round herself; he is in a black domino which opens to show his evening dress underneath.]

NORA [*still in the doorway, struggling with him*]: No, no, I don't want to go in – I want to go back upstairs. It's far too early to leave.

HELMER: But, my darling Nora –

NORA: Oh, please, Torvald – I do beg you. . . . Just one more hour!

HELMER: Not a single minute, Nora dear – you know what we agreed. Now come along in, you'll catch cold out here. [*In spite of her resistance he brings her gently into the room.*]

MRS LINDE: Good evening.

NORA: Kristina!

HELMER: Why, Mrs Linde – here so late?

MRS LINDE: Yes, forgive me, but I did want to see Nora in her costume.

NORA: Have you been sitting here waiting for me?

MRS LINDE: Yes, I'm afraid I didn't get here in time – you'd already gone upstairs – and I felt I really couldn't go away without seeing you.

HELMER [*taking* NORA'S *shawl off*]: Yes, just look at her! She's worth seeing, if you ask *me*! Isn't she lovely, Mrs Linde?

MRS LINDE: She certainly is.

HELMER: Remarkably lovely, isn't she? And that's what everybody at the dance thought, too. But this sweet little thing's dreadfully obstinate. What are we to do with her? You'd hardly believe it, but I practically had to use force to get her away.

NORA: You'll be very sorry you didn't let me stay, Torvald – even for just half an hour longer.

HELMER: Just listen to her, Mrs Linde! She danced her tarantella; it was a huge success – and rightly so, even if it *was*, perhaps, a trifle too realistic – I mean, a little more so than was, strictly speaking, artistically necessary. . . . But never mind, it was a success – a huge success. Could I let her stay after that, and spoil the effect? No thank you; I put my arm round my lovely little Capri girl – I might almost say my *capricious* little Capri girl – we made a quick turn of the room, a bow all round, and then, as they say in the novels, the beautiful vision was gone! An exit should always be well-timed, Mrs Linde; but that's something I simply cannot get Nora to see! Phew, it's warm in here. [*He throws his domino on a chair and opens the door to his room.*] Hullo, it's all dark! Oh yes, of course. . . . Excuse me – [*He goes in and lights the candles.*]

NORA [*in a rapid and breathless whisper*]: Well?

MRS LINDE [*softly*]: I've had a talk with him.

NORA: Yes?

MRS LINDE: Nora, you must tell your husband everything.

NORA [*dully*]: I knew it.

MRS LINDE: You've nothing to fear from Krogstad. But you *must* tell your husband.

NORA: I'll never tell him.

MRS LINDE: Then the letter will.

NORA: Thank you, Kristina; now I know what I must do. . . . Sh!

HELMER [*coming in again*]: Well, Mrs Linde, have you been admiring her?

MRS LINDE: Yes, indeed . . . and now I must say good night.

HELMER: What, already? Is this yours, this knitting?

MRS LINDE [*taking it*]: Oh yes, thank you – I nearly forgot it.

HELMER: So you knit?

MRS LINDE: Oh yes.

HELMER: You know, it'd be much better if you did embroidery.

MRS LINDE: Oh? Why?

HELMER: It's so much more graceful. I'll show you. You hold embroidery like this, in your left hand, and you work the needle with your right – in long easy sweeps. Isn't that so?

MRS LINDE: Yes, I suppose so.

HELMER: But knitting's quite another matter – it can't help being ungraceful. Look here – arms held tightly in, needles going up and down – it has an almost Chinese effect. . . . That really was an excellent champagne they gave us to-night. . . .

MRS LINDE: Well, good night. And Nora – don't be obstinate any longer.

HELMER: That's quite right, Mrs Linde.

MRS LINDE: Good night, Mr Helmer.⁹

HELMER [*seeing her to the door*]: Good night – good night. I hope you get home safely. I'd be very glad to . . . but then you haven't far to go, have you? Good night – good night.

[*She goes. He shuts the door after her and comes back.*] Well, I thought she'd never go – she's a terrible bore, that woman.

NORA: Aren't you tired out, Torvald?

HELMER: No, not in the least.

NORA: Not sleepy?

HELMER: Not a bit – in fact, I feel particularly lively. What about you? Yes, you do look tired out – why, you're half asleep.

NORA: Yes, I'm very tired – I could fall asleep here and now.

HELMER: There you are – there you are! You see how right I was not to let you stay any longer.

NORA: You're always right, Torvald, whatever you do.

HELMER [*kissing her on the forehead*]: Now my little skylark's talking like a reasonable being. Did you notice how cheerful Rank was this evening?

NORA: Oh, was he? I didn't get a chance to talk to him.

HELMER: I hardly did; but I haven't seen him in such good spirits for a long time. [*He looks at* NORA *for a moment, then goes to her.*] Ah, it's wonderful to be back home again, all alone with you. . . . How fascinating you are, you lovely little thing.

NORA: Don't look at me like that, Torvald.

HELMER: Mayn't I look at my dearest treasure? At all the beauty that belongs to no one but me – that's all my very own?

NORA [*going round to the other side of the table*]: You mustn't say things like that tonight.

HELMER [*following her:*] I see you still have the tarantella in your blood – it makes you more enchanting than ever. Listen – the party's beginning to break up. [*Softly*] Nora – soon the whole house'll be quiet . . .

NORA: Yes, I hope so.

HELMER: Yes, you do, don't you, my own darling Nora? I'll tell you something: when I'm out with you at a party, do you know why I hardly talk to you – don't come near you – and only steal a glance at you every now and then . . . do you know why? It's because I pretend that we're secretly in love – engaged in secret – and that no one dreams that there's anything between us.

NORA: Oh yes, yes, I know that you're always thinking of me.

HELMER: And when it's time to go, and I'm putting your shawl over your lovely young shoulders – round your exquisite neck – then I imagine that you're my little bride, that we've just come from the wedding, and that I'm bringing you back to my home for the first time – that for the first time I shall be alone with you – all alone with your young trembling loveliness. All the evening I've been longing for nothing but you. When I watched you swaying and beckoning in the tarantella, it set my blood on fire till I couldn't bear it any longer. That's why I brought you home so early –

NORA: No, Torvald, go away. Leave me alone – I don't want –

HELMER: What's all this? So my little Nora's playing with me! 'Don't want'? I'm your husband, aren't I?

[*There is a knock on the front door.*]

NORA [*startled*]: Listen!

HELMER [*going to the hall*]: Who is it?

RANK [*outside*]: It's I – may I come in for a moment?

HELMER [*angrily, under his breath*]: Oh, what does he want now? [*Aloud*] Wait a minute. [*He goes and opens the door.*] Ah, it's nice of you not to pass our door without looking in.

RANK: I thought I heard you talking, and I felt I'd like to see you. [*He lets his eye roam quickly round the room.*] Ah yes, this dear familiar place; you two must be very happy and comfortable here.

HELMER: It looked as if you were pretty happy upstairs, too.

RANK: Wonderfully – why not? Why shouldn't one enjoy everything the world has to offer – at any rate, as much as one can – and for as long as one can? The wine was superb!

HELMER: Especially the champagne.

RANK: You thought so too, did you? It's quite incredible the amount I managed to put away!

NORA: Torvald drank a good deal of champagne tonight, too.

RANK: Oh?

NORA: Yes, and that always puts him in high spirits.

RANK: Well, why shouldn't a man have a pleasant evening after a good day's work?

HELMER: A good day's work? I'm afraid I can't claim that.

RANK [*slapping him on the back*]: Ah, but *I* can!

NORA: Dr Rank . . . then you must have been working on a scientific test today?

RANK: Exactly.

HELMER: Well, well! Little Nora talking about scientific tests!

NORA: And am I to congratulate you on the result?

RANK: You may indeed.

NORA: It was good, then?

RANK: The best possible result – for doctor *and* patient. . . . Certainty.

NORA [*quickly, probing*]: Certainty?

RANK: Complete certainty. So why shouldn't I give myself a jolly evening after that?

NORA: Yes, of course you must, Dr Rank.

HELMER: I quite agree – as long as you don't have to pay for it the next morning.

RANK: Ah well, you don't get anything for nothing in this life.

NORA: Dr Rank – you like fancy-dress parties, don't you?

RANK: Yes, when there are lots of pretty costumes.

NORA: Then tell me – what are you and I going to wear at our next?

HELMER: Little scatterbrain – thinking about the next dance already!

RANK: You and I? Yes, I can tell you – you shall be a mascot.

HELMER: Ah, but what costume would suggest *that*?

RANK: Your wife could go in what she wears every day. . .

HELMER: Very charmingly put. But don't you know what you'll wear?

RANK: Oh yes, my dear fellow, I'm quite certain about *that*.

HELMER: Well?

RANK: At the next fancy-dress party, I shall be invisible.

HELMER: What an odd idea!

RANK: There's a big black hat – you've heard of the Invisible Hat? – you put it on, and then no one can see you.

HELMER [*hiding a smile*]: Well, perhaps you're right.

RANK: But I'm quite forgetting what I came for. Give me a cigar, Helmer – one of the black Havanas.

HELMER: With the greatest pleasure [*offering him his case*].

RANK [*taking one and cutting the end*]: Thanks.

NORA [*striking a match*]: Let me give you a light.

RANK: Thank you.

    [*She holds the match while he lights the cigar.*]
    And now – good-bye.

HELMER: Good-bye – good-bye, my dear fellow.

NORA: Sleep well, Dr Rank.

RANK: Thank you for that wish.

NORA: Wish me the same.

RANK: You? Well, if you want me to. . . . Sleep well. And – thank you for the light. . . . [*With a nod to them both, he goes.*]

HELMER [*subdued*]: He's had too much to drink.

NORA [*absently*]: Perhaps.

[HELMER, *taking his keys from his pocket, goes out to the hall.*]

NORA: Torvald – what do you want out there?

HELMER: I must empty the letter-box, it's almost full; there won't be room for tomorrow's paper.

NORA: Are you going to work tonight?

HELMER: You know perfectly well I'm not. Here, what's this? Someone's been at the lock!

NORA: At the lock?

HELMER: Yes, they certainly have. What can this mean? I shouldn't have thought that the maid – Here's a broken hairpin – Nora, it's one of yours!

NORA [*quickly*]: Perhaps the children . . .

HELMER: Then you must break them of that sort of thing. Ugh – ugh – There, I've got it open all the same. [*Emptying the letter-box and calling into the kitchen*] Helena? Helena, put out the lamp at the front door. [*He shuts the front door and comes into the room with the letters in his hand.*]

HELMER: Look – just look what a lot there are! [*Looking through them*] Whatever's this?

NORA [*at the window*]: The letter! No, Torvald, no!

HELMER: Two visiting-cards – from Rank.

NORA: From Dr Rank?

HELMER [*looking at them*]: 'S. Rank, M.D.'[10] They were on top – he must have put them in as he left.

NORA: Is there anything on them?

HELMER: There's a black cross over the name . . . look. What a gruesome idea – it's just as if he were announcing his own death.

NORA: That's what he's doing.

HELMER: What? Do you know about it? Has he told you something?

NORA: Yes, when these cards came, it would be to say good-bye to us; he's going to shut himself up to die.

HELMER: My poor old friend. Of course I knew that he wouldn't be with me much longer – but so soon ...! And to go away and hide, like a wounded animal ...

NORA: If it *must* be, then it's best to go without a word, isn't it, Torvald?

HELMER [*pacing up and down*]: He'd come to be so much a part of our lives. I can't realize that he's gone. With all his loneliness and suffering, he seemed like a background of clouds that set off the sunshine of our happiness. Well, perhaps it's all for the best – for him, at any rate. [*Coming to a halt*] And maybe for us too, Nora, now that you and I have no one but each other. [*Putting an arm round her*] Oh, my darling, I feel as if I can't hold you close enough. You know, Nora, I've often wished that you could be threatened by some imminent danger so that I could risk everything I had – even my life itself – to save you.

NORA [*freeing herself, and speaking firmly and purposefully*]: Now you must read your letters, Torvald.

HELMER: No, no, not tonight. I want to be with my darling wife.

NORA: When your friend's dying ...?

HELMER: Yes, you're right – it's upset us both. Something ugly has come between us – the thought of death and decay. We must try to shake it off. . . . And until we do, let us keep apart.

NORA [*putting her arms round his neck*]: Good night, Torvald – good night.

HELMER [*kissing her on the forehead*]: Good night, Nora – sleep well, my little songbird. Now I'll go and read my letters. [*He takes the bundle into his room, shutting the door behind him.*]

NORA [*wild-eyed, groping round her she seizes* HELMER'S *domino and pulls it round herself. She speaks in hoarse, rapid, broken whispers*]: I shall never see him again! Never – never – never! [*She throws the shawl over her head.*] And never see the children again either – never, never again. The water's black, and cold as ice – and deep . . . so deep. . . . Oh, if only it were all over! He has it now – he's reading it. . . . Oh no, no – not yet! Good-bye, Torvald – good-bye, my children –

[*She is about to rush out through the hall, when* HELMER *flings his door open and stands there with the open letter in his hand.*]

HELMER: Nora!

NORA [*with a loud cry*]: Ah . . .!

HELMER: What is all this? Do you know what's in this letter?

NORA: Yes, I know. Let me go – let me out!

HELMER [*holding her back*]: Where are you going?

NORA [*struggling to free herself*]: You shan't save me, Torvald!

HELMER [*taken aback*]: It's true! So what it says here is true? How terrible! No, no, it's not possible – it *can't* be true.

NORA: It *is* true. I've loved you more than anything in the world.

HELMER: Now don't let's have any silly excuses.

NORA [*taking a step towards him*]: Torvald . . .!

HELMER: You wretched woman – what have you done?

NORA: Let me go. You *shan't* take the blame – I won't let you suffer for me.

HELMER: We won't have any melodrama. [*Locking the front door*] Here you shall stay until you've explained yourself. Do you realize what you've done? Answer me – do you realize?

NORA [*looking fixedly at him, her expression hardening as she speaks*]: Yes, now I'm beginning to realize everything.

HELMER [*pacing about the room*]: What a terrible awakening! For these last eight years you've been my joy and my pride –

and now I find that you're a liar, a hypocrite – even worse
– a criminal! Oh, the unspeakable ugliness of it all! Ugh!
[NORA *looks fixedly at him without speaking. He stops in
front of her.*]
I might have known that something of this sort would
happen – I should have foreseen it. All your father's shiftless character – Be quiet! – all your father's shiftless character has come out in you. No religion, no morality, no
sense of duty ... So this is what I get for condoning his
fault! I did it for your sake, and this is how you repay
me!

NORA: Yes – like this.

HELMER: You've completely wrecked my happiness, you've
ruined my whole future! Oh, it doesn't bear thinking of.
I'm in the power of a man without scruples; he can do what
he likes with me – ask what he wants of me – order me
about as he pleases, and I dare not refuse. And I'm brought
so pitifully low all because of a shiftless woman!

NORA: Once I'm out of the way, you'll be free.

HELMER: No rhetoric, please! Your father was always ready
with fine phrases too. How would it help me if you were
'out of the way', as you call it? Not in the least! He can still
see that the thing gets about, and once he does, I may very
well be suspected of having been involved in your crooked
dealings. They may well think that I was behind it – that
I put you up to it. And it's you that I have to thank for all
this – and after I've cherished you all through our married
life. *Now* do you realize what you've done to me?

NORA [*calm and cold*]: Yes.

HELMER: It's so incredible that I can't grasp it. But we must
try to come to some understanding. Take off that shawl –
take it off, I tell you. Somehow or other I must try to
appease him – the thing must be hushed up at all costs. As
for ourselves – we must seem to go on just as before ... but
only in the eyes of the world of course. You will remain

here in my house – that goes without saying – but I shall not allow you to bring up the children ... I shouldn't dare trust you with them. Oh, to think that I should have to say this to someone I've loved so much – someone I still ... Well, that's all over – it must be; from now on, there'll be no question of happiness, but only of saving the ruin of it – the fragments – the mere façade ...

[*There is a ring at the front door.*]

HELMER [*collecting himself*]: What's that – at this hour? Can the worst have – Could he ...? Keep out of sight, Nora – say that you're ill.

[NORA *remains motionless.* HELMER *goes and opens the hall door.*]

MAID [*at the door, half-dressed*]: There's a letter for the Mistress.

HELMER: Give it to me. [*He takes the letter and shuts the door.*] Yes, it's from him. You're not to have it – I shall read it myself.

NORA: Yes, read it.

HELMER [*by the lamp*]: I hardly dare – it may mean ruin for both of us. No, I *must* know! [*Tearing open the letter, he runs his eye over a few lines, looks at a paper that is enclosed, then gives a shout of joy.*] Nora!

[*She looks at him inquiringly.*]

Nora! Wait, I must just read it again. . . . Yes, it's true; I'm saved! Nora, I'm saved!

NORA: And I?

HELMER: You too, of course. We're both saved – both you and I. Look, he's sent you back your bond. He says that he regrets ... and apologizes ... a fortunate change in his life. . . . Oh, never mind what he says – we're saved, Nora, no one can touch you now. Oh Nora, Nora – Wait, first let me destroy the whole detestable business. [*Casting his eye over the bond*] No, I won't even look at it – I shall treat the whole thing as nothing but a bad dream. [*Tearing the bond and the two letters in pieces, he throws them on the stove, and watches them burn.*] There! Now it's all gone. He said in his letter that since Christmas Eve you'd ... Oh, Nora, these three days must have been terrible for you.

NORA: They've been a hard struggle, these three days.

HELMER: How you must have suffered – seeing no way out except ... No, we'll put all those hateful things out of our minds. Now we can shout for joy, again and again: 'It's all over – it's all over!' Listen, Nora – you don't seem to realize – it's all over. What's the matter? Such a grim face? Poor little Nora, I see what it is: you simply can't believe that I've forgiven you. But I have, Nora, I swear it – I've forgiven you everything. I know now that what you did was all for love of me.

NORA: That is true.

HELMER: You loved me as a wife *should* love her husband. It was just that you hadn't the experience to realize what you were doing. But do you imagine that you're any less dear to me for not knowing how to act on your own? No, no, you must simply rely on me – I shall advise you and guide you. I shouldn't be a proper man if your feminine helplessness didn't make you twice as attractive to me. You must forget all the hard things that I said to you in that first dreadful moment when it seemed as if the whole world was falling about my ears. I've forgiven you, Nora, I swear it – I've forgiven you.

NORA: Thank you for your forgiveness. [*She goes out through the door to the right.*]

HELMER: No, don't go. [*He looks in.*] What are you doing out there?

NORA [*off*]: Taking off my fancy-dress.

HELMER [*at the open door*]: Yes, do. Try to calm down and set your mind at peace, my frightened little songbird. You can rest safely, and my great wings will protect you. [*He paces up and down by the door.*] Oh, Nora, how warm and cosy our home is; it's your refuge, where I shall protect you like a hunted dove that I've saved from the talons of a hawk. Little by little, I shall calm your poor fluttering heart, Nora, take my word for it. In the morning you'll look on all this quite differently, and soon everything will be just as it used to be. There'll be no more need for me to tell you that I've forgiven you – you'll feel in your heart that I have. How can you imagine that I could ever think of rejecting – or even reproaching – you? Ah, you don't know what a real man's heart is like, Nora. There's something indescribably sweet and satisfying for a man to know deep down that he has forgiven his wife – completely forgiven her, with all his heart. It's as if that made her doubly his – as if he had brought her into the world afresh! In a sense, she has become both his wife and his child. So from now on, that's what you shall be to me, you poor, frightened, helpless, little darling. You mustn't worry about anything, Nora – only be absolutely frank with me, and I'll be both your will and your conscience. . . . Why, what's this? Not in bed? You've changed your clothes!

NORA [*in her everyday things*]: Yes, Torvald, I've changed my clothes.

HELMER: But why? At *this* hour!

NORA: I shan't sleep tonight.

HELMER: But, my dear Nora –

NORA [*looking at her watch*]: It's not so very late. Sit down here, Torvald – you and I have a lot to talk over. [*She sits down at one side of the table.*]

HELMER: Nora – what is all this? Why do you look so stern?

NORA: Sit down – this'll take some time. I have a lot to talk to you about.

HELMER [*sitting across the table from her*]: Nora, you frighten me – I don't understand you.

NORA: No, that's just it – you don't understand me. And I've never understood you – until tonight. No, you mustn't interrupt – just listen to what I have to say. Torvald, this is a reckoning.

HELMER: What do you mean by that?

NORA [*after a short pause*]: Doesn't it strike you that there's something strange about the way we're sitting here?

HELMER: No ... what?

NORA: We've been married for eight years now. Don't you realize that this is the first time that we two – you and I, man and wife – have had a serious talk together?

HELMER: Serious? What do you mean by that?

NORA: For eight whole years – no, longer than that – ever since we first met, we've never exchanged a serious word on any serious subject.

HELMER: Was I to keep forever involving you in worries that you couldn't possibly help me with?

NORA: I'm not talking about worries; what I'm saying is that we've never sat down in earnest together to get to the bottom of a single thing.

HELMER: But, Nora dearest, what good would that have been to you?

NORA: That's just the point – you've never understood me. I've been dreadfully wronged, Torvald – first by Papa, and then by you.

HELMER: What? By your father and me? The two people who loved you more than anyone else in the world.

NORA [*shaking her head*]: You've never loved me, you've only found it pleasant to be in love with me.

HELMER: Nora – what are you saying?

NORA: It's true, Torvald. When I lived at home with Papa, he used to tell me his opinion about everything, and so I had the same opinion. If I thought differently, I had to hide it from him, or he wouldn't have liked it. He called me his little doll, and he used to play with me just as I played with my dolls. Then I came to live in your house –

HELMER: That's no way to talk about our marriage!

NORA [*undisturbed*]: I mean when I passed out of Papa's hands into yours. You arranged everything to suit your own tastes, and so I came to have the same tastes as yours ... or I pretended to. I'm not quite sure which ... perhaps it was a bit of both – sometimes one and sometimes the other. Now that I come to look at it, I've lived here like a pauper – simply from hand to mouth. I've lived by performing tricks for you, Torvald. That was how you wanted it. You and Papa have committed a grievous sin against me: it's your fault that I've made nothing of my life.

HELMER: That's unreasonable, Nora – and ungrateful. Haven't you been happy here?

NORA: No, that's something I've never been. I thought I had, but really I've never been happy.

HELMER: Never ... happy?

NORA: No, only gay. And you've always been so kind to me. But our home has been nothing but a play-room. I've been your doll-wife here, just as at home I was Papa's doll-child. And the children have been my dolls in their turn. I liked it when you came and played with me, just as they liked it when I came and played with them. That's what our marriage has been, Torvald.

HELMER: There is some truth in what you say, though you've exaggerated and overstated it. But from now on, things will be different. Play-time's over, now comes lesson-time.

NORA: Whose lessons? Mine or the children's?

HELMER: Both yours and the children's, Nora darling.

NORA: Ah, Torvald, you're not the man to teach me to be a real wife to you –

HELMER: How can you say that?

NORA: – and how am I fitted to bring up the children?

HELMER: Nora!

NORA: Didn't you say yourself, a little while ago, that you daren't trust them to me?

HELMER: That was in a moment of anger – you mustn't pay any attention to that.

NORA: But you were perfectly right – I'm not fit for it. There's another task that I must finish first – I must try to educate myself. And you're not the man to help me with that; I must do it alone. That's why I'm leaving you.

HELMER [*leaping to his feet*]: What's that you say?

NORA: I must stand on my own feet if I'm to get to know myself and the world outside. That's why I can't stay here with you any longer.

HELMER: Nora – Nora . . . !

NORA: I want to go at once. I'm sure Kristina will take me in for the night.

HELMER: You're out of your mind. I won't let you – I forbid it.

NORA: It's no good your forbidding me anything any longer. I shall take the things that belong to me, but I'll take nothing from you – now or later.

HELMER: But this is madness . . .

NORA: Tomorrow I shall go home – to my old home, I mean – it'll be easier for me to find something to do there.

HELMER: Oh, you blind, inexperienced creature . . . !

NORA: I must try to *get* some experience, Torvald.

HELMER: But to leave your home – your husband and your children. . . . You haven't thought of what people will say.

NORA: I can't consider that. All I know is that this is necessary for me.

HELMER: But this is disgraceful. Is this the way you neglect your most sacred duties?

NORA: What do you consider is my most sacred duty?

HELMER: Do I have to tell you that? Isn't it your duty to your husband and children?

NORA: I have another duty, just as sacred.

HELMER: You can't have. What duty do you mean?

NORA: My duty to myself.

HELMER: Before everything else, you're a wife and a mother.

NORA: I don't believe that any longer. I believe that before everything else I'm a human being – just as much as you are . . . or at any rate I shall try to become one. I know quite well that most people would agree with you, Torvald, and that you have warrant for it in books; but I can't be satisfied any longer with what most people say, and with what's in books. I must think things out for myself and try to understand them.

HELMER: Shouldn't you first understand your place in your own home? Haven't you an infallible guide in such matters – your religion?

NORA: Ah, Torvald, I don't really know what religion is.

HELMER: What's that you say?

NORA: I only know what Pastor Hansen taught me when I was confirmed. He told me that religion was this, that, and the other. When I get away from all this, and am on my own, I want to look into that too. I want to see if what Pastor Hansen told me was right – or at least, if it is right for me.

HELMER: This is unheard-of from a young girl like you. But if religion can't guide you, then let me rouse your conscience. You must have *some* moral sense. Or am I wrong? Perhaps you haven't.

NORA: Well, Torvald, it's hard to say; I don't really know – I'm so bewildered about it all. All I know is that I think quite differently from you about things; and now I find that the law is quite different from what I thought, and I simply can't convince myself that the law is right. That a woman shouldn't have the right to spare her old father on his deathbed, or to save her husband's life! I can't believe things like that.

HELMER: You're talking like a child; you don't understand the world you live in.

NORA: No, I don't. But now I mean to go into that, too. I must find out which is right – the world or I.

HELMER: You're ill, Nora – you're feverish. I almost believe you're out of your senses.

NORA: I've never seen things so clearly and certainly as I do tonight.

HELMER: Clearly and certainly enough to forsake your husband and your children?

NORA: Yes.

HELMER: Then there's only one possible explanation . . .

NORA: What?

HELMER: You don't love me any more.

NORA: No, that's just it.

HELMER: Nora! How can you say that?

NORA: I can hardly bear to, Torvald, because you've always been so kind to me – but I can't help it. I don't love you any more.

HELMER [*with forced self-control*]: And are you clear and certain about that, too?

NORA: Yes, absolutely clear and certain. That's why I won't stay here any longer.

HELMER: And will you also be able to explain how I've forfeited your love?

NORA: Yes, I can indeed. It was this evening, when the miracle didn't happen – because then I saw that you weren't the man I'd always thought you.

HELMER: I don't understand that. Explain it.

NORA: For eight years I'd waited so patiently – for, goodness knows, I realized that miracles don't happen every day. Then this disaster overtook me, and I was completely certain that now the miracle would happen. When Krogstad's letter was lying out there, I never imagined for a moment that you would submit to his conditions. I was completely certain that you would say to him 'Go and publish it to the whole world!' And when that was done . . .

HELMER: Well, what then? When I'd exposed my own wife to shame and disgrace?

NORA: When that was done, I thought – I was completely certain – that you would come forward and take all the blame – that you'd say '*I*'m the guilty one.'

HELMER: Nora!

NORA: You think that I should never have accepted a sacrifice like that from you? No, of course I shouldn't. But who would have taken my word against yours? That was the miracle I hoped for . . . and dreaded. It was to prevent *that* that I was ready to kill myself.

HELMER: Nora, I'd gladly work night and day for you, and endure poverty and sorrow for your sake. But no man would sacrifice his *honour* for the one he loves.

NORA: Thousands of women have.

HELMER: Oh, you're talking and thinking like a stupid child.

NORA: Perhaps . . . But you don't talk or think like the man I could bind myself to. When your first panic was over – not about what threatened me, but about what might happen to *you* – and when there was no more danger, then, as far as you were concerned, it was just as if nothing had happened at all. I was simply your little songbird, your doll, and from now on you would handle it more gently than ever because it was so delicate and fragile. [*Rising*] At that moment, Torvald, I realized that for eight years I'd been living here with a strange man, and that I'd borne him three children. Oh, I can't bear to think of it – I could tear myself to little pieces!

HELMER [*sadly*]: Yes. I see – I see. There truly is a gulf between us. . . . Oh, but Nora, couldn't we somehow bridge it?

NORA: As I am now, I'm not the wife for you.

HELMER: I could change . . .

NORA: Perhaps – if your doll is taken away from you.

HELMER: But to lose you – to lose you, Nora! No, no, I can't even imagine it . . .

NORA [*going out to the right*]: That's just why it *must* happen. [*She returns with her outdoor clothes, and a little bag which she puts on a chair by the table.*]

HELMER: Nora! Not now, Nora – wait till morning.

NORA [*putting on her coat*]: I couldn't spend the night in a strange man's house.

HELMER: But couldn't we live here as brother and sister?

NORA [*putting her hat on*]: You know quite well that that wouldn't last. [*She pulls her shawl round her.*] Good-bye, Torvald. I won't see my children – I'm sure they're in better hands than mine. As I am now, I'm no good to them.

HELMER: But some day, Nora – some day . . .?

NORA: How can I say? I've no idea what will become of me.

HELMER: But you're my wife – now, and whatever becomes of you.

NORA: Listen, Torvald: I've heard that when a wife leaves her husband's house as I'm doing now, he's legally freed from all his obligations to her. Anyhow, *I* set you free from them. You're not to feel yourself bound in any way, and nor shall I. We must both be perfectly free. Look, here's your ring back – give me mine.

HELMER: Even that?

NORA: Even that.

HELMER: Here it is.

NORA: There. Now it's all over. Here are your keys. The servants know all about running the house – better than I did. Tomorrow, when I've gone, Kristina will come and pack my things that I brought from home; I'll have them sent after me.

HELMER: Over! All over! Nora, won't you ever think of me again?

NORA: I know I shall often think of you – and the children, and this house.

HELMER: May I write to you, Nora?

NORA: No . . . you must never do that.

HELMER: But surely I can send you –

NORA: Nothing – nothing.

HELMER: – or help you, if ever you need it?

NORA: No, I tell you, I couldn't take anything from a stranger.

HELMER: Nora – can't I ever be anything more than a stranger to you?

NORA [*picking up her bag*]: Oh, Torvald – there would have to be the greatest miracle of all . . .

HELMER: What would that be – the greatest miracle of all?

NORA: Both of us would have to be so changed that – Oh, Torvald, I don't believe in miracles any longer.

HELMER: But I'll believe. Tell me: 'so changed that . . .'?

NORA: That our life together could be a real marriage. Good-bye. [*She goes out through the hall.*]

HELMER [*sinking down on a chair by the door and burying his face in his hands*]: Nora! Nora! [*He rises and looks round.*] Empty! She's not here any more! [*With a glimmer of hope*] 'The greatest miracle of all . . .'?

[*From below comes the noise of a door slamming.*][11]

THE LADY FROM THE SEA

CHARACTERS

DR WANGEL, a country doctor
MRS ELLIDA WANGEL, his second wife
BOLETTA } his daughters by his
HILDE, a young girl } first marriage
ARNHOLM, a schoolmaster
LYNGSTRAND
BALLESTED
A STRANGER
Young people from the town, tourists, and summer visitors

The action takes place during the summer in a small town on a fjord in northern Norway

ACT ONE

To the left is Dr Wangel's house, with a large built-in veranda. In front of it, and all around, is a garden, and before the veranda is a flagstaff. In the garden to the right stands an arbour with a table and chairs.

At the back is a hedge with a little gate, and beyond it a road with trees on either side along the water's edge. Between the trees can be seen the fjord, and high mountains with peaks in the distance. It is a warm summer morning, and brilliantly clear.

> [BALLESTED, *a middle-aged man in an old velvet jacket with a broad-brimmed artist's hat, stands at the foot of the flagstaff disentangling the cords. The flag is lying on the ground. A little way off is an easel with a canvas standing on it, while beside it are a camp-stool, brushes, palette, and a box of colours.*
>
> BOLETTA WANGEL *comes through the open french window out to the veranda; she has a large vase of flowers which she puts on the table.*]

BOLETTA: Well, Ballested, have you got it to work?

BALLESTED: Oh yes, Miss Boletta, there wasn't much the matter with it. May I ask – does this mean visitors?

BOLETTA: Yes, we're expecting Mr Arnholm, the headmaster, this morning; he arrived in town last night.

BALLESTED: Arnholm? Wait a minute – wasn't the tutor who was here a year or two ago called Arnholm?

BOLETTA: Yes, that's the man.

BALLESTED: Well, well – so he's in these parts again.

BOLETTA: That's why we want the flag up.

BALLESTED: Well, that's very natural.

> [BOLETTA *goes back into the garden-room. A moment or two*

later, LYNGSTRAND *comes along the road from the right;
he stops, interested, when he sees the easel and painting gear.
He is a slim young man, delicate-looking, and poorly but neatly
dressed.*]

LYNGSTRAND [*across the hedge*]: Good morning.

BALLESTED [*turning*]: Oh – good morning [*He hoists the flag.*]
Aha! Up goes the balloon! [*He makes the cords fast, and then
turns busily to the easel.*] Good morning, my dear sir; I don't
think I have the pleasure.

LYNGSTRAND: You're an artist, aren't you?

BALLESTED: Of course I am. Why shouldn't I be?

LYNGSTRAND: I can see you are. Might I come in for a
moment?

BALLESTED: Do you want to have a look?

LYNGSTRAND: Yes, I'd like to.

BALLESTED: There isn't really much to see yet, but please
come in.

[LYNGSTRAND *comes in through the gate.*]

It's the fjord I'm doing – there, between the islands.

LYNGSTRAND: Yes, I can see it is.

BALLESTED: I haven't put the figure in yet, though – you
can't get a model anywhere in this town.

LYNGSTRAND: Oh, you're having a figure, too?

BALLESTED: Yes, on this rock in the foreground I'm going to
put a dying mermaid.

LYNGSTRAND: Why does she have to be dying?

BALLESTED: She's strayed in from the open sea, and now she
can't find her way back. And the water's brackish, you see,
so here she lies – dying.

LYNGSTRAND: Ah, I see.

BALLESTED: It was the lady of the house here who gave me
the idea of painting something of the sort.

LYNGSTRAND: What are you going to call it when it's
finished?

BALLESTED: I think I shall entitle it *The Mermaid's Death.*

LYNGSTRAND: Good idea! I'm sure it'll make a very nice picture.

BALLESTED [*looking at him*]: Are you in that line yourself, perhaps?

LYNGSTRAND: A painter, you mean?

BALLESTED: Yes.

LYNGSTRAND: No, I'm going to be a sculptor. My name's Hans Lyngstrand.

BALLESTED: A sculptor, eh? Well, sculpting's quite a nice refined art too. I think I've spotted you in the street once or twice. 'Been staying in these parts long?

LYNGSTRAND: Only a fortnight, but I'm going to try to stay till the end of the summer.

BALLESTED: You like the bathing, eh?

LYNGSTRAND: Yes; I want to build up my strength a bit.

BALLESTED: You're delicate, eh?

LYNGSTRAND: Yes, I suppose I am rather. But it's nothing serious – only a little trouble with my breathing.

BALLESTED: Pooh, that's nothing. What you want's a chat with a good doctor.

LYNGSTRAND: Yes, I thought if I got a chance I'd speak to Dr Wangel here.

BALLESTED: That's right. [*Looking out to the left*] Ah, here comes another steamer – jammed full of trippers. 'Wonderful how the tourist traffic's grown this last year or two.

LYNGSTRAND: Yes, the place does seem to be busy.

BALLESTED: And we're full up with summer visitors too. I'm sometimes afraid all these strangers'll spoil our little town.

LYNGSTRAND: You belong here, do you?

BALLESTED: Well – not exactly ... but I've acclam – acclimatized myself; after all this time I really feel I'm almost a part of the place.

LYNGSTRAND: You've lived here a long time, then?

BALLESTED: 'Been here close on eighteen years now. 'First

came here with Skive's Theatrical Touring Company, but we ran into financial trouble, so the company broke up and scattered to the four winds.

LYNGSTRAND: But you stayed?

BALLESTED: Yes, I stayed ... and it's all turned out for the best. You see, in those days I was just a scene-painter.

[BOLETTA comes out with a rocking-chair, which she puts on the veranda.]

BOLETTA [calling into the garden-room]: Hilde, see if you can find the embroidered footstool for Father.

LYNGSTRAND [coming to the veranda and bowing]: Good morning, Miss Wangel.

BOLETTA: Oh ... Good morning, Mr Lyngstrand. Excuse me a moment, I must just ... [she goes back into the house.]

BALLESTED: You know the family, then?

LYNGSTRAND: Not really; I've met the daughters once or twice at people's houses, and I've talked to Mrs Wangel. The last time there was a concert in the bandstand up at the Look-Out, she told me I might come and call.

BALLESTED: Well, you know, you ought to cultivate their acquaintance.

LYNGSTRAND: Yes, I've been meaning to pay a visit, but I couldn't think of a suitable excuse.

BALLESTED: An excuse? Whatever for? [Looking out to the left] Confound it, the steamer's at the pier already. [Collecting his things] I must get down to the hotel – perhaps some of the new arrivals may need me. I do a bit of hairdressing too, as a matter of fact.

LYNGSTRAND: You're certainly a man of many parts.

BALLESTED: Oh, in these small towns a man must ac-climatize himself to everything. Should you require anything in the hairdressing line – a little pomade and so forth – you've only got to ask for Ballested the dancing-master.

LYNGSTRAND: Dancing-master?

BALLESTED: Or the President of the local Brass Band, if you

prefer it. We've got a concert up at the Look-Out this evening. Good-bye – good-bye.

[*He goes, with his painting things, through the wicket gate and then out to the left.* HILDE *comes out with the footstool, and* BOLETTA *brings more flowers.* LYNGSTRAND *bows to* HILDE *from the garden.*]

HILDE [*at the balustrade, not returning his bow*]: Boletta said you'd ventured into the garden today.

LYNGSTRAND: Yes, I took the liberty of coming in for a moment.

HILDE: I suppose you've been out for your morning walk?

LYNGSTRAND: Well, it wasn't much of a walk today.

HILDE: Have you been bathing, then?

LYNGSTRAND: Yes, I had a short dip. I saw your mother down there – just going into her bathing-hut.

HILDE: Who?

LYNGSTRAND: Your mother.

HILDE: Really? [*She puts the footstool in front of the rocking-chair.*]

BOLETTA: Did you see anything of Father's boat out on the fjord?

LYNGSTRAND: I did see a sailing-boat.

BOLETTA: That would have been Father; he's been to see some patients on the islands. [*She arranges things on the table.*]

LYNGSTRAND [*coming one step up the veranda stairs*]: My goodness, what a lot of flowers!

BOLETTA: Yes, doesn't it look nice?

LYNGSTRAND: Lovely, yes. It must be some sort of family celebration.

HILDE: That's just what it is.

LYNGSTRAND: I thought so. Your father's birthday, perhaps?

BOLETTA [*cautioning* HILDE]: Ahem!

HILDE [*ignoring her*]: No, it's Mother's.

LYNGSTRAND: Ah really – your mother's?

BOLETTA [*in an angry whisper*]: Hilde – no!

HILDE [*also whispering*]: Leave me alone. [*To* LYNGSTRAND] Well, I suppose you'll be going back to lunch now.[1]

LYNGSTRAND [*retreating from the steps*]: – Er – yes, I ought to think about getting something to eat.

HILDE: I'm sure the cooking's very good at the hotel.

LYNGSTRAND: Oh, I'm not at the hotel any more; it was too expensive for me.

HILDE: Where are you now, then?

LYNGSTRAND: I'm at Mrs Jensen's.

HILDE: Which Mrs Jensen?

LYNGSTRAND: The midwife.

HILDE: Well, if you'll excuse me, Mr Lyngstrand, I've a great deal to do, so . . .

LYNGSTRAND: Oh, I shouldn't have said that.

HILDE: Said what?

LYNGSTRAND: What I said just now.

HILDE [*looking him up and down with distaste*]: I really don't know what you mean.

LYNGSTRAND: No, no, of course not. Well – I must be saying good-bye . . . for the present.

BOLETTA [*coming to the steps*]: Good-bye, Mr Lyngstrand. I hope you'll excuse us today. But some other day, when you have time, and if you feel like it, I hope, you'll drop in and see Father and – and the rest of us.

LYNGSTRAND: Oh – thank you. Yes, I should like to – very much. [*He bows and goes out through the garden gate. As he passes along the road to the right, he bows towards the veranda again.*]

HILDE [*under her breath*]: Adieu, Monsieur. Give my love to old Mother Jensen!

BOLETTA [*shaking her by the arm and speaking quietly*]: Hilde! You *are* a naughty girl! That was a silly thing to do – he might have heard you.

HILDE: Pooh! Do you think I care?

BOLETTA [*looking out to the right*]: Ah, here's Father.
[DR WANGEL, *in outdoor clothes and with a little handbag,
comes along the footpath from the right.*]

WANGEL: Well, girls, here I am again! [*He comes through the
wicket-gate.*]

BOLETTA [*going down into the garden to meet him*]: Oh, it's nice
to have you back, Father.

HILDE [*also joining him*]: Have you finished for the day now?

WANGEL: Oh no, I still have to go down to the surgery for a
bit. By the way, do you know if Mr Arnholm's arrived
yet?

BOLETTA: Yes, we sent down to the hotel to find out. He got
here last night.

WANGEL: You haven't seen him yet, then?

BOLETTA: No, but he's sure to come here during the morning.

WANGEL: Yes, he's bound to.

HILDE [*tugging at him*]: Look, Father!

WANGEL [*looking at the veranda*]: Yes, I see. It *does* look festive.

BOLETTA: We've done them nicely, haven't we?

WANGEL: You certainly have. Is – is anybody in?

HILDE: No, she's gone out to –

BOLETTA [*quickly interrupting*]: Mother's gone down to
bathe.

WANGEL [*gives* BOLETTA *an affectionate look and pats her on the
head. Then, rather hesitantly*]: Er – look here, girls – are you
going to keep these decorations up the whole day? And
the flag, too?

HILDE: But, Father, you know we are.

WANGEL: Oh . . . Look, don't you think –

BOLETTA [*mischievously*]: But don't you *see*? All this is in
Mr Arnholm's honour. I mean, when an old friend like that
comes to pay you his respects . . .

HILDE [*smiling and shaking him*]: After all, Father, he *was*
Boletta's tutor!

WANGEL [*with a wry smile*]: You're a pair of little minxes, you really are! After all, it is only natural to keep her memory green. But all the same . . . Here, Hilde – [*giving her his bag*] take this down to the surgery. But look, girls – how shall I put it? – I don't really approve – not the way you do it, I mean. . . . Making a yearly custom of it like this. . . . Still, I don't quite see how else you could do it. . . .

[HILDE *is about to take the bag through the garden to the left when she stops and turns.*]

HILDE [*pointing*]: Look, there's someone coming up the hill now. It must be Mr Arnholm.

BOLETTA [*looking down the hill*]: What, that man? Hilde, *really*! You surely don't think – why he's practically middle-aged!

WANGEL: Wait a minute, my dear, I do believe – yes, I'm sure it is.

BOLETTA [*with a look of surprise*]: Good heavens, I think you're right.

[ARNHOLM, *in smart morning-dress, with gold spectacles and a light cane, appears on the road from the left. He looks rather tired. As he sees them in the garden, he gives a friendly bow and comes through the gate.*]

WANGEL [*going to meet him*]: Well, my dear Arnholm, it's splendid to see you back here again!

ARNHOLM: Thank you, Doctor, it's very kind of you to say so. [*They shake hands and come across the garden together.*] And the children too! [*Looking at them as he takes their hands*] I should never have recognized either of them!

WANGEL: I can well believe it.

ARNHOLM: Well, perhaps Boletta . . . yes, I should have known Boletta.

WANGEL: Oh, surely not. Why, it must be almost nine years since you saw her last. Yes, there've been a great many changes here since then.

ARNHOLM [*looking round*]: Oh, I shouldn't say that. The trees have grown a good deal, I admit – and that arbour's new –

WANGEL: Well, I didn't mean just on the surface –

ARNHOLM [*smiling*]: And of course you have two great grown-up daughters about the house now.

WANGEL: Well, only one of them's grown up!

HILDE [*under her breath*]: Oh, Father – *really*!

WANGEL: And now I suggest we go and sit on the veranda, it's cooler there. After you.

ARNHOLM: Thank you, Doctor.

[*They go up;* WANGEL *gives* ARNHOLM *the rocking-chair.*]

WANGEL: There! Now you can just sit quietly and rest; you look rather tired after your journey.

ARNHOLM: Oh, it's nothing. Now that I'm *here* again . . .

BOLETTA [*to her father*]: Shall we put some soda-water and syrup in the garden-room? It'll soon be too hot out here.

WANGEL: A good idea, girls. Syrup and soda – and perhaps a little brandy.

BOLETTA: Brandy too?

WANGEL: Just a little, in case anyone wants it.

BOLETTA: All right. Hilde, aren't you taking the bag down to the surgery?

[BOLETTA *goes into the garden-room, shutting the door after her.* HILDE *takes the bag and goes across the garden and behind the house to the left.*]

ARNHOLM [*who has been watching Boletta*]: What a lovely – what lovely girls they've grown into!

WANGEL [*sitting*]: Yes, haven't they?

ARNHOLM: With Boletta, it's quite amazing. And with Hilde too. But tell me about yourself, my dear Doctor. Are you going to stay here for the rest of your life?

WANGEL: Well, it certainly looks like it. I was born and bred here, as they say; and I was very happy here with my wife, till she was taken from us so young. . . . Well, you knew her when you were here, Arnholm.

ARNHOLM: Yes – yes . . .

WANGEL: And now I'm very happy with my second wife. Yes, on the whole I must say that fate has been very good to me.

ARNHOLM: But you've no children by your second marriage?

WANGEL: We had a little boy, two – nearly three – years ago . . . but not for long – he died when he was only a few months old.

ARNHOLM: Isn't your wife at home today?

WANGEL: She should be back very soon now; she's gone down to bathe. At this time of year she goes every single day, whatever the weather.

ARNHOLM: Isn't she well, then?[2]

WANGEL: She's not exactly ill, but her nerves have been very bad – on and off, that is – these last few years. I really don't know what to make of it. But do you know, once she gets into the sea she's perfectly well and happy.

ARNHOLM: Yes, I remember.

WANGEL [*with an almost imperceptible smile*]: Ah yes, you knew Ellida in the days when you were teaching out on Skjoldvik.[3]

ARNHOLM: Yes, indeed; she often came to call on the Pastor, and I usually met her when I went to the lighthouse to see her father.

WANGEL: Then you'll realize what a deep impression the life out there made on her. The people in the town here can't understand it at all; they call her 'the Lady from the Sea'.

ARNHOLM: Really?

WANGEL: Yes . . . Look, Arnholm, my dear fellow, do have a talk with her about the old days – it'd do her so much good.

ARNHOLM [*looking at him doubtfully*]: Do you really think so?

WANGEL: Yes, I'm sure it would.

ELLIDA'S VOICE [*from outside the garden to the right*]: Are you there, Wangel?[4]

WANGEL [*getting up*]: Yes, dear.

[MRS ELLIDA WANGEL, *in a big light wrap and with her wet hair hanging over her shoulders, comes from among the trees by the arbour.* ARNHOLM *rises.*]

WANGEL [*holding out his hands to her with a smile*]: Ah, here's our mermaid!

ELLIDA [*coming quickly up to the veranda and grasping his hands*]: Thank goodness you're back safely. When did you get home?

WANGEL: Just now – a few minutes ago. [*Pointing to* ARNHOLM] But aren't you going to greet an old friend?

ELLIDA [*holding out her hand to* ARNHOLM]: Ah, how are you? Do forgive me for being out when –

ARNHOLM: Oh, please! Don't stand on ceremony with me.

WANGEL: How was the water today – nice and fresh?

ELLIDA: Fresh? Good heavens, the water's never fresh here – it's dull and tepid. Ugh, here in the fjords the water's sluggish.

WANGEL: Sluggish?

ELLIDA: Yes, sluggish. And I believe it makes *us* sluggish, too.

WANGEL [*smiling*]: Well, that's a fine advertisement for a watering-place!

ARNHOLM: I believe, Mrs Wangel, that you have a special affinity with the sea, and everything to do with it.

ELLIDA: Yes, perhaps . . . I almost think so myself. Oh look, how pretty the girls have made everything for you.

WANGEL [*embarrassed*]: Er – [*Looking at his watch*] well, it's time I was off . . .

ARNHOLM: Is this really for me?

ELLIDA: It must be; we aren't decorated like this every day. Oh . . . the heat's stifling under this roof! [*She goes down into the garden.*] Come over here, at least there's a little air here. [*She sits in the arbour.*]

ARNHOLM [*following her*]: I find the air here quite fresh.

ELLIDA: Oh, you're used to the stuffy atmosphere of the capital. I hear it's perfectly terrible there in the summer.

WANGEL [*who has also gone down into the garden*]: Well, Ellida dear, I must leave *you* to entertain our friend for a little.

ELLIDA: Have you some work to do?

WANGEL: Yes, I must go down to the surgery, and then I must change. But I shan't be long.

ARNHOLM [*sitting in the arbour*]: There's no need to hurry, my dear Doctor; I'm sure Mrs Wangel and I will manage to pass the time!

WANGEL [*nodding*]: Of course you will. Well – good-bye for the present. [*He goes out through the garden to the left.*]

ELLIDA [*after a short pause*]: It's a pleasant place to sit, here, isn't it?

ARNHOLM: Very, at the moment.

ELLIDA: They call this *my* arbour, because it was I who planned it – or at least, Wangel did, to please me.

ARNHOLM: Do you usually sit out here?

ELLIDA: Yes, most of the day.

ARNHOLM: With the girls, I expect.

ELLIDA: No, the girls usually sit on the veranda.

ARNHOLM: And the Doctor?

ELLIDA: Oh, he goes from one to the other; sometimes he's here with me, and sometimes he's over there with the children.

ARNHOLM: And do you like that?

ELLIDA: I think it suits us all, that way. We can always call across to each other – when we feel we have anything to say.

ARNHOLM [*after thinking for a moment*]: The last time we ran into each other – out at Skjoldvik, I mean . . . Hm – that's a long time ago now. . . .

ELLIDA: Yes, it's a good ten years since you were out there with us.

ARNHOLM: Yes, just about. When I remember you out there

at the lighthouse ... The old Pastor used to call you 'the
Heathen' because he said your father had called you after a
ship instead of giving you a proper Christian name ...5

ELLIDA: Well?

ARNHOLM: I should never have expected to come here and
find you married to Dr Wangel.

ELLIDA: In those days, Wangel wasn't ... In those days, the
girls' first mother – their real mother, I mean – was still
alive.

ARNHOLM: Oh, I know. But even apart from that – even if
he'd been perfectly free – I should never have expected
this.

ELLIDA: Nor should I – never in the world. Not in those
days.

ARNHOLM: The Doctor's such a fine man. So upright – so
kindhearted and good to everyone –

ELLIDA [*warmly and sincerely*]: Yes, he really is.

ARNHOLM: – but it seems to me that you and he must be
poles apart.

ELLIDA: Yes, you're right – we are.

ARNHOLM: Then how did it happen? How?

ELLIDA: Oh, you mustn't ask me about that, my dear Arnholm; I couldn't explain it – and even if I could, you
wouldn't understand a single word of it.

ARNHOLM: H'm. ... [*Dropping his voice*] Have you ever
told him anything about me? I mean, of course, about that
fruitless proposal that I was once rash enough to make to
you?

ELLIDA: No. Do you think I would? I haven't told him a
word about – about what you said.

ARNHOLM: I'm glad. I was rather embarrassed at the thought
that –

ELLIDA: There's no need to be. I simply told him what is
perfectly true – that I liked you very much, and that you
were the best friend that I had out there.

ARNHOLM: Thank you very much. But do tell me – why did you never write to me after I went away?

ELLIDA: I thought that perhaps it might hurt you to hear from someone who – who'd not been able to agree to what you wanted. I thought it would be like reopening an old wound.

ARNHOLM: Mm! Yes, perhaps you were right.

ELLIDA: But why did *you* never write?

ARNHOLM [*looking at her with a half-reproachful smile*]: I? Take the first step? And perhaps have you think that I was trying again? Not after a rebuff like that.

ELLIDA: No, I see what you mean. And haven't you ever thought of proposing to anyone else?

ARNHOLM: No. I've been faithful to my memories.

ELLIDA [*half joking*]: Oh nonsense – never cling to old unhappy memories. It seems to me you'd do much better to think of getting happily married.

ARNHOLM: I should have to be quick about it then, Mrs Wangel; remember I'm past thirty-seven already, I'm sorry to say.

ELLIDA: Then that's all the more reason for not wasting time. [*She is silent for a moment, then, in a low voice, she says earnestly*] Listen, my dear Arnholm, I'm going to tell you something now that, even to save my life, I couldn't have told you at the time.

ARNHOLM: What's that?

ELLIDA: That when you made what you just called 'that fruitless proposal', I *couldn't* have given you any other answer than I did.

ARNHOLM: I know. You could only offer me friendship – I know that.

ELLIDA: But you don't know that I was heart and soul in love with someone else.

ARNHOLM: Even then?

ELLIDA: Exactly.

ARNHOLM: But that's impossible – you've got the times wrong. I'm sure you can't have known Wangel in those days.

ELLIDA: I'm not talking about Wangel.

ARNHOLM: Not Wangel? But in those days – out on Skjold-vik ... I can't think of *anybody* out there whom I could imagine you possibly falling in love with.

ELLIDA: No, I'm sure you can't. The whole thing was utter madness.

ARNHOLM: Tell me more about it.

ELLIDA: Isn't it enough for you to know that I wasn't free at the time. And you know that now.

ARNHOLM: And if you *had* been free?

ELLIDA: Well?

ARNHOLM: Would you have answered my letter differently?

ELLIDA: How can I say? When Wangel came, my answer was different.

ARNHOLM: Then what is the good of telling me that you weren't free?

ELLIDA [*rising nervously, as if in distress*]: Because I must have someone to tell. No, don't get up.

ARNHOLM: Then your husband doesn't know about it?

ELLIDA: I told him at the beginning that I had once been in love. He never wanted to know any more, and we've never referred to it since. Anyhow, it was really nothing more than a mad impulse, and it was all over so soon – in a way, at least.

ARNHOLM [*rising*]: Only 'in a way'? Not altogether?

ELLIDA: Yes, altogether! Oh, good heavens, my dear Arn-holm, it isn't in the least like you think. It's something so completely incomprehensible that I don't know how to explain it – you'd only think I was ill or out of my mind.

ARNHOLM: We've always been good friends – now you really must tell me the whole story.

ELLIDA: Oh ... I'll try. But how anyone so matter-of-fact as you will be able to understand how – [*she looks round, and breaks off.*] Wait – there's somebody coming.

[LYNGSTRAND *walks along the road from the left, and comes into the garden. He has a flower in his buttonhole and carries a fine big bouquet with silk ribbons, wrapped in paper. He hesitates, standing uncertainly in front of the veranda.*]

ELLIDA [*from the arbour*]: Are you looking for the girls, Mr Lyngstrand?

LYNGSTRAND [*turning*]: Oh – good morning, Mrs Wangel. [*He bows and goes over to her.*] No, I'm not. It isn't the young ladies; I came to see you, Mrs Wangel. You did say I might come and call.

ELLIDA: So I did; we're always glad to see you.

LYNGSTRAND: Thank you. And as I was lucky enough to hear that today is a special occasion . . .

ELLIDA: Oh, you heard about it?

LYNGSTRAND: Oh yes. So may I take the liberty of presenting you with these? [*He bows formally and offers her the bouquet.*]

ELLIDA [*with a smile*]: But, my dear Mr Lyngstrand, wouldn't it be better if you gave your lovely flowers to Mr Arnholm yourself? After all, it's in his honour that –

LYNGSTRAND [*looking uncertainly from one to the other*]: Oh . . . excuse me, but I don't know this gentleman. I just – I came on account of the birthday, Mrs Wangel.

ELLIDA: The birthday? But there must be some mistake, Mr Lyngstrand; it's nobody's birthday here.

LYNGSTRAND [*with a knowing smile*]: Ah, I know all about it. But I didn't realize that it was such a secret.

ELLIDA: But what do you know?

LYNGSTRAND: That it's your – your birthday, Mrs Wangel.[6]

ELLIDA: Mine?

ARNHOLM [*with an inquiring look at her*]: Today? No, surely not.

ELLIDA [*to* LYNGSTRAND]: Whatever made you think that?

LYNGSTRAND: It was Miss Hilde who let it out. I was up here for a while earlier this morning, and I asked the young ladies why they were decorating the place so, with flowers and the flag . . .

ELLIDA: Well?

LYNGSTRAND: And Miss Hilde said, 'Ah, today is Mother's birthday.'

ELLIDA: Mother's? Oh, I see.

ARNHOLM: Ah! [*He and* ELLIDA *exchange meaning glances.*] Well, Mrs Wangel, since this young man seems to know all about it . . .

ELLIDA [*to* LYNGSTRAND]: Yes – now that you know . . .

LYNGSTRAND [*offering her the bouquet again*]: May I wish you many happy returns of the day?

ELLIDA [*taking the flowers*]: Thank you very much.

[ELLIDA, ARNHOLM, *and* LYNGSTRAND *sit down in the arbour.*]

All this – about my birthday – was meant to be a secret, Mr Arnholm.

ARNHOLM: So I see . . . not for us outsiders!

ELLIDA [*putting the flowers on the table*]: That's it – not for outsiders.

LYNGSTRAND: I promise faithfully I won't breathe a word to a soul.

ELLIDA: Oh! I didn't mean it like that. But how are you? I think you're looking better.

LYNGSTRAND: Yes, I think I'm getting on splendidly; and next year, if I can go south . . .

ELLIDA: And you *will*, so the girls were telling me.

LYNGSTRAND: Yes, because I have a very good friend in Bergen who's been looking after me, and he's promised to help me to go next year.

ELLIDA: How did you meet him?

LYNGSTRAND: Oh, it was a great piece of luck. I once went to sea in one of his ships.

ELLIDA: Oh did you? So you were fond of the sea in those days?

LYNGSTRAND: No, not in the least – but after my Mother died, Father didn't want me hanging about at home so he sent me to sea. On our way home we were wrecked in the English Channel – and that was lucky for me.

ARNHOLM: In what way?

LYNGSTRAND: Because that was how I got my lesion – here in my chest – through being so long in the icy water before they picked me up. So I had to give up the sea. Oh yes, it was really very lucky.

ARNHOLM: Oh, do you think so?

LYNGSTRAND: Yes, because my lesion isn't really dangerous, and now I can be a sculptor, like I've always really wanted. Just think! To work in that lovely clay – to feel it gently taking shape under your fingers!

ELLIDA: And what are you going to model? Mermaids and mermen? Or old vikings?

LYNGSTRAND: No, nothing like that. As soon as I can manage it, I want to try to do something really big – what's known as a 'group'.

ELLIDA: Ah yes; and what is the group to be?

LYNGSTRAND: Oh, it'd be something from my own ex-perience.

ARNHOLM: Yes, that's always best.

ELLIDA: But what is it to be?

LYNGSTRAND: Well, I thought there'd be a young woman – a sailor's wife – lying asleep, and strangely restless. She's dreaming – I think I'll be able to do it so that you can see she's dreaming . . .

ARNHOLM: Won't there be anything else?

LYNGSTRAND: Yes, there'll be one other figure – more of a *shape*, you might say. It's her husband. She's been unfaith-ful to him while he was away. And now he's been drowned at sea.

ARNHOLM: Oh, you mean . . .?

ELLIDA: He's been drowned?

LYNGSTRAND: Yes, drowned on the voyage. But the extraordinary thing is that he's come home in spite of that. It's night-time, and there he is standing by the bed, looking at her. He'll stand there, dripping wet, the way they are when they've been pulled out of the sea.

ELLIDA [*leaning back in her chair*]: What an extraordinary idea! [*Shutting her eyes*] Yes, I can see it all so vividly.

ARNHOLM: But how on earth, Mr – er . . .? You said it was to be something you'd experienced yourself.

LYNGSTRAND: But I *have* experienced it – in a sort of way.

ARNHOLM: You've known of a dead man who . . .?

LYNGSTRAND: Well, I don't mean that I've actually *known* it – not in real life, you understand. But all the same . . .

ELLIDA [*eager and excited*]: Tell me eveything you know about it – I want to hear it all.

ARNHOLM [*smiling*]: Yes, that *would* interest you – anything with the tang of the sea in it!

ELLIDA: Tell me about it, Mr Lyngstrand.

LYNGSTRAND: Well, when our ship was due to sail for home – from a place called Halifax, it was – we had to leave our bos'n behind in hospital, so we signed on an American in his place. Well, this new bos'n –

ELLIDA: The American?

LYNGSTRAND: Yes – one day he got the Captain to lend him a bundle of old newspapers. He was always poring over them – he wanted to learn Norwegian, he said.

ELLIDA: Go on.

LYNGSTRAND: Well, one evening we'd run into bad weather and all hands were on deck – except this bos'n and me. He'd sprained his ankle and couldn't walk, and I wasn't very well, so I was lying in my bunk. Well, he was sitting there in the fo'c'sle reading over one of the old newspapers –

ELLIDA: Yes?

LYNGSTRAND: And as he sat there I suddenly heard him give a sort of groan, and when I looked at him I saw his face was as white as chalk. And he went and screwed the paper up tight, and then he tore it into little pieces . . . and all without a sound!

ELLIDA: Didn't he say anything? Didn't he talk at all?

LYNGSTRAND: Not at the time. But after a while, as if he was talking to himself, he said: 'Married! To another man – while I was away!'

ELLIDA [half to herself – shutting her eyes]: Did he say that?

LYNGSTRAND: Yes – and do you know, he said it in perfectly good Norwegian? He must have had a real gift for foreign languages, that man.

ELLIDA: And then? What happened after that?

LYNGSTRAND: Well, now comes the extraordinary part. I shall never forget it as long as I live. He went on – still very quietly – 'But she's mine, and she always will be, and she shall come with me, even if I have to come like a drowned man from the depths of the sea to fetch her!'

ELLIDA [pouring a glass of water with a shaking hand]: Oh . . . How hot it is today!

LYNGSTRAND: And he said it with such determination that I felt he might really be able to do it.

ELLIDA: Have you any idea – what became of him?

LYNGSTRAND: Oh, he's certainly dead now, Mrs Wangel.

ELLIDA [quickly]: What makes you think that?

LYNGSTRAND: Because after that we were wrecked in the English Channel. I got away in the long-boat with the captain and five others, but the mate took the dinghy, with the American and another man . . .

ELLIDA: And they've never been heard of since?

LYNGSTRAND: Not a single word; my friend said so in a letter the other day. That's just why I'm so anxious to make a group of it. I can see the sailor's faithless wife so vividly, and then the avenger, who's drowned but who still comes home from the sea. I can see them both so clearly.

ELLIDA: So can I. [*Rising*] Let's go in. No, we'll go and join Wangel – I find the heat stifling here! [*She comes out of the arbour.*]

LYNGSTRAND [*who has also risen*]: I'm afraid *I* shall have to be on my way. I only looked in to wish you many happy returns.

ELLIDA: Well, if you must. [*Holding out her hand*] Good-bye, and thank you for the flowers.

[LYNGSTRAND *bows and goes out to the left through the wicket-gate.*]

ARNHOLM [*getting up and going over to* ELLIDA]: My dear Mrs Wangel, I can see that this has upset you.

ELLIDA: Yes, I suppose it has, in a way – though I . . .

ARNHOLM: But, in your heart, you must have expected it.

ELLIDA [*looking at him in amazement*]: Expected?

ARNHOLM: I should have thought so.

ELLIDA: Expected a man to come back – to come back like that?

ARNHOLM: What on earth? Was it that sculptor's ridiculous yarn . . .?

ELLIDA: Perhaps it isn't so ridiculous after all, my dear Arnholm.

ARNHOLM: Was it all this nonsense about a dead man that upset you so? I thought it was –

ELLIDA: What did you think?

ARNHOLM: Naturally I thought you were only using that as a blind – that what really hurt you was to find out that an anniversary was being kept here in secret – that your husband and his children were cherishing memories that you have no part in.

ELLIDA: No, no – that doesn't matter. I've no right to monopolize my husband.

ARNHOLM: I should have thought you had.

ELLIDA: Yes ... but in fact I haven't. That's just the point; I have a life myself, in which they have no part.

ARNHOLM: *You?* Are you trying to say that you – that you don't really love your husband?

ELLIDA: Oh, I do, I do. I've come to love him with all my heart. That's why this is so terrible – so inexplicable, so utterly unthinkable!

ARNHOLM: Now you really must trust me with the entire story. Won't you, Mrs Wangel?

ELLIDA: My dear friend, I can't. Not now, at any rate. Later perhaps.

[BOLETTA *comes out on the veranda and down into the garden.*]

BOLETTA: Father's coming in from the surgery – shall we all go and sit in the garden-room?

ELLIDA: Yes, let us.

[WANGEL, *having changed his clothes, comes with* HILDE *from behind the house to the left.*]

WANGEL: Well, here I am, free at last. Now it'd be nice to have a glass of something cool.

ELLIDA: Wait a minute ... [*She goes into the arbour and fetches the bouquet.*]

HILDE: Oh look – what lovely flowers! Where did you get them?

ELLIDA: Lyngstrand gave them to me, Hilde dear.

HILDE [*surprised*]: Lyngstrand?

BOLETTA [*uneasily*]: Has Lyngstrand been here? Again?

ELLIDA [*with a little smile*]: Yes, he came back with these – to wish me many happy returns of the day.

BOLETTA [*glancing at Hilde*]: Oh –

HILDE [*muttering*]: The idiot!

WANGEL [*to* ELLIDA – *painfully embarrassed*]: Hm! yes – Well, you see – Ellida, my dearest, let me explain ...

ELLIDA [*interrupting*]: Come along girls, let's put these in water with the others. [*She goes up on to the veranda.*]

BOLETTA [*quietly to* HILDE]: There – she's really good-hearted after all.

HILDE [*under her breath, looking furious*]: Fiddlesticks! She's only putting it on to please Father.

WANGEL [*up on the veranda, pressing* ELLIDA'S *hand*]: Thank you – thank you for that – from the bottom of my heart, Ellida.

ELLIDA [*arranging the flowers*]: Oh well – why shouldn't I join in and keep – Mother's birthday?

ARNHOLM: Hm!...

[*He goes up to* WANGEL *and* ELLIDA. BOLETTA *and* HILDE *stay down in the garden.*]

ACT TWO

Up at the 'Look-Out', a wooded height behind the town. Rather to the back is a cairn with a weather-vane. Round the cairn, as well as in the foreground, large stones have been placed as seats. Far below in the background can be seen the outer fjord, with islands and jutting headlands. The open sea cannot be seen. It is dusk on a summer evening; there is a reddish-golden haze in the air, spreading over the mountain peaks far into the distance. From below, in the background, the faint sound of part-singing can be heard.

> [*Young people from the town, and ladies and gentlemen in intimate talk, come up in couples from the right, pass the cairn, and go out to the left.*
> *After a moment,* BALLESTED *enters, as guide to a party of foreign tourists and their ladies; he is laden with their wraps and satchels.*]

BALLESTED [*pointing up with his stick*]: Sehen Sie, meine Herr-schaften, over there *liegt eine andere* hill. *Das wollen wir besteigen,* too, *und* now *herunter –*
> [*He goes on in French, and leads the party off to the right.*[7]
> HILDE *comes quickly up the right-hand slope; she pauses and looks back; a moment later,* BOLETTA *comes up the same way.*]

BOLETTA: But, my dear, why should we run away from Lyngstrand?

HILDE: Because I can't bear going so slowly on the hills. Just look at him – simply *crawling* up!

BOLETTA: Oh, but you know how ill he is.

HILDE: Do you think it's really serious?

BOLETTA: Yes, I certainly do.

HILDE: He went to consult Father this afternoon – I wonder what *he* thinks of him.

BOLETTA: Father told me he has patches on both lungs; he won't live very long, Father says.

HILDE: Did he? Well, that's exactly what I've been thinking.

BOLETTA: Well, for heaven's sake don't let him notice anything.

HILDE: As if I would! [*Dropping her voice*] There! Now Hans has managed to clamber up. 'Hans', indeed – you've only to look at him, haven't you? – to know that he's called 'Hans'!

BOLETTA [*in a whisper*]: Behave yourself! I mean it!
[LYNGSTRAND *comes from the right with a parasol in his hand.*]

LYNGSTRAND: Please forgive me, ladies, for not being able to keep up with you.

HILDE: So you've got a parasol now?

LYNGSTRAND: It's your mother's – she said I might use it as a stick, seeing I haven't brought one.

BOLETTA: Are they still down there – Father and the others?

LYNGSTRAND: Yes, your father's gone into the restaurant for a moment, but the others are sitting outside listening to the music. But your mother said they'll be coming up here presently.

HILDE [*who is standing looking at him*]: I suppose you're tired out now.

LYNGSTRAND: Yes, I rather think I *am* a little tired – I feel perhaps I ought to sit down for a bit. [*He sits on one of the stones in the foreground to the right.*]

HILDE [*standing in front of him*]: You know there'll be dancing down at the bandstand later on?

LYNGSTRAND: Yes, I did hear it mentioned.

HILDE: I'm sure you enjoy dancing, don't you?

BOLETTA [*who has begun picking wild flowers in the heather*]: Oh Hilde, do let Mr Lyngstrand get his breath!

LYNGSTRAND: Yes, Miss Hilde, I should like dancing – if only I could.

HILDE: Oh, I see. Didn't you ever learn, then?

LYNGSTRAND: No, as a matter of fact, I didn't; but that wasn't what I meant – I meant that I can't because of my chest.

HILDE: Oh, you mean this 'lesion' that you say you have?

LYNGSTRAND: Yes, that's right.

HILDE: Aren't you awfully sorry that you have a 'lesion' like that?

LYNGSTRAND: Oh no, I can't really say that I am. [*Smiling*] I think it's because of it that everyone's so nice and kind and friendly to me.

HILDE: And of course it isn't really serious.

LYNGSTRAND: No, not in the least – your father doesn't seem to think so, either.

HILDE: And it'll clear up just as soon as you get abroad?

LYNGSTRAND: Oh yes, it'll clear up.

BOLETTA [*carrying flowers*]: Look, Mr Lyngstrand, here's one for your buttonhole.

LYNGSTRAND: Oh, thank you so much, Miss Wangel – it's ever so nice of you.

HILDE [*looking down to the right*]: The others are coming up the path.

BOLETTA [*also looking down*]: I hope they know where to turn off. No, they're going the wrong way.

LYNGSTRAND [*getting up*]: I'll run down to the turning and call to them.

HILDE: You'll have to call pretty loud.

BOLETTA: No, it isn't worth it – you'll only tire yourself out again.

LYNGSTRAND: Oh, downhill's easy. [*He goes out to the right.*]

HILDE: Downhill, yes. [*Looking after him*] He's even jumping! It hasn't occurred to him that he'll have to come up again!

BOLETTA: Poor boy!

HILDE: If Lyngstrand were to propose to you, would you accept him?

BOLETTA: You must be mad!

HILDE: Oh, I mean, of course, if he hadn't got his 'lesion' and weren't going to die soon. Would you accept him *then*?

BOLETTA: I think *you'd* better have him.

HILDE: I'm blessed if I would. Why, he hasn't a bean – he can't even keep himself.

BOLLETA: Then why do you always go about with him?

HILDE: Oh, only because of his 'lesion'.

BOLETTA: I haven't noticed that you pity him much.

HILDE: Oh, I don't. But I find it so fascinating.[8]

BOLETTA: What?

HILDE: To watch him – and to get him to say it isn't serious, and that he's going abroad, and going to be an artist. He really believes it, and he's so ridiculously happy about it – and it's never going to happen – never in the world – because he isn't going to live long enough. I find that a very exciting thought.

BOLETTA: Exciting!

HILDE: Yes, I find it exciting – I don't mind admitting it.

BOLETTA: Oh, Hilde, you really are a horrid child!

HILDE: That's just what I want to be – out of sheer spite. [*Looking down*] Ah, at last! Arnholm doesn't much like climbing! [*Turning*] By the way, what do you think I noticed about Arnholm at lunch?

BOLETTA: Well?

HILDE: Just imagine – he's going bald – right on the top of his head!

BOLETTA: Nonsense. He certainly isn't.

HILDE: He is. What's more, he's got wrinkles – round his eyes. Good heavens, Boletta, to think that you were so in love with him when he was your tutor here!

BOLETTA [*smiling*]: Yes, just fancy! I remember once crying my eyes out because he said Boletta was an ugly name.

HILDE: Did you really? [*Looking down again*] I say, just look there. 'The Lady from the Sea' is walking with him now –

not with Father – and chattering away. I wonder if those two are a bit gone on each other.

BOLETTA: You ought to be ashamed of yourself, really you ought! How can you go and talk about her like that? Just when we were beginning to get on so well with her –

HILDE: Were we? You're imagining things, my girl. Oh no, we'll never get on with her; she isn't our sort, and we aren't hers. Goodness knows what made Father bring her into the family. I shouldn't be a bit surprised if, one of these fine days, she went raving mad!

BOLETTA: Mad? How can you say such a thing?

HILDE: Well, it wouldn't be surprising – her mother went mad. She died mad, I know that for a fact.

BOLETTA: Good gracious, is there anything you don't go poking your nose into? Now you're not to go talking about that – for Father's sake. Now, be a good girl – do you hear, Hilde?

[WANGEL, ELLIDA, ARNHOLM, *and* LYNGSTRAND *come up from the right.*]

ELLIDA [*pointing out to the back*]: It's out that way.

ARNHOLM: Oh yes, of course, it must be.

ELLIDA: *That's* where the sea is.

BOLETTA [*to* ARNHOLM]: Don't you think it's pretty up here?

ARNHOLM: It's wonderful – a magnificent view!

WANGEL: Yes. Haven't you ever been up here before?

ARNHOLM: No, never. In my day I doubt if one could get here – there wasn't any path.

WANGEL: And no gardens either – this has all been laid out in the last few years.

BOLETTA: There's an even better view from Crow's-Nest Hill – over there.

WANGEL: Shall we go there, Ellida?

ELLIDA [*sitting on a stone to the right*]: I don't think I will, thanks. You others go, I'll sit here and wait for you.

WANGEL: Then I'll stay with you – the girls can take Mr Arnholm.

BOLETTA: Would you like to come with us, Mr Arnholm?

ARNHOLM: Yes, very much. Is there a path up there too?

BOLETTA: Oh yes, a nice wide one.

HILDE: Wide enough for two people to walk quite comfortably arm in arm.

ARNHOLM [*joking*]: Is there indeed, Miss Hilde? [*To* BOLETTA] Shall we see if she's right?

BOLETTA [*suppressing a smile*]: Yes, let's.
    [*They go out arm in arm to the left.*]

HILDE [*to* LYNGSTRAND]: Shall we go too?

LYNGSTRAND: Arm in arm?

HILDE: Why not? I don't mind.

LYNGSTRAND [*taking her arm with a happy laugh*]: This is rather a lark!

HILDE: A 'lark'?

LYNGSTRAND: Yes, we look just as if we were engaged.

HILDE: I'm sure you've never walked arm in arm with a lady before, Mr Lyngstrand.
    [*They go out to the left.*]

WANGEL [*standing by the cairn*]: Now we have a moment to ourselves, Ellida dear.

ELLIDA: Yes, come and sit here by me.

WANGEL [*sitting*]: It's so quiet and peaceful here. Now we can talk.

ELLIDA: What about?

WANGEL: About you – and about *us*, Ellida. I realize that things can't go on like this.

ELLIDA: What else do you suggest, then?

WANGEL: Perfect trust, my dear. And a proper life together, as we used to have.

ELLIDA: Oh, if only we could. But that's so utterly impossible.

WANGEL: I think I understand. Yes, from certain things you've let fall from time to time, I think I do.

ELLIDA [*vehemently*]: You don't! Don't say that: you *can't* understand!

WANGEL: But I do. You have an honest nature, Ellida – and great loyalty . . .

ELLIDA: Yes, I think I have.

WANGEL: So that if you are to be really happy in any relationship, it must be a full and perfect one.

ELLIDA [*looking eagerly at him*]: Yes? Well?

WANGEL: You weren't meant to be a man's second wife.

ELLIDA: What makes you think that *now*?

WANGEL: The idea has often crossed my mind, but today I knew for certain. That anniversary that the children kept – you looked on me as a sort of accomplice in it. Well, yes . . . A man can't just wipe out his memories – at least, *I* can't, I'm not made like that.

ELLIDA: I know you're not. Oh, I know that so well.

WANGEL: But you're wrong, all the same. To you, it's almost as if the children's mother were still alive – as if she were still here with us, invisibly. You feel that my heart is divided between her and you, and the thought of it shocks you – you almost feel there's something immoral in our relationship. That's why you can't – or won't – live with me any longer as my wife.

ELLIDA [*rising*]: Have you realized that? Seen it all so clearly?

WANGEL: Yes, today I really understood it at last – through and through.

ELLIDA: 'Through and through'? No, you mustn't think that.

WANGEL [*rising*]: Dear Ellida – I know quite well that there's more behind it.

ELLIDA [*anxiously*]: You know that there's more?

WANGEL: Yes. There's the fact that you can't bear this place. You feel that the mountains shut you in, and that depresses you. There's not enough light for you here; our horizon is too narrow; the air's too weak and relaxing for you.

ELLIDA: Yes, you're perfectly right ... night and day, summer and winter, I'm haunted by this irresistible longing for the sea.

WANGEL: I know that, too, Ellida dear. [*Putting his hand on her head*] That's why this poor sick child shall go back to her own home again.

ELLIDA: What do you mean?

WANGEL: It's quite simple – we'll go away.

ELLIDA: Away?

WANGEL: Yes. Somewhere out by the open sea – somewhere where you can find a home after your own heart.

ELLIDA: Oh, my dear, you mustn't think of it. It's quite impossible – you'd never be happy anywhere in the world but here.

WANGEL: Never mind about that. Besides, do you think I could be happy here – without you?

ELLIDA: But I am here – and I shall stay. You're not without me.

WANGEL: Am I not, Ellida?

ELLIDA: Oh, don't let's talk about that. Everything that you live for is here – all that you long for – your whole life's work – is here.

WANGEL: As I said, never mind about that. We're leaving here – we'll go out there somewhere. Now that's quite settled, Ellida dear.

ELLIDA: But how do you think that would help?

WANGEL: You'd get back your health and your peace of mind.

ELLIDA: I doubt it. And what about you? Think of yourself as well – what would you get from it?

WANGEL: I should win you back, my dear.

ELLIDA: You wouldn't. No, no, you never would, Wangel. That's what's so terrible to think of – so heartbreaking.

WANGEL: That remains to be seen. If you have these ideas
here, then there's no other answer for you than to go away
– and the sooner the better. Now it's quite settled, do you
hear?

ELLIDA: No. Heaven knows, I'd rather tell you the whole
thing, just as it happened.

WANGEL: Yes – tell me.

ELLIDA: You see, I can't have you making yourself miserable
on my account – especially when it won't do us any good.

WANGEL: You've given me your word that you'll tell me
everything – just as it happened.

ELLIDA: I'll tell you as well as I can – and all that I feel I
know about it. Come and sit beside me.

[*They sit on one of the stones.*]

WANGEL: Well, Ellida?

ELLIDA: That day out there when you came and asked me if
I would marry you, you told me quite frankly and openly
about your first marriage. You said it had been so happy.

WANGEL: And so it was.

ELLIDA: Yes, my dear, I'm sure it was – that's not the reason
I mention it now. I only want to remind you that I was
frank with you in turn. I told you, quite unreservedly, that
I had once been in love with another man – and that we
had become – in a way – engaged.

WANGEL: In a way?

ELLIDA: Yes, something of the kind. But it lasted such a short
time. He went away. And after a while, I ended it. I told
you all that.

WANGEL: But, Ellida dear, why do you want to bring all that
up now? After all, it doesn't really concern me; and I've
never once so much as asked you who he was.

ELLIDA: No, you haven't. You're always so considerate to
me.

WANGEL [*smiling*]: Well, as it happens – it wouldn't be so very
difficult to guess his name.

ELLIDA: His name?

WANGEL: Out there, round Skjoldvik, there weren't many to choose from – I might say there was really only one.

ELLIDA: You think it was Arnholm?

WANGEL: Yes . . . Wasn't it?

ELLIDA: No.

WANGEL: No? Then I simply can't imagine –

ELLIDA: Do you remember a big American ship coming into Skjoldvik that autumn for repairs?

WANGEL: I certainly do. That was the ship where the Captain was found murdered in his cabin one morning. I had to go out and do the post-mortem.

ELLIDA: Yes, so you did.

WANGEL: He'd been murdered by the second mate.

ELLIDA: You can't say that – it was never proved.

WANGEL: There wasn't much doubt about it. Why else should he have gone and drowned himself as he did?

ELLIDA: He didn't drown himself – he slipped away in a ship bound for the north.

WANGEL [surprised]: How do you know that?

ELLIDA [with an effort]: You see, Wangel, that second mate was the man I was engaged to.

WANGEL [starting up]: What? But that's impossible!

ELLIDA: It's true. He was the man.

WANGEL: But, Ellida, how in the world could you do such a thing? How could you accept a man like that – an utter stranger? What was his name?

ELLIDA: In those days he called himself Friman. Afterwards he signed his letters Alfred Johnston.

WANGEL: Where did he come from?

ELLIDA: From Finnmark, he said.[9] But he was born over in Finland; he crossed the border as a child – with his father, I think.

WANGEL: He was a Kvæn, then?

ELLIDA: Yes, that's what they're called.

WANGEL: What else do you know about him?

ELLIDA: Only that he went to sea when he was very young.
And that he'd been on long voyages.

WANGEL: And nothing else?

ELLIDA: No. We never seemed to talk about that sort of
thing.

WANGEL: What did you talk about, then?

ELLIDA: Mostly about the sea . . .

WANGEL: Oh? The sea?

ELLIDA: About its storms and its calms . . . dark nights at
sea . . . and the sea sparkling in the sunshine. But we talked
mostly about the whales and the dolphins – and the seals
that lie out on the rocks basking in the noonday warmth.
And we talked about the gulls and the skuas and all the
other seabirds. . . . And, do you know, it's an extraordinary
thing, but as we talked like this he seemed to me to have
something in common with the birds and beasts of the sea.

WANGEL: But *you*?

ELLIDA: Yes, I almost believed that I had, too.

WANGEL: I see. . . . And so you became engaged?

ELLIDA: Yes. He said that I must.

WANGEL: 'Must'? Hadn't you a will of your own?

ELLIDA: Not when I was with him. That was what seemed
so incredible afterwards.

WANGEL: Were you with him much?

ELLIDA: No, not very often. He came out one day to see the
lighthouse; that was how I got to know him. After that,
we met once or twice; and then there was the business
about the Captain, and he had to go away.

WANGEL: Yes, I want to hear a little more about that.

ELLIDA: Early one morning, before it was light, I got
a note from him, saying that I must go to him out on
Bratthammer – you know, the headland between Skjoldvik and the lighthouse.

WANGEL: Yes, yes, I know it.

ELLIDA: He wrote that I was to come at once, because he wanted to talk to me.

WANGEL: And you went?

ELLIDA: Yes, I couldn't help myself. . . . Well – then he told me that he'd stabbed the Captain that night.

WANGEL: He actually said so? Admitted it frankly?

ELLIDA: Yes. But he said he had only done what was right and proper.

WANGEL: Right and proper? Why had he stabbed him, then?

ELLIDA: He wouldn't tell me – he said it wasn't fit for me to hear.

WANGEL: And you simply took his word for it?

ELLIDA: It never occurred to me not to. And anyhow, he had to go away. Then, just as he was going to say good-bye . . . Well, you'd never imagine what he did.

WANGEL: Oh? Then tell me.

ELLIDA: He took a key-chain out of his pocket, and he pulled from his finger a ring he always wore; then from me he took a little ring that I had, and he slipped the two rings on the key-chain. Then he said that we must be married to the sea.

WANGEL: Married . . .?

ELLIDA: Yes, that was what he said. Then, with all his strength, he flung the chain with the two rings as far as he could out to sea.[10]

WANGEL: But, Ellida – you agreed?

ELLIDA: Yes . . . you see – at the time it seemed so right. And then, thank heaven, he went away.

WANGEL: But after he'd gone . . .?

ELLIDA: Oh, I soon came to my senses again, you can be sure of that. I saw how mad – how utterly ridiculous – the whole thing had been.

WANGEL: But you mentioned letters. So you've heard from him since?

ELLIDA: Yes, I've heard from him. First I had a few short

lines from Archangel simply saying that he was going over to America, and giving me an address where I could write to him.

WANGEL: And did you?

ELLIDA: Oh yes, at once. Of course I told him that everything must be over between us. And that he mustn't think of me any more than I should think of him.

WANGEL: But he wrote again in spite of that?

ELLIDA: Yes, he wrote again.

WANGEL: And what did he say in answer to what you'd told him?

ELLIDA: Not a word. It was as if I'd never broken with him. He wrote, quite coolly and calmly, that I was to wait for him. He would let me know when he was ready for me, and then I was to go to him at once.

WANGEL: He wouldn't release you?

ELLIDA: No. So I wrote again – almost word for word what I'd written before. Rather more strongly perhaps.

WANGEL: Did he give in then?

ELLIDA: Oh no – far from it. He wrote back just as calmly as ever – not a word about my breaking with him. So then I saw that it was useless and I never wrote to him again.

WANGEL: And you heard nothing more from him?

ELLIDA: Yes, I've had three letters from him since. He wrote to me once from California, and another time from China. The last letter I had from him was from Australia, saying that he was going to the gold mines. But since then I've heard nothing from him.

WANGEL: The man must have had an extraordinary power over you, Ellida.

ELLIDA: Oh yes, yes . . . he is – terrible!

WANGEL: But now you mustn't think about him again – ever. Dearest Ellida, promise me that. And now we must try another cure for you. Fresh air – fresher than we get here up the fjord – salt, fresh, sea air. What do you say to that?

ELLIDA: Oh, you mustn't talk like that – you mustn't even think of it. It wouldn't help me! I'm quite sure it wouldn't. I could never throw it off, even out there.

WANGEL: What? My dear, what do you mean?

ELLIDA: I mean this terrible thing . . . this inexplicable power that he has over my mind . . .

WANGEL: But you have thrown it off – long ago. When you broke with him. That was all over long ago.

ELLIDA [*starting up*]: No, that's just it. It is not over.

WANGEL: Not over?

ELLIDA: No, Wangel, it's not over. And I'm afraid that it never will be – as long as I live.

WANGEL [*in a strangled voice*]: Do you mean to say that, in your heart of hearts, you've never been able to forget this stranger?

ELLIDA: I *had* forgotten him. But then – it was as if he'd come back again.

WANGEL: When was that?

ELLIDA: It's about three years ago now – a little more perhaps. It was when I was expecting the child.

WANGEL: Ah – just then? Yes, Ellida, now I'm beginning to understand so many things.

ELLIDA: You're wrong, my dear. I don't think anyone in the world could understand this thing that's happened to me.

WANGEL [*giving her a pained look*]: And to think that all these last three years you've been in love with another man. Not with me at all – with someone else!

ELLIDA: Oh, you're so wrong! I don't love anyone but you.

WANGEL [*quietly*]: Then why, all this time, have you not wanted to live with me as my wife?

ELLIDA: Because of – the fear that I have of the stranger.

WANGEL: Fear . . . ?

ELLIDA: Yes, fear. A fear so terrible that I think it could only come from the sea. Because now, Wangel, I'll tell you –

[*The young townspeople come back from the left, bow, and go out to the right. With them come* ARNHOLM, BOLETTA, HILDE, *and* LYNGSTRAND.]

BOLETTA [*as they pass*]: Well! Are you still up here?

ELLIDA: Yes, it's so lovely and cool right up here.

ARNHOLM: *We*'re going down to dance.

WANGEL: Splendid. We'll be down soon, too.

HILDE: *Au revoir*, then.

ELLIDA: Mr Lyngstrand – just a minute . . .

[LYNGSTRAND *waits.* ARNHOLM, BOLETTA, *and* HILDE *go out to the right.*]

ELLIDA [*to* LYNGSTRAND]: Are you going to dance too?

LYNGSTRAND: No, Mrs Wangel, I think I'd better not.

ELLIDA: No, you ought to be careful. That chest of yours – it isn't really better yet.

LYNGSTRAND: Not quite. No.

ELLIDA [*rather hesitantly*]: How long is it since you went on that voyage?

LYNGSTRAND: When I got my lesion?

ELLIDA: Yes, the voyage you were talking about this morning.

LYNGSTRAND: Oh, it must be about – let me see – yes, it's a good three years ago now.

ELLIDA: Three years . . .

LYNGSTRAND: Or just over. We left America in February, and we were wrecked in March. We were caught by the spring gales.

ELLIDA [*looking at* WANGEL]: And that was just the time when . . .

WANGEL: But, Ellida dear –

ELLIDA: Well, don't let us keep you, Mr Lyngstrand. You go. But don't dance.

LYNGSTRAND: No, I'll just watch. [*He goes out to the right.*]

WANGEL: Ellida dear - why were you asking him about that voyage?

ELLIDA: Johnston was in that ship – I'm sure of it.

WANGEL: What makes you think so?

ELLIDA [*not answering him*]: During the voyage he found out that I'd married someone else while he was away. And it was at that very moment that this thing descended on me.

WANGEL: This fear?

ELLIDA: Yes. I suddenly see him – actually standing there, right in front of me ... or rather, a little to one side. He never looks at me – he's simply there.

WANGEL: What do you feel he looks like?

ELLIDA: Just as when I last saw him.

WANGEL: Ten years ago.

ELLIDA: Yes – out on Bratthammer. What I see most clearly is his tie-pin, with a great milky pearl in it that seems to glare at me like the eye of a dead fish.

WANGEL: Good lord – you're more ill than I thought. More ill than even you realize, Ellida.

ELLIDA: Yes, yes. Help me if you can. I can feel it closing in on me – nearer and nearer.

WANGEL: And you've been going about like this for three whole years – suffering like this in secret, and never telling me!

ELLIDA: But I couldn't! It's only now that I've had to speak – for your own sake. If I'd told you all this before, I should have had to tell you – the unspeakable thing ...

WANGEL: The unspeakable thing?

ELLIDA: No, no – don't ask me! Just one other thing, and that's all: Wangel – how can we explain the mystery of the child's eyes?

WANGEL: My own darling Ellida, I assure you it was only your imagination. The child's eyes were perfectly normal – just like any other child's.

ELLIDA: No, they weren't. You must have seen it! The child's eyes changed colour with the sea – when the fjord was calm and sunny, so were his eyes; but when it was stormy – oh, I saw it even if you couldn't!

WANGEL [*humouring her*]: Well – possibly. But even if that was true – what of it?

ELLIDA [*softly, coming closer*]: I've seen eyes like that before.

WANGEL: Oh? Where?

ELLIDA: Out on Bratthammer, ten years ago.

WANGEL [*recoiling a step*]: What do you mean?

ELLIDA [*in a trembling whisper*]: The child had the stranger's eyes.

WANGEL [*with an involuntary cry*]: Ellida . . .!

ELLIDA [*desperately beating her head with her hands*]: Now you can see why I can never – why I dare not – live with you again as your wife! [*She suddenly turns and rushes down the slope to the right.*]

WANGEL [*hurrying after her and calling*]: Ellida! Ellida! My poor unhappy Ellida!

ACT THREE

A remote corner of Dr Wangel's garden. It is a damp, marshy place, overgrown with huge old trees. On the right, the edge of a dark pool can be seen. A low picket-fence separates the garden from a footpath, with the fjord in the background. In the far distance, across the fjord, are mountain ridges and peaks. It is late afternoon – almost evening.

[BOLETTA *is sitting sewing on a stone seat to the left with a few books and a workbasket on it.* HILDE *and* LYNGSTRAND, *both with fishing-tackle, are standing at the edge of the pool.*]

HILDE [*with a gesture to* LYNGSTRAND]: Don't move – I can see a big one!

LYNGSTRAND [*looking*]: Where?

HILDE [*pointing*]: Can't you see? Just down there. And – good heavens, look there's another. [*Looking through the trees*] Oh, now he'll come and frighten them away!

BOLETTA [*looking up*]: Who will?

HILDE: Your headmaster, my girl!

BOLETTA: Mine?

HILDE: Yes, he was never mine, thank goodness.

ARNHOLM [*coming from the right, through the trees*]: Are there fish in the pond still?

HILDE: Yes, there are some very old carp.

ARNHOLM: What, are those old carp still alive?

HILDE: Yes, they're real veterans, but we're going to try to put paid to some of them.

ARNHOLM: You'd do better to try out in the fjord.

LYNGSTRAND: No, the pond – it's more mysterious, in a manner of speaking.

HILDE: Yes, it's much more fascinating here. Have you just been in the sea?

ARNHOLM: Yes, I've just come from the bathing-place.

HILDE: I expect you stayed in the pool?

ARNHOLM: Yes, I'm not much of a swimmer.

HILDE: Can you swim on your back?

ARNHOLM: No.

HILDE: I can [*To* LYNGSTRAND] Let's try over on the other side.

[*They go off round the pool to the right.*]

ARNHOLM [*going to Boletta*]: So you're sitting all alone, Boletta?

BOLETTA: Yes, I generally do.

ARNHOLM: Isn't your mother out in the garden?

BOLETTA: No, she's probably out for a walk with Father.

ARNHOLM: How is she this afternoon?

BOLETTA: I don't really know, I forgot to ask.

ARNHOLM: What are those books you have there?

BOLETTA: Oh, one's a book on botany, the other's a geography.

ARNHOLM: Do you like that sort of thing?

BOLETTA: Yes, when I can find the time; but of course the housework has to come first.

ARNHOLM: But doesn't your mother – your stepmother – help you with that?

BOLETTA: No, that's my job. I had to do it during the two years that Father was alone, and I've gone on with it ever since.

ARNHOLM: But you're still as fond of reading as ever?

BOLETTA: Yes, I read all the serious books I can lay my hands on. I'd like to know a little about the world – we're so completely cut off here from all that's going on. . . . Well, almost completely.

ARNHOLM: But, my dear Boletta, don't say that.

BOLETTA: But it's true. We seem to live much the same sort of life as those carp down there in the pond. There's the fjord quite close to them, with great shoals of fish swim-

ming freely in and out, but these poor tame domesticated
fish know nothing about it, and they can never join them.

ARNHOLM: I don't think they'd do very well out there.

BOLETTA: Oh, it doesn't seem to me they'd be very much
worse off.

ARNHOLM: Besides, you can't say that you're really cut off
from the world here – not during the summer, at any rate.
Why, nowadays this has really become quite a meeting-
place for the fashionable world – it's almost a junction, with
so much coming and going!

BOLETTA [smiling]: Oh yes, when you only come and go
yourself, it's easy for you to make fun of us.

ARNHOLM: I? Make fun? Whatever makes you think that?

BOLETTA: All this about a meeting-place and a junction for
the fashionable world – it's only what you've heard the
people round here saying. They're always talking like that.

ARNHOLM: Yes, I must admit I *have* noticed that.

BOLETTA: It isn't really true, you know – not for us who live
here all the year round. What good does it do us if the great
world outside passes through here on its way to see the
Midnight Sun? We can't join them, and there's certainly no
Midnight Sun for us. No, we just have to go on living in
our carp pond.

ARNHOLM [sitting beside her]: Boletta dear, tell me, isn't there
something – something special, I mean – that you long for
here at home?

BOLETTA: Oh yes, perhaps there is.

ARNHOLM: What is it? What do you long for particularly?

BOLETTA: Chiefly to get away.

ARNHOLM: More than anything else?

BOLETTA: Yes. And then I'd like to learn a little more – really
to get to *know* about everything.

ARNHOLM: When I was teaching you, your father often said
that you ought to go to college.

BOLETTA: Yes – poor Father, he says so many things. But

when it comes to the point, Father has very little real energy.

ARNHOLM: No, I'm afraid you're right, he hasn't. But haven't you ever talked to him about it? Really seriously, I mean?

BOLETTA: No, not really.

ARNHOLM: But you know, you ought to, Boletta – before it's too late. Why don't you?

BOLETTA: Oh, I suppose it's because I haven't much real energy either. That's one way I certainly take after Father.

ARNHOLM: Hm! aren't you being rather unfair to yourself?

BOLETTA: No – unfortunately. Besides, Father has very little time to think about me or my future – and not much inclination, either. He won't be bothered with that sort of thing if he can help it. He's so completely taken up with Ellida.

ARNHOLM: With . . . ? How?

BOLETTA: I mean that he and my stepmother – [breaking off]. Well, you can see that father and mother live in a world of their own.

ARNHOLM: Well, that's all the more reason for you to try to get away from here.

BOLETTA: Yes, but I don't feel I have the right to do that – not to forsake Father.

ARNHOLM: But, my dear Boletta, you'll have to leave him some time, in any case; so it seems to me that the sooner the better.

BOLETTA: Yes, I suppose there's nothing else for it. I must consider myself too – I must try to find a post of some sort. When Father dies I shall have nobody to depend on. . . . But, poor Father, I dread the thought of leaving him.

ARNHOLM: Dread?

BOLETTA: Yes, for his sake.

ARNHOLM: But, good heavens, there's your stepmother; she'll stay with him.

BOLETTA: Yes, that's true. But she isn't able to do all the

things that Mother did so well. There are so many things that she doesn't notice – or perhaps that she *won't* notice – or that she doesn't care about. I don't know which.

ARNHOLM: Hm! . . . I think I see what you mean.

BOLETTA: Poor Father. In some ways he's very weak – perhaps you've noticed. He hasn't really enough work to take up all his time, and she's so completely unable to help him . . . though he's no one but himself to blame for that.

ARNHOLM: Why do you think that?

BOLETTA: Oh, Father always likes to see happy faces round him; he says there must be sunshine and happiness in the house. So I'm afraid he often gives her – medicine that doesn't do her any good in the long run.

ARNHOLM: Do you really think so?

BOLETTA: Yes, I can't help thinking so, because sometimes she's so strange. [*Vehemently*] But isn't it unfair that I should have to stay at home, because really it's no earthly use to Father – and I do feel I have a duty to myself as well.

ARNHOLM: You know, my dear Boletta, we'll have to talk this over.

BOLETTA: Oh, what's the use? I expect I was meant to stay here in the carp pond.

ARNHOLM: Not at all – it all depends on you.

BOLETTA [*eagerly*]: Do you think so?

ARNHOLM: Yes. Take my word for it, the whole thing's entirely in your own hands.

BOLETTA: Oh, if only it were! Will you put in a good word for me with Father?

ARNHOLM: Of course. But first, my dear Boletta, I must have a very frank and open talk with you. [*Looking out to the left*] Sh! – don't say anything – we'll talk about it later.

[ELLIDA *comes from the left; she is hatless, but wears a large shawl over her head and shoulders.*]

ELLIDA [*in restless animation*]: Oh, it's delightful here – really lovely.

ARNHOLM [*rising*]: Have you been out for a walk?

ELLIDA: Yes, I had a glorious long walk with Wangel; now we're going for a sail.

BOLETTA: Won't you sit down?

ELLIDA: No thanks, I won't sit.

BOLETTA [*moving along the seat*]: There's plenty of room.

ELLIDA [*pacing about*]: No, no, I couldn't sit – I really couldn't.

ARNHOLM: Your walk's certainly done you good – you seem much more cheerful.

ELLIDA: Oh yes, I feel wonderful – so completely happy – and so safe – so safe! [*Looking out to the left*] What's that great steamer coming in?

BOLETTA [*getting up to look*]: It must be the big English ship.

ARNHOLM: She's stopping out at the moorings. Does she usually put in here?

BOLETTA: Only for half an hour. Then she goes on up the fjord.

ELLIDA: And then tomorrow she sails away again, out into the open sea – far across the sea. Imagine going with her! To be able to do that . . . just to be able to!

ARNHOLM: Haven't you ever been on a long sea voyage, Mrs Wangel?

ELLIDA: No . . . never. Only little trips here in the fjord.

BOLETTA [*with a sigh*]: No, we have to put up with the dry land.

ARNHOLM: Well, it's our natural element.

ELLIDA: No, I don't believe that at all.

ARNHOLM: Not the dry land?

ELLIDA: No, I don't believe it is. I think that if only men had chosen from the very beginning to live on the sea – or even *in* the sea – we should have reached a perfection quite different from our present state – both better and happier.[11]

ARNHOLM: Do you really believe that?

ELLIDA: Yes, why shouldn't it be true? I've often talked to Wangel about it . . .

ARNHOLM: Well, what does he say?

ELLIDA: He thinks I might be right.

ARNHOLM [*joking*]: Well, who knows? But what's done is done. We've taken the wrong road once and for all, and become land-beasts instead of sea-beasts. All things considered, it's too late now to put it right!

ELLIDA: Yes, that's true, unfortunately – and I believe that mankind knows it too, and it haunts us like a secret sorrow. Take my word for it, that's at the root of all human misery, I'm sure it is.

ARNHOLM: But, my dear Mrs Wangel, I've never noticed that mankind is so very miserable; on the contrary, I should say that most people have a pleasant, happy life, full of deep, spontaneous joy.

ELLIDA: Oh no – that isn't true. Our joy is something like the joy we get in the long light summer days – it implies the darkness that is to come, and that implication casts its shadow over all human joy, just as the drifting clouds cast their shadows over the fjord. It lies there so blue and shining, and then –

BOLETTA: Now, you shouldn't give way to sad thoughts like that. You were so bright and cheerful just now.

ELLIDA: Yes, so I was – this is really very silly of me. [*Looking round restlessly*] If only Wangel would come – he promised me faithfully, yet he doesn't come. He must have forgotten; dear Mr Arnholm, won't you see if you can find him for me?

ARNHOLM: Of course I will.

ELLIDA: Tell him he must come quickly, because now I can't see him . . .

ARNHOLM: Not see him?

ELLIDA: Oh, you don't understand; when he's not with me, I quite often can't remember what he looks like, and then I feel as if I'd lost him altogether – and that upsets me terribly. Please hurry. [*She wanders over towards the pond.*]

BOLETTA [*to* ARNHOLM]: I'll go with you; you wouldn't
know where . . .

ARNHOLM: Don't worry, I'll manage.

BOLETTA [*dropping her voice*]: No, no, I'm worried – I'm
afraid he's on board the steamer.

ARNHOLM: Afraid?

BOLETTA: He generally goes to see if there's anyone he knows
on board, and then he gets in the bar . . .

ARNHOLM: Ah – come along, then. [*He and* BOLETTA *go out
to the left.*]

[ELLIDA *stands for a while gazing into the pool, now and then
talking to herself in broken phrases. Outside, on the footpath
beyond the garden fence, a* STRANGER *in travelling clothes
comes from the left. He has bushy reddish hair and beard. On
his head is a Scottish cap, and over his shoulder a satchel on a
strap.*]

STRANGER [*goes slowly along the fence and looks into the garden.
When he catches sight of* ELLIDA, *he stops and, looking at her
intently, says softly*]: Good evening, Ellida.

ELLIDA [*she turns and calls*]: Ah, my dear – here you are at
last.[12]

STRANGER: Yes, at last.

ELLIDA [*looking at him in surprise and horror*]: Who are *you*?
Are you looking for someone?

STRANGER: You know I am, my dear.[13]

ELLIDA [*taken aback*]: I beg your pardon? How dare you speak
to me like that? Who is it you're looking for?

STRANGER: I'm looking for you.

ELLIDA [*with a shudder*]: Oh . . .! [*She looks at him for a moment, staggers back, and gives a stifled cry.*] Your eyes! Your
eyes!

STRANGER: So you're beginning to recognize me at last, my
dear? I knew you at once, Ellida.

ELLIDA: Your eyes! Don't look at me like that – I shall call
for help.

STRANGER: Quiet, quiet! Don't be afraid – I'm not going to hurt you.

ELLIDA [*covering her eyes with her hand*]: Don't look at me like that, I tell you!

STRANGER [*leaning his arms on the fence*]: I came on that English steamer.

ELLIDA [*with a frightened glance at him*]: What do you want with me?

STRANGER: I promised you that I'd come back as soon as I could.

ELLIDA: Go away – go away again! Never – never come back here! I wrote and told you that it must be all over between us – forever. You know that.

STRANGER [*unperturbed, without answering*]: I wanted to come to you before, my dear, but I couldn't. Now at last I've been able, and here I am, Ellida.

ELLIDA: What do you want with me? What are you thinking of? Why have you come here?

STRANGER: You know why – I've come to fetch you.

ELLIDA [*shrinking away in terror*]: To fetch me? Is *that* what you mean to do?

STRANGER: Yes, it is.

ELLIDA: But you must know that I'm married.

STRANGER: Yes, I know that.

ELLIDA: And in spite – in spite of that, you've come to – fetch me?

STRANGER: I have indeed.

ELLIDA [*clasping her hands to her head*]: Oh this is terrible – appalling . . .

STRANGER: Don't you want to come, my love?

ELLIDA [*wildly*]: Don't look at me like that!

STRANGER: I'm asking you – don't you want to come?

ELLIDA: No, no, no! I won't – never in the world! I won't, I tell you. I neither can nor will. [*Low*] I dare not.

STRANGER [*climbing over the fence into the garden*]: Very

283

well, Ellida – but before I go, just let me tell you one thing.

ELLIDA [*tries to escape but cannot; she stands as if paralysed with terror, supporting herself on a tree-stump by the pond*]: Don't touch me. Don't come near me – stay where you are. Don't touch me, I say!

STRANGER [*cautiously taking a few steps towards her*]: You needn't be afraid of me, Ellida.

ELLIDA [*covering her eyes with her hands*]: Don't look at me like that!

STRANGER: Don't be afraid. Don't.

[DR WANGEL *comes through the garden from the left.*]

WANGEL [*still among the trees*]: I'm sorry if I've kept you waiting.

ELLIDA [*running to him, she clings tightly to his arm and cries*]: Oh, Wangel, save me – save me if you can!

WANGEL: Ellida – what in heaven's name . . .?

ELLIDA: Save me, Wangel! Don't you see him? *He's* standing there!

WANGEL [*looking at him*]: That man? [*Going towards him*] May I ask who you are, and what you're doing in this garden?

STRANGER [*indicating* ELLIDA *with a nod*]: I want to talk with her.

WANGEL: Oh, indeed? So it was you? [*To* ELLIDA] They told me up at the house that a stranger had been asking for you.

STRANGER: Yes, that was I.

WANGEL: And what do you want with my wife? [*Turning*] Do you know him, Ellida?

ELLIDA [*in a low voice, wringing her hands*]: Know him? Oh yes, yes.

WANGEL [*quickly*]: Well?

ELLIDA: Oh, Wangel, this is the man – this is the very man I told you of.

WANGEL: What? You mean to say . . . ? [*Turning*] Are you the Johnston who once . . . ?

STRANGER: Well, you can call me Johnston. I don't mind, but it's not what I call myself.

WANGEL: Not?

STRANGER: Not any more, no.

WANGEL: And what can you want with my wife? You must surely know that the lighthouse-keeper's daughter was married long ago, and you must know whom she married.

STRANGER: I've known that for over three years.

ELLIDA [*excited*]: How did you find out?

STRANGER: I was on my way home to you when I came across an old newspaper – it was from these parts, and in it was the account of your marriage.

ELLIDA [*looking straight in front of her*]: My marriage . . . So that was why . . .

STRANGER: I couldn't believe it. Because when we linked our rings, Ellida, that was a marriage too.

ELLIDA [*covering her face with her hands*]: Ah!

WANGEL: How dare you . . . ?

STRANGER: Had you forgotten?

ELLIDA [*crying out, conscious of his gaze*]: Don't stand and look at me so!

WANGEL [*placing himself between them*]: You'll deal with me, not with her. Well, to put it bluntly, since you know the circumstances, what business have you here? Why have you come to find my wife?

STRANGER: I promised Ellida that I should come to her as soon as I could.

WANGEL: Kindly stop calling her 'Ellida'.

STRANGER: And Ellida promised faithfully to wait till I came.

WANGEL: You keep using my wife's Christian name. We don't do that sort of thing here.

STRANGER: I know that. But since *I* have the first claim on her . . .

WANGEL: You? But –

ELLIDA [*cowering behind* WANGEL]: Oh, he'll never let me go!

WANGEL: You say that she belongs to you?

STRANGER: Has she told you about the two rings – Ellida's and mine?

WANGEL: She has, but what of it? She put an end to that long ago. You had her letters, so you know that perfectly well.

STRANGER: Ellida and I agreed that linking our rings should be as binding in every way as a marriage.

ELLIDA: But I won't have it, I tell you. I never want to hear from you again. Don't look at me like that! I won't have it, do you hear?

WANGEL: You must be mad if you think you can come here and base any claim on such a childish piece of tomfoolery.

STRANGER: That is true. I have no claim – not in your sense of the word.

WANGEL: What will you do then? You surely don't imagine that you can take her from me by force, against her will!

STRANGER: No, what would be the use of that? If Ellida wants to come with me, she must come of her own free will.

ELLIDA [*starting, and crying out*]: Of my own free will?[14]

WANGEL: Do you really imagine . . .?

ELLIDA [*to herself*]: My own free will . . .

WANGEL: You must be out of your mind! Go away – We have nothing more to say to you!

STRANGER [*looking at his watch*]: It will soon be time for me to go aboard again. [*Coming a step nearer*] Well, Ellida . . .? I've done what I had to do. [*Still nearer*] I've kept the promise that I gave you.

ELLIDA [*imploringly, as she shrinks away*]: Oh, don't touch me!

STRANGER: You have till tomorrow night to think it over.

WANGEL: There's nothing to think over, so clear out!

STRANGER [*still to* ELLIDA]: I'm going up the fjord with the steamer, but I shall be back tomorrow night, and I shall come and see you again. You must wait for me here in the garden – I'd rather settle this with you alone, you understand.

ELLIDA [*low-voiced and trembling*]: Oh, Wangel, do you hear . . .?

WANGEL: Now, keep calm – we shall find a way to stop him.

STRANGER: Good-bye, Ellida, for the present. Tomorrow night, then.

ELLIDA [*entreating*]: Oh no . . . no! Don't come tomorrow night! Never come here again!

STRANGER: And if by then you feel you want to come away with me over the sea . . .

ELLIDA: Oh, don't look at me like that!

STRANGER: I only want to say that, if you do, you must be ready to start.

WANGEL: Go up to the house, Ellida.

ELLIDA: I can't. Oh, help me – save me, Wangel!

STRANGER: Because remember this – if you don't come with me tomorrow, it will all be over.

ELLIDA [*trembling as she looks at him*]: All over? For ever?

STRANGER [*with a nod*]: Nothing can change it then, Ellida. I shall never come back to this country. You will never see me again, and never hear from me. It will be as if I were dead, and lost to you for ever.

ELLIDA [*catching her breath*]: Oh . . .!

STRANGER: So think carefully before you decide. Good-bye. [*He climbs back over the fence, and then stops to say:*] Yes, Ellida, be ready to leave tomorrow night, because that is when I shall come to fetch you. [*He goes calmly and leisurely along the path and out to the right.*]

ELLIDA [*looking after him for a while*]: Of my own free will, he said. Do you realize? He said that I should go with him of my own free will.

WANGEL: Gently, gently, now. He's gone, and you'll never see him again.

ELLIDA: Oh, how can you say that? He's coming back tomorrow night.

WANGEL: Let him come. Whatever happens, you'll not need to see him.

ELLIDA [*shaking her head*]: Oh, Wangel, don't imagine that you can stop him.

WANGEL: Well, my dear, just leave it all to me.

ELLIDA [*thoughtfully, not listening to him*]: When he's been here – tomorrow night . . .? And when he has sailed away with his ship across the sea . . .?

WANGEL: Well?

ELLIDA: Will he really never – never come back?

WANGEL: No, Ellida; you can be quite sure of that. After this, what could he do here – now that he's learned from your own lips that you'll have nothing more to do with him? The whole thing is finished.

ELLIDA [*to herself*]: Tomorrow, then . . . or never.

WANGEL: And if he should ever decide to come here again –

ELLIDA [*eagerly*]: Then what?

WANGEL: Then we should be able to deal with him.

ELLIDA: Oh, you can't be sure of that.

WANGEL: We shall be able, I tell you. If there's no other way to set you free from him, then he must answer for the murder of the Captain.

ELLIDA [*vehemently*]: No, no, you can't do that! We know nothing about the murder of the Captain – nothing at all.

WANGEL: Nothing? Why he actually confessed to you.

ELLIDA: No, we know nothing about it. If you say anything, I shall deny it. He's not to be shut in – he belongs out there on the open sea. He belongs out there!

WANGEL [*slowly, looking at her*]: Oh, Ellida – Ellida!

ELLIDA [*clinging to him passionately*]: Oh, my dear, faithful love – save me from that man.

WANGEL [*gently, disengaging himself*]: Come along – come with me.

[LYNGSTRAND *and* HILDE, *both with fishing-tackle, come round the pond from the right.*]

LYNGSTRAND [*hurrying over to* ELLIDA]: Oh, Mrs Wangel, we've got something extraordinary to tell you!

ELLIDA: What is it?

LYNGSTRAND: Just fancy – we've seen the American!

WANGEL: The American?

HILDE: Yes, I saw him, too.

LYNGSTRAND: He went round behind the garden, and now he's boarded the big English ship.

WANGEL: But how did you recognize him?

LYNGSTRAND: I sailed with him once. I was quite sure he'd been drowned, and now here he is as large as life!

WANGEL: Do you know anything more about him?

LYNGSTRAND: No, but I'm sure he's come back to be revenged on his faithless wife.

WANGEL: What do you mean?

HILDE: Lyngstrand wants to use him for a statue.

WANGEL: What on earth are you talking about?

ELLIDA: I'll explain it all later.

[ARNHOLM *and* BOLETTA *come from the left along the path outside the garden fence.*]

BOLETTA [*calling into the garden*]: Come and look – the English ship's just sailing up the fjord.

[*A great ship glides slowly by in the distance.*]

LYNGSTRAND [*to* HILDE, *by the gate*]: He'll surely find her tonight.

HILDE [*nodding*]: The faithless wife, yes.

LYNGSTRAND: Fancy – just at midnight!

HILDE: Oh, I do think it's exciting!

ELLIDA [*watching the ship*]: Tomorrow . . .

WANGEL: But then never again.

ELLIDA [*softly, trembling*]: Oh, Wangel – save me from myself!

WANGEL [*watching her anxiously*]: Ellida ... I think – you're keeping something from me.

ELLIDA: Yes ... the fascination ...

WANGEL: Fascination?

ELLIDA: That man is like the sea.

[*She goes, slowly and thoughtfully, across the garden and out to the left;* WANGEL, *watching her intently, walks uneasily by her side.*]

ACT FOUR

Dr Wangel's garden-room. There are doors to the left and right, with, at the back between two windows, an open french window leading to the veranda, with part of the garden visible below. To the left is a sofa with a table in front of it; to the right, a piano, and beyond it a large stand for plants. In the middle of the floor is a round table surrounded by chairs, and on it a rose bush in flower, with other pots of plants about the room.
It is morning.

> [BOLETTA *is in the room, sitting on the sofa by the table to the left. She is working at her embroidery.*
> LYNGSTRAND *is sitting on a chair at the upper end of the table.* BALLESTED *sits in the garden painting, while* HILDE *stands and watches beside him.*]

LYNGSTRAND [*after sitting silently for a while with his elbows on the table, watching* BOLETTA *at work*]: It must be very difficult to sew a border like that, Miss Wangel.

BOLETTA: Oh, not really – as long as you don't lose count.

LYNGSTRAND: Count? Oh, do you have to count?

BOLETTA: Yes, the stitches. Like this.

LYNGSTRAND: So you do – just fancy! Really it's almost a kind of art. Do you do your own design?

BOLETTA: Yes, if I have something to copy.

LYNGSTRAND: Not without a copy?

BOLETTA: No.

LYNGSTRAND: So it's not really an art after all.

BOLETTA: No it's more a sort of – handicraft.

LYNGSTRAND: Still, I should think you could learn art.

BOLETTA: Even if I haven't any talent?

LYNGSTRAND: Even then – if you could always be with a *real* artist.

BOLETTA: Do you think I'd be able to learn from him?

LYNGSTRAND: Not exactly 'learn', in the ordinary way. I think it would come gradually – a kind of miracle, almost, Miss Wangel.

BOLETTA: That would be wonderful.

LYNGSTRAND [*after a moment*]: Have you ever thought – I mean, have you ever thought really seriously about marriage, Miss Wangel?

BOLETTA [*giving him a glance*]: About . . .? No.

LYNGSTRAND: *I* have.

BOLETTA: Really?

LYNGSTRAND: Yes, I often think about things like that – and marriage in particular. And I've read a great many books on the subject. I think marriage might almost be regarded as a sort of miracle. . . . The way the woman is gradually transformed till she comes to resemble her husband.

BOLETTA: You mean she comes to share his interests?

LYNGSTRAND: Yes, that's right.

BOLETTA: Ah, but his abilities – his skill and his talents?

LYNGSTRAND: Ah yes . . . perhaps even them, too.

BOLETTA: Do you believe, then, that everything that a man has read – or thought out for himself – can be passed on to his wife like that?

LYNGSTRAND: Yes, I think so. Very gradually. Just like a miracle. But I'm sure it could only happen with a true marriage – one that's affectionate and really happy.

BOLETTA: Hasn't it ever occurred to you that a man might be influenced by his wife in the same way? Grow like her, I mean.

LYNGSTRAND: A man? Oh no – I've never thought *that*.

BOLETTA: But why not a man just as much as a woman?

LYNGSTRAND: Oh no – because a man has his work to live

for – that's what gives a man such stability, Miss Wangel. A *man* has his vocation.

BOLETTA: Every man?

LYNGSTRAND: Well, no. I was thinking mostly of artists.

BOLETTA: Do you think it's right for an artist to marry?

LYNGSTRAND: Oh, I think so – if he can find someone whom he really loves, then –

BOLETTA: Still, I think he ought to live just for his art.

LYNGSTRAND: Oh, of course he should. But he can do that perfectly well, and still get married.

BOLETTA: But what about her?

LYNGSTRAND: Her? Who?

BOLETTA: The woman he marries. What should *she* live for?

LYNGSTRAND: She should live for his art, too. I should think *that* ought to make a woman really happy.

BOLETTA: Mm – I'm not so sure . . .

LYNGSTRAND: Oh yes, Miss Wangel, believe me. There's not only the honour and glory that she gets from being his wife – in fact, I should say that's the least of it. . . . It's that she can help him to create; she can make his work easier – by being with him and looking after him, and making his life really comfortable. I think that would give a woman enormous pleasure.

BOLETTA: Oh, you don't realize how selfish you are!

LYNGSTRAND: I – selfish? Great heavens! Oh, if only you knew me a little better. . . . [*Bending closer to her*] Miss Wangel – when I'm gone – in a very little while now –

BOLETTA [*with a look of sympathy*]: Now you mustn't start getting morbid.

LYNGSTRAND: I really don't see what's so morbid about it.

BOLETTA: What do you mean, then?

LYNGSTRAND: I shall be going away in a month's time. First I shall go home, and after that, I shall go to the south.

BOLETTA: Oh yes – of course.

LYNGSTRAND: Will you think of me sometimes, Miss Wangel?

BOLETTA: Of course I will.

LYNGSTRAND [*happily*]: Promise?

BOLETTA: Yes, I promise.

LYNGSTRAND: Word of honour, Miss Wangel?

BOLETTA: My word of honour. [*With a change of mood*] Oh, but what's the use of all this? It won't do any good.

LYNGSTRAND: How can you say that? It would be so wonderful for me to know that you were at home here thinking of me.

BOLETTA: Is that all?

LYNGSTRAND: Well, I haven't really gone into it any deeper –

BOLETTA: Nor have I. There's so much against it – in fact, I think there's everything against it.

LYNGSTRAND: Oh, there might easily be some miracle or other – a lucky stroke of fortune, or something. Because I'm convinced that I'm lucky.

BOLETTA [*eagerly*]: Yes . . . you *do* believe that?

LYNGSTRAND: Oh, I believe it with all my heart. And then in a year or two, when I come back as a famous sculptor, with plenty of money and really cured –

BOLETTA: Yes, of course. We hope you will.

LYNGSTRAND: You can be sure of it. Especially if you keep your word and think kindly of me while I'm away in the south. And you've promised you will.

BOLETTA: Yes, I know. [*Shaking her head*] But it won't do any good, all the same.

LYNGSTRAND: Oh yes, Miss Boletta. At the very least it will mean that I shall get on much more easily and quickly with my work.

BOLETTA: Do you think so?

LYNGSTRAND: Yes, I'm certain I shall. And I feel it'll be very inspiring for you too – here in this out-of-the-

way place – to know that in a way you're helping me to
create.

BOLETTA [*looking at him*]: But you? What about you?

LYNGSTRAND: I . . .?

BOLETTA [*looking into the garden*]: Sh! – let's talk about something else. Here comes the headmaster.

[ARNHOLM *appears in the garden to the left; he stops to talk to* BALLESTED *and* HILDE.]

LYNGSTRAND: Are you fond of your old tutor, Miss Boletta?

BOLETTA: Fond of him?

LYNGSTRAND: Yes, I mean do you like him very much?

BOLETTA: Oh yes, I do. He's the sort of friend that I can always go to for advice and he's always ready to help if he can.

LYNGSTRAND: Isn't it odd that he's never married?

BOLETTA: Does it strike you as odd?

LYNGSTRAND: Yes, because they say he's quite well off.

BOLETTA: Yes, I expect he is. But I don't think it can have been very easy for him to find anyone who'd have him.

LYNGSTRAND: Why not?

BOLETTA: Well, he says himself that nearly all the girls he knows have been his pupils.

LYNGSTRAND: What difference does that make?

BOLETTA: Well, good heavens, you don't marry a man who's been your tutor!

LYNGSTRAND: Don't you think a young girl could love her tutor?

BOLETTA: Not once she's really grown up.

LYNGSTRAND: Well, fancy that!

BOLETTA [*warning him*]: Sh! – careful.

[BALLESTED, *having collected his gear, carries it out through the garden to the right, helped by* HILDE. ARNHOLM *comes up across the veranda and into the room.*]

ARNHOLM: Good morning, Boletta my dear. Good morning, Mr – er . . .

[*With a glance of irritation, he nods coldly to* LYNGSTRAND, *who rises and bows.*]

BOLETTA [*rising and going over to* ARNHOLM]: Good morning, Mr Arnholm.

ARNHOLM: How is everybody here today?

BOLETTA: Very well, thank you.

ARNHOLM: Has your stepmother gone down to bathe?

BOLETTA: No, she's up in her room.

ARNHOLM: Isn't she well?

BOLETTA: I don't know. She's locked her door.

ARNHOLM: Oh? Really?

LYNGSTRAND: Mrs Wangel seemed very upset about that American yesterday.

ARNHOLM: What do you know about that?

LYNGSTRAND: I told Mrs Wangel that I'd actually seen him in the flesh outside the garden.

ARNHOLM: Ah – just so.

BOLETTA [*to* ARNHOLM]: You and Father sat up very late last night.

ARNHOLM: Yes, we did rather; we had something serious to discuss.

BOLETTA: Did you manage to talk to him about me at all?

ARNHOLM: No, Boletta my dear, I didn't – he had something else on his mind.

BOLETTA [*sighing*]: Yes – he always has.

ARNHOLM [*with a meaning look*]: But later on today we'll have another talk about it. Where's your father now – has he gone out?

BOLETTA: Yes, he'll be down at the surgery; I'll go and fetch him.

ARNHOLM: No, don't do that. I'd rather go to him.

BOLETTA [*listening towards the left*]: Wait a minute, Mr Arnholm; I think that's Father on the stairs. He must have been upstairs looking after her.

[DR WANGEL *comes in through the door on the left.*]

WANGEL [*holding out his hand to* ARNHOLM]: Ah, my dear Arnholm – you here already? It's good of you to come so early – there are still several things I'd like to talk over with you.

BOLETTA [*to* LYNGSTRAND]: Shall we go and join Hilde in the garden?

LYNGSTRAND: Yes, I should like that, Miss Wangel.
[*He and* BOLETTA *go down into the garden, and out through the trees.*]

ARNHOLM [*watching them go, then turning to* WANGEL]: Do you know much about that young man?

WANGEL: No, nothing at all.

ARNHOLM Don't you think he's seeing rather a lot of the girls?

WANGEL: Is he? I hadn't really noticed.

ARNHOLM: I think you should keep an eye on that sort of thing.

WANGEL: Yes, I'm sure you're right – but, good heavens, what's a poor chap to do? The girls are so used to looking after themselves, they won't listen to a word – either from me or from Ellida.

ARNHOLM: Not from her either?

WANGEL: No – and anyhow, I really can't expect her to attend to things like that – she's not up to it . . . [*Breaking off.*] But that isn't what we were going to talk about. Tell me, have you thought any more about what I told you?

ARNHOLM: Since I left you last night, I've thought about nothing else.

WANGEL: And what do you think should be done?

ARNHOLM: My dear friend, it seems to me that you, as a doctor, should know better than me.

WANGEL: Ah, but you don't know how difficult it is for a doctor to come to a right decision about a patient whom he really loves. Besides, this is no ordinary illness . . . It's not a case for an ordinary doctor – or any ordinary medicine.

ARNHOLM: How is she today?

WANGEL: I've just been up to see her, and she seemed quite calm. But underneath all her moods, there's something that I simply can't fathom – something hidden, that makes her so changeable all of a sudden, so unstable, so capricious.

ARNHOLM: That's only natural in her morbid state of mind.

WANGEL: It's not just that. Fundamentally, it's something that was born in her. The trouble is that Ellida comes of seafaring stock.

ARNHOLM: My dear Doctor, what exactly do you mean by that?

WANGEL: Haven't you ever noticed that the people who live by the open sea are like a race apart? It's almost as if the sea were a part of their lives; there are surges – yes, and ebbs and flows too – in all their thoughts and feelings. They can never bear to be separated from it – oh, I should have thought about that before. It was really a crime against Ellida to take her from out there and bring her here.

ARNHOLM: Do you really believe that?

WANGEL: I'm coming to believe it more and more; but I should have known it from the first. Really I *did* know it, even then, but I wouldn't admit it to myself. I loved her so much, you see, so I thought only of myself – it was unpardonably selfish of me.

ARNHOLM: Hm! – all men are a bit selfish in those circumstances; all the same, I've never noticed that vice in you, Doctor.

WANGEL [*restlessly pacing the room*]: It's true – and, what's more, I've gone on in the same way ever since. I'm so very much older than she is – I should have been like a father to her. I should have guided her; I should have done all I could to cultivate and improve her mind. But I'm afraid I've done absolutely nothing. I didn't take the trouble, you see, because I preferred her just as she was. So things became worse and worse for her, and I simply didn't know what to do. [*Dropping his voice*] That was why, in desperation, I wrote and asked you to come here.

ARNHOLM [*looking at him in surprise*]: What? Was *that* why you wrote?

WANGEL: Yes – but don't let anyone know.

ARNHOLM: But what in the world ...? My dear Doctor, I don't see what good you thought I could be.

WANGEL: No, of course you're right – I was on the wrong tack. I thought that Ellida had once been in love with you, and that she was still secretly rather fond of you. I thought perhaps it might do her good to see you again and talk over the old days when she was at home.

ARNHOLM: Then it was your wife that you meant, when you wrote that there was someone here waiting – and perhaps longing to see me?

WANGEL: Yes, who else?

ARNHOLM [*quickly*]: No, no, you're right – it was just that I misunderstood.

WANGEL: Naturally you would. As I said, I was completely on the wrong tack.

ARNHOLM: And you call yourself selfish!

WANGEL: Oh, I had so much to atone for, that I felt I daren't neglect any action that might relieve her mind a little.

ARNHOLM: What do you think is the real explanation of this power that that stranger has over her?

WANGEL: Ah, my dear friend, there may be aspects of that question that aren't capable of explanation.

ARNHOLM: Something that's inexplicable in itself, you mean? Completely inexplicable?

WANGEL: In our present state of knowledge, at any rate.

ARNHOLM: Do you believe in that sort of thing?

WANGEL: I don't believe or disbelieve; I simply don't know. That's why I leave it alone.

ARNHOLM: Tell me one thing, though: that curiously uncanny assertion of hers that the child's eyes –

WANGEL [*vehemently*]: I don't believe a word of that – I refuse to believe anything of the sort. That must be sheer imagination on her part – nothing else.

ARNHOLM: When you saw the man yesterday, did you notice his eyes?

WANGEL: I did indeed.

ARNHOLM: And you didn't see any resemblance?

WANGEL [*evasively*]: Well ... good heavens, what can I say? The light wasn't good at the time ... and then Ellida had told me so much about the likeness beforehand – I don't think I could possibly have looked at him impartially.

ARNHOLM: Yes ... I see that. But then there was the other point: that all this fear and unrest descended on her just at the time when this stranger seems to have been on his way home.

WANGEL: Well, you see ... that's another thing that she may have imagined, or persuaded herself into, since the day before yesterday. It didn't strike her as suddenly – as spontaneously, as she maintains now. But when she heard from this young Lyngstrand that Johnston – or Friman, or whatever he calls himself now – was on his way home in March three years ago, she evidently convinced herself that her mental unrest started just at that time.

ARNHOLM: But didn't it?

WANGEL: Not at all. Signs of it were noticeable long before. It's true that she did – quite by chance – have rather a severe attack in March just three years ago –

ARNHOLM: Well, then –

WANGEL: But the circumstances – her condition at the time – would easily account for that.

ARNHOLM: You might take it either way.

WANGEL [*wringing his hands*]: But not to be able to help her! Not to know how to advise her. ... Not to know which way to turn ...

ARNHOLM: Suppose you were to decide to move – to go somewhere else, where she could live in surroundings where she might feel more at home?

WANGEL: My dear man, do you think I haven't suggested that? I proposed that we should move out to Skjoldvik, but she wouldn't.

ARNHOLM: Not even that?

WANGEL: No. She doesn't believe it would help – and she may be right.

ARNHOLM: Hm . . . do you think so?

WANGEL: Yes, and there's another thing – now that I come to think it over, I don't really see how I could manage it. I feel it would be most unfair to the girls to move to such an out-of-the-way place. After all they must live in a place where there's at least *some* chance of their getting married one day.

ARNHOLM: Married? Are you thinking about that already?

WANGEL: Yes, good heavens, I must take that into account too. But then, on the other hand, when I think how my poor Ellida's suffering . . . Oh my dear Arnholm, in many ways I really seem to be in a cleft stick!

ARNHOLM: Perhaps there's no need for you to worry so much on Boletta's account . . . [*Breaking off.*] I wonder where she – where they've gone. [*He goes to the open door and looks out.*]

WANGEL [*over by the piano*]: Oh, I'd willingly make any sacrifice at all – for all three of them – if only I *knew* . . .

[ELLIDA *comes in from the door on the left.*]

ELLIDA [*quickly, to* WANGEL]: You won't go out this morning, will you?

WANGEL: No, no, of course I won't. I'm staying at home with you. [*Pointing to* ARNHOLM, *who approaches*] But you haven't said good morning to our friend.

ELLIDA [*turning*]: Oh, I didn't see you, Mr Arnholm. [*Giving him her hand*] Good morning.

ARNHOLM: Good morning, Mrs Wangel. So you haven't been for your usual bathe today?

ELLIDA: No, no – that's out of the question today. But won't you sit down for a moment?

ARNHOLM: Not just now, thank you very much. [*Catching* WANGEL's *eye*] I promised the girls I'd join them in the garden.

ELLIDA: Goodness knows if you'll be able to find them; I never know where they get to.

WANGEL: They're probably down by the pond.

ARNHOLM: Oh, I expect I shall run them to earth. [*He nods and goes across the veranda and out through the garden to the right.*]

ELLIDA: What's the time, Wangel?

WANGEL [*looking at his watch*]: Just after eleven.

ELLIDA: Just after eleven. And between eleven and half past to-night the steamer will be here. Oh, if only it were all over.

WANGEL [*going to her*]: Ellida dear, there's something I want to ask you.

ELLIDA: What is it?

WANGEL: The night before last – up at the Look-Out – you told me that, during the last three years, you'd often seen him, as clear as daylight, before your eyes.

ELLIDA: Yes, so I have. You can take my word for it.

WANGEL: Well – how did you see him?

ELLIDA: How did I see him?

WANGEL: I mean, what did he look like, when you thought you saw him?

ELLIDA: But, my dear Wangel, you've seen for yourself what he looks like.

WANGEL: And he looked just like that in your imagination?

ELLIDA: Yes, he did.

WANGEL: Exactly as you saw him in reality last night?

ELLIDA: Yes, exactly.

WANGEL: Then how was it that you didn't recognize him at once?

ELLIDA [*startled*]: Didn't I?

WANGEL: No; afterwards you said yourself that you had no idea at first who this strange man was.

ELLIDA [*impressed*]: I really believe you're right. Isn't that an extraordinary thing, Wangel – to think that I shouldn't know him at once?

WANGEL: It was only by his eyes, you said –

ELLIDA: Ah yes – his eyes . . . his eyes.

WANGEL: Well now, up at the Look-Out you told me that he always appeared to you just as he was when you parted out there ten years ago.

ELLIDA: Did I say that?

WANGEL: Yes.

ELLIDA: Well, I suppose he looked much the same then as he does now.

WANGEL: No. The night before last, on the way home, you described him quite differently. You said that ten years ago he was clean-shaven. He was dressed quite differently, too. And there was a tie-pin with a pearl in it. The man yesterday hadn't anything of the sort.

ELLIDA: No – he hadn't . . .

WANGEL [*watching her intently*]: Now, Ellida my dear, try to think. Or – perhaps you can't remember now exactly how he looked when you stood on Bratthammer together.

ELLIDA [*thoughtfully, closing her eyes for a while*]: Not very clearly. No – isn't that odd? – today I can't remember him at all.

WANGEL: Not really so odd. Now that you've seen a new – and real – figure, it has blotted out the old one so that you can't see it any more.

ELLIDA: Do you think so, Wangel?

WANGEL: Yes, and it's blotted out all your morbid imaginings too. That's why it's a good thing that you've seen the reality.

ELLIDA: Good? Do you call it good?

WANGEL: Yes. What has happened might act as a cure for you.

ELLIDA [*sitting on the sofa*]: Wangel, come here and sit by me – I must tell you what I think.

WANGEL: Yes, Ellida dear, tell me. [*He sits on a chair at the far side of the table.*]

ELLIDA: It was really a great misfortune – for both of us – that you and I should have come together.

WANGEL: What are you saying?

ELLIDA: Oh yes, it was – and it was bound to be. It couldn't have led to anything but unhappiness – not after the way we came together.

WANGEL: What was the matter with the way . . .?

ELLIDA: Listen, Wangel, it's no good our going on lying to ourselves – and to each other

WANGEL: But do we? You say we lie?

ELLIDA: Yes, we do. Or at any rate we won't admit the truth. Because the truth – quite purely and simply – is that you came out there and – and bought me.

WANGEL: Bought . . .! You say 'bought'?

ELLIDA: Oh, I was every bit as bad as you. I agreed to the deal – I sold myself to you.

WANGEL [*with a hurt look*]: Ellida – how can you have the heart to say that?

ELLIDA: But what else could I call it? You couldn't bear your empty house any longer, so you were looking for a new wife –

WANGEL: And a new mother for my children, Ellida.

ELLIDA: Yes, that too, perhaps – among other things. Though you had absolutely no idea whether I was fitted for that post – you'd only seen me, to speak to, once or twice. But you'd taken a fancy to me, so –

WANGEL: Well, call it that if you like.

ELLIDA: While I, for my part . . . there I was, helpless and bewildered and utterly alone. It was only natural that I should accept – when you came and offered to provide for me for the rest of my life.

WANGEL: My dear Ellida, I certainly didn't think of it as 'providing for you'. I asked you frankly if you would share what little I had with myself and the children.

ELLIDA: Yes, you did. But even so, I ought never to have accepted – not at any price should I have sold myself. The meanest work, the direst poverty would have been better – if it was of my own choice – my own free will.

WANGEL [rising]: Then the five – no, six – years that we've been together have meant nothing at all to you?

ELLIDA: Oh, you mustn't think that, Wangel. No one could wish for more than you have given me – but the trouble is that I didn't come to live with you of my own free will.

WANGEL [looking at her]: Not of – of your own free will?

ELLIDA: No, it was not of my own free will that I came away with you.

WANGEL [low]: Ah . . . I remember that phrase from yesterday.

ELLIDA: It's all contained in that phrase. It's thrown a new light on my life. Now I see it clearly.

WANGEL: What do you see?

ELLIDA: I see that our life together is not a true marriage.

WANGEL [bitterly]: You're right there! The life we lead now is not a true marriage.

ELLIDA: Nor was it before – never. Not from the very first. [Looking straight to her front] The other . . . that might have been a real marriage.

WANGEL: What do you mean – the other?

ELLIDA: Mine – with him.

WANGEL [looking at her in amazement]: I simply don't understand you.

ELLIDA: Oh, Wangel, my dear, don't let's lie to each other – or to ourselves either.

WANGEL: No, of course not. But where is this leading?

ELLIDA: You see – we can never get away from the fact that a promise freely given is just as binding as a marriage.

WANGEL: But what in the world . . .?

ELLIDA [*rising impetuously*]: Give me permission to leave you, Wangel.

WANGEL: Ellida! Ellida . . .

ELLIDA: Yes, yes – just let me have that. I tell you it couldn't end any other way – not after the way that you and I came together.

WANGEL [*hiding his pain*]: Is there such a gulf between us?

ELLIDA: There had to be – it couldn't have been otherwise.

WANGEL [*looking sadly at her*]: So all the time we've been together, I've never really won you – you've never been mine.

ELLIDA: Oh, Wangel – how gladly I would love you if only I could. But I'm quite sure that that could never happen.

WANGEL: A divorce, then? A formal, legal divorce – is that what you want?

ELLIDA: My dear, you don't understand me at all. It isn't the formalities that I mind about – that sort of thing doesn't seem to me to matter. What I want is that you and I should release each other of our own free wills.

WANGEL [*bitterly, nodding slowly*]: To break our agreement – I see.

ELLIDA [*eagerly*]: Exactly – to break our agreement.

WANGEL: But afterwards, Ellida? Have you thought what will happen – to both of us? What's to become of our lives – yours as well as mine?

ELLIDA: We mustn't consider that. The future must look after itself, as best it can. The most important thing, Wangel, is that you should do as I beg and implore you – simply set me free . . . give me back my complete freedom.

WANGEL: Ellida, this is a terrible thing that you're asking of me. At least give me time to think it over before I decide. Let us talk it over more thoroughly – and give yourself a chance to realize what you're doing.

ELLIDA: But we simply haven't the time for that. I must have my freedom this very day!

WANGEL: Why today especially?

ELLIDA: Because it's tonight that he's coming.

WANGEL [*with a start*]: Coming? He? What has the stranger to do with this?

ELLIDA: I want to be completely free when I meet him.

WANGEL: But – but what do you mean to do *then*?

ELLIDA: I don't want to have the excuse that I'm another man's wife – that I have no choice. Because there'd be no decision in that.

WANGEL: You talk of choice, Ellida? Choice? Choice in a thing like this?

ELLIDA: Yes; I must have choice. Whichever I do, I must *choose*. I must be able to let him go away alone . . . or – to go with him.

WANGEL: Do you realize what you're saying? Go with him? Put your whole life in his hands?

ELLIDA: But didn't I put my whole life in *your* hands? Un-hesitatingly?

WANGEL: Possibly . . . But he – he's a complete stranger – a man you know almost nothing about!

ELLIDA: Perhaps I knew even less about you – but I went with you all the same.

WANGEL: At least you had some idea of the sort of life that you were going to. But now . . . just think – what do you know now? Absolutely nothing! You don't even know who he is – or what he is.

ELLIDA [*looking straight ahead*]: That is true. *That* is the terrible thing.

WANGEL: Yes – it is . . . terrible.

ELLIDA: That is why I feel that I *must* do it.

WANGEL [*looking at her*]: Because it means something terrible to you?

ELLIDA: Yes – exactly.

WANGEL [*nearer*]: Tell me, Ellida – what do you really mean by the terrible thing?

ELLIDA [*thinking*]: The terrible thing ... It's something that frightens me and yet fascinates me.

WANGEL: Fascinates?

ELLIDA: Fascinates above all, I think.

WANGEL [*slowly*]: You *are* like the sea.

ELLIDA: That is terrible, too.

WANGEL: And there is something terrrible in *you*. You frighten and yet fascinate ...

ELLIDA: Do you feel that, Wangel?

WANGEL: In spite of everything, I've never really known you – never completely. I'm beginning to see that now.

ELLIDA: That is why you must set me free – free me from every tie with you and yours. I am not the woman that you took me for – you know that yourself now. Now we can part as friends – and of our own free will.

WANGEL [*sadly*]: It might be best for both of us – to part. But even so, I can't do it – for me, you are like the terrible thing, Ellida – you have the same overpowering fascination.

ELLIDA: Do I?

WANGEL: Let us try to get through this day wisely – to act calmly and sensibly. I *dare* not let you go today – I have no right to – for your own sake, Ellida. I claim a duty and a right to protect you.

ELLIDA: Protect? What is there to protect me from? There's no force from outside that's threatening me. The terrible thing lies deeper, Wangel ... it is the terrible fascination within my own mind – and what can you do against that?

WANGEL: I can support you and give you courage to fight against it.

ELLIDA: Yes ... if I *want* to fight against it.

WANGEL: But don't you?

ELLIDA: Ah, that's something that I don't even know my-self.

WANGEL: It will all be settled tonight, Ellida dear –

ELLIDA [breaking out]: Yes, think of it! The turning-point o my whole life – so near!

WANGEL: – and then tomorrow –

ELLIDA: Yes, tomorrow ... Perhaps I shall have denied my true destiny!

WANGEL: Your true...?

ELLIDA: A whole lifetime of freedom wasted. For me – and perhaps for him, too.

WANGEL [quietly, gripping her by the wrists]: Ellida, do you love this stranger?

ELLIDA: Love him? Oh, how can I say? I only know that, to me, he is the terrible thing, and that –

WANGEL: Well?

ELLIDA [breaking free]: – and that it's with him that I feel I belong.

WANGEL [bowing his head]: I'm beginning to understand a little.

ELLIDA: Then what help have you against this? What advice can you give me?

WANGEL [looking at her sadly]: Tomorrow – he will have gone. The danger will have lifted. Then I will consent to let you go – to break our agreement, Ellida.

ELLIDA: Oh, Wangel ... tomorrow will be too late.

WANGEL [looking towards the garden]: The children! At least let us spare the children – as long as we can.

[ARNHOLM, BOLETTA, HILDE, and LYNGSTRAND come from the garden. LYNGSTRAND takes his leave and goes off to the left; the others come into the room.]

ARNHOLM: Ah, we've been making plans, let me tell you!

HILDE: We're going out on the fjord tonight, and –

BOLETTA: No, don't give it away!

WANGEL: We've been making plans too.

ARNHOLM: Really?

WANGEL: Ellida's going out to Skjoldvik tomorrow – for a while.

BOLETTA: Going away?

ARNHOLM: Well, that's an excellent idea, Mrs Wangel.

WANGEL: She wants to go home – to the sea.

HILDE [*rushing to her*]: You're going away? Leaving us?

ELLIDA [*surprised*]: Why, Hilde, what's the matter?

HILDE [*collecting herself*]: Oh nothing. [*Under her breath, turning away*] Go if you want to!

BOLETTA [*worried*]: Father, you're going, too – to Skjoldvik. I can see you are.

WANGEL: No, certainly not. I might run over there now and then, while –

BOLETTA: But you'll come back here to us?

WANGEL: Oh yes.

BOLETTA: Now and then – yes!

WANGEL: I'm afraid it can't be helped, my dear. [*He goes across the room.*]

ARNHOLM [*whispering*]: We'll talk later, Boletta.
[*He goes over to* WANGEL, *and they talk quietly together by the door.*]

ELLIDA [*quietly to* BOLETTA]: What was the matter with Hilde? She seemed quite upset.

BOLETTA: Haven't you ever realized what it is that Hilde has been longing for all this time?

ELLIDA: Longing for?

BOLETTA: Ever since you came to this house.

ELLIDA: No . . . what?

BOLETTA: Just one word of affection from you.

ELLIDA: Ah . . .! If I had a duty *here* . . .
[*She clasps her hands to her head, staring fixedly in front of herself, as if preyed on by warring thoughts and feelings.* WANGEL *and* ARNHOLM *come forward, still whispering.* BOLETTA

goes and looks into the side-room to the right, then holds the door open.]

BOLETTA: Lunch is on the table, Father, if you're ready.

WANGEL [*with forced cheerfulness*]: Is it, my dear? That's splendid. After you, Arnholm. We'll go in and drink a parting toast to 'the Lady from the Sea'.

[*They go through the door to the right.*]

The far corner of Dr Wangel's garden, by the carp pond. The summer twilight is falling.

[ARNHOLM, BOLETTA, LYNGSTRAND, *and* HILDE, *in a boat, are pushing themselves along the bank from the left.*]

HILDE: Look, we can easily jump ashore here.

ARNHOLM: No, no, don't!

LYNGSTRAND: I can't jump, Miss Hilde.

HILDE: How about you, Mr Arnholm – can't you jump either?

ARNHOLM: I'd rather not.

BOLETTA: Let's land at the steps of the bathing-hut.

[*They punt themselves off to the right.*

At the same time, BALLESTED *appears on the footpath to the right, carrying music and a french horn. He greets the boating-party, and turns to talk to them. Their answers come back from farther and farther away.*]

BALLESTED: What did you say ...? Yes of course, it's in honour of the English steamer – it's the last time she'll be here this year. ... Well, don't be too long, if you want to hear the music. [*Calling*] What ...? [*Raising his voice*] I can't hear what you're saying!

[ELLIDA, *with a shawl over her head, comes in from the left, followed by* DR WANGEL.]

WANGEL: But, Ellida dear, I assure you there's plenty of time.

ELLIDA: No, no, there isn't. He might be here at any moment.

BALLESTED [*from outside the fence*]: Ah, good evening, Doctor; good evening, Mrs Wangel.

WANGEL [*seeing him*]: Ah, Ballested – Is there to be music tonight again?

BALLESTED: Yes – our brass band believes in making itself heard: there are all sorts of festive occasions at this time of year. Tonight it's in honour of the English ship.

ELLIDA: The English ship – has she been sighted already?

BALLESTED: Not yet – but she slips out from between the islands, and she's on us before you can say 'knife'!

ELLIDA: Yes – she is.

WANGEL [*half to* ELLIDA]: This is her last trip – she won't be back after tonight.

BALLESTED: Yes, it's sad, isn't it, Doctor? That's just why, as I say, we want to do something in her honour. Ah yes, the happy summer days are drawing to a close. 'Soon the ice will bar the way', as it says in the play.

ELLIDA: 'The ice will bar the way' – yes.

BALLESTED: A melancholy thought. These last few months we've all been as happy as sandboys in the summer sun. It's hard to reconcile one's self to the dark days. At first, at any rate – for one can always exclim – *ac*climatize one's self, Mrs Wangel. Yes, one certainly can. [*He bows, and goes out to the left.*]

ELLIDA [*looking out over the fjord*]: Oh, this dreadful waiting! These last unbearable minutes before I must decide!

WANGEL: Are you still determined to talk to him yourself?

ELLIDA: I *must* talk to him myself. I shall make my choice of my own free will.

WANGEL: You have *no* choice, Ellida. I won't allow it.

ELLIDA: No one can stop me from choosing – not you, nor anyone else. You can forbid me to go with him, or follow him, if that is what I choose. You can keep me here by force, against my will. Yes, you can do that. But you cannot stop me choosing – in my innermost heart . . . choosing him instead of you – if that has to be my choice.

WANGEL: No, you are right – I can't stop that.

ELLIDA: And I have nothing whatever to hinder me; here at home there's nothing in the world to hold me. Oh, Wangel, I have no roots whatever in your house. The children don't belong to me – not in their hearts, I mean – they never have done. When I go away – if I do go – whether it's with him tonight, or out to Skjoldvik tomorrow – I'll not have a single key to hand over, no orders to give about anything at all. I'm so utterly without roots in your house. Even from the very beginning I've been like a complete outsider here.

WANGEL: But *you* wanted it to be like that.

ELLIDA: I didn't. I had no leanings one way or the other. I simply let everything stay just as I found it the day I came. It was you who wanted it that way, and no one else.

WANGEL: I thought that would be the best for you.

ELLIDA: Yes, I know you did, Wangel; and now we have to pay for it – it's taking its revenge. Because now there's nothing here to hold me, nothing to help me, nothing to give me strength. I have no ties with what should have been our most precious possession.

WANGEL: I do realize that, Ellida. That's why, from tomorrow, you shall have your freedom again and be able to live your own life.

ELLIDA: You call it my own life! No, my own life – my *true* life – went astray when I joined it to yours. [*Wringing her hands in pain and agitation*] And now tonight – in half an hour – the man whom I failed will be here. The man to whom I ought to have been as completely faithful as he has been to me. And now he's coming to offer me my last and only chance to live my own true life – the life that frightens yet fascinates me – and that I *cannot* renounce, not of my own free will.

WANGEL: But that's just why you need your husband – and your doctor, too – to take the choice out of your hands, and to act for you.

ELLIDA: Yes, Wangel, I do see that. Oh, you mustn't think that there aren't times when I feel how safe and peaceful it would be if I could cling to you, and try to defy all those things that frighten and fascinate me . . . But I can't do that – no, no, I can't.

WANGEL: Look, Ellida, let's go for a little walk together.

ELLIDA: I wish I could, but I dare not – he said I was to wait for him here.

WANGEL: Do come – you have plenty of time still.

ELLIDA: Do you really think so?

WANGEL: Yes, plenty.

ELLIDA: Then just for a little.

[*They go out in front to the right, just as* ARNHOLM *and* BOLETTA *appear on the upper bank of the pond.*]

BOLETTA [*noticing them as they go*]: Look there!

ARNHOLM [*quietly*]: Sh! – let them go.

BOLETTA: Have you any idea what's been going on between them these last few days?

ARNHOLM: Have you noticed anything?

BOLETTA: I certainly have.

ARNHOLM: I mean – anything in particular?

BOLETTA: Yes . . . several things. Haven't you?

ARNHOLM: Well, I don't really know . . .

BOLETTA: Of course you have, only you won't admit it.

ARNHOLM: I think it'll be good for your stepmother to go on this little trip.

BOLETTA: Do you?

ARNHOLM: Yes, I feel it would be a good thing for everybody if she were to get away for a while now and then.

BOLETTA: If she goes home to Skjoldvik tomorrow, she'll certainly never come back to us.

ARNHOLM: My dear Boletta, how can you say such a thing?

BOLETTA: I'm quite certain I'm right, you wait and see. She won't come back – at any rate as long as Hilde and I are here.

ARNHOLM: Hilde too?

BOLETTA: Well, perhaps Hilde wouldn't matter so much – she's practically a child still. And in her heart of hearts, I believe she adores Ellida. But you know, it's different with me – a stepmother who's not much older than I am –

ARNHOLM: My dear Boletta, it might not be so very long before you leave home yourself.

BOLETTA [*eagerly*]: Do you think so? Have you spoken to Father about it?

ARNHOLM: Yes, I have.

BOLETTA: Well – what did he say?

ARNHOLM: Well, just at the moment your father has rather a lot on his mind.

BOLETTA: There! What did I tell you?

ARNHOLM: But I did find out this much – you mustn't expect any help from him.

BOLETTA: No . . .?

ARNHOLM: He told me quite clearly how he stood, and he felt that anything of that kind was quite impossible for him.

BOLETTA [*reproachfully*]: And you have the heart to stand there and make fun of me!

ARNHOLM: I certainly haven't made fun of you, my dear Boletta. It's entirely up to you whether you come away from here or not.

BOLETTA: What do you think is up to me?

ARNHOLM: Whether you come out into the world – learn all the things that you really want to, and take part in all the things that you've been longing for while you've been at home here . . . to live your life in happier circumstances. What do you say, Boletta?

BOLETTA [*clasping her hands*]: Oh, but good heavens, that simply wouldn't be possible. If Father can't – or won't – help, I've no one else in the world to turn to.

ARNHOLM: Couldn't you bring yourself to accept a helping hand from your old – your former tutor?

BOLETTA: From you, Mr Arnholm? Would you really . . .?

ARNHOLM: Stand by you? Yes, very gladly – both in word and deed, you can depend on that. Will you accept? Well? Do you consent?

BOLETTA: Do I consent? To get away and see the world, to learn something really worth while – all the wonderful things that I've always looked on as quite impossible. . . .

ARNHOLM: Yes, now you can really do all those things – if you only want to.

BOLETTA: And you'll help me to attain such unbelievable happiness? Oh no – how *can* I accept so much from a stranger.

ARNHOLM: You can accept it from *me*, Boletta – you can accept anything from me.

BOLETTA [*seizing his hands*]: Yes, I really think I can. I don't know how it is, but – [*Impulsively*] Oh, I could laugh and cry from sheer happiness! Oh, I'm really going to live after all – I'd begun to be afraid that life would pass me by.

ARNHOLM: You needn't be afraid of that, Boletta dear. But now you must tell me quite frankly if you have any ties here – any ties at all.

BOLETTA: Ties? No, I haven't.

ARNHOLM: Not the very slightest?

BOLETTA: No, none at all . . . although, of course, Father's a tie in a way – and so is Hilde, but –

ARNHOLM: Well, you would have to leave your father sooner or later; and one day Hilde, too, will be wanting to live her own life – it's only a question of time. But apart from that, there's nothing to keep you here? No commitment of any sort?

BOLETTA: No, none whatever – as far as that's concerned, I can go away whenever I like.

ARNHOLM: Then if that's so, Boletta dear, you shall come away with me.

BOLETTA [*clapping her hands*]: Oh, thank heaven! It's wonderful to think of!

ARNHOLM: I hope you have complete faith in me?

BOLETTA: Oh, I have.

ARNHOLM: And you can really put yourself and your whole future into my hands, Boletta? You do feel that, don't you?

BOLETTA: But of course – why shouldn't I? How can you doubt it? My old tutor – my tutor from the old days, I mean.

ARNHOLM: Not only because of that. I wasn't really concerned with that any longer. But – well – since you are free, Boletta, and have no ties to hold you ... I'm asking if you would be willing ... willing to be joined to me – for life.

BOLETTA [*shrinking back in fear*]: Oh – what are you saying?

ARNHOLM: For life, Boletta. Will you be my wife?

BOLETTA [*almost to herself*]: No, no – I couldn't! It's quite impossible.

ARNHOLM: Would it really be so completely impossible for you to –

BOLETTA: But you can't really mean what you've been saying, Mr Arnholm. [*Looking at him*] Or – were you thinking of that all the time? When you offered to do so much for me?

ARNHOLM: Boletta, listen for a moment – I seem to have taken you by surprise.

BOLETTA: But it *must* surprise me – a thing like that – coming from you.

ARNHOLM: Perhaps you're right. You didn't know – you couldn't have known – that it was for your sake that I've travelled up here.

BOLETTA: You came here – for my sake?

ARNHOLM: Yes, Boletta, I did. Last spring I had a letter from your father, and in it there was something that led me to believe – er – that your memories of your former tutor ... were a little more than just friendly.

BOLETTA: How could Father write a thing like that?

ARNHOLM: That wasn't what he meant at all. But in the meantime, I'd become used to the idea that here was a young girl longing for me to come back – no, Boletta dear, let me finish – and, you see, when a man like me is – no longer in his first youth, a thought like that – or an illusion, if you prefer it – makes a tremendous impression on him. I began to feel a real – a grateful affection for you. It seemed to me that I must go and see you again, and tell you that I felt for you – all that I imagined that you felt for me.

BOLETTA: But now, when you know that it isn't like that – that it was all a mistake . . .?

ARNHOLM: It makes no difference, Boletta. The picture of you that I have in my heart will always be coloured – and enhanced – by what I thought then. I don't expect you can understand, but that's the truth.

BOLETTA: I never thought that anything like this could happen.

ARNHOLM: But now that you know it can ... what do you say, Boletta? Could you make up your mind to – well, to be my wife?

BOLETTA: But, Mr Arnholm, it seems so utterly impossible. You were my tutor – I could never think of you as anything else.

ARNHOLM: Very well ... If you feel that you *can't* ... The situation is still the same, dear Boletta.

BOLETTA: How do you mean?

ARNHOLM: Naturally I still stand by what I told you. I shall make sure that you get away from here, and out into the world. You shall learn the things that you long to, you shall live your own life – in security, Boletta, and I shall see that your later years are secure too, Boletta. You'll always have a good, tried, faithful friend in me – you can rely on that.

BOLETTA: But, good heavens, Mr Arnholm, all that's quite impossible now.

ARNHOLM: Is *that* impossible, too?

BOLETTA: Yes, surely you can see that it is. After all that you have said to me – and after my answer . . . Oh, you must see yourself that I couldn't possibly take so much from you – that I couldn't accept anything at all from you – not after this.

ARNHOLM: Then would you rather stay here at home, and let life pass you by?

BOLETTA: Oh, I can't bear to think of it.

ARNHOLM: Will you give up all hope of seeing anything of the world outside – throw away the chance to do all those things that you say yourself you've longed for? Can you know that life could hold so infinitely much for you, and yet renounce it like this? Think Boletta, think!

BOLETTA: Oh . . . you are so right, Mr Arnholm.

ARNHOLM: And then, when your father isn't here any more, you might find yourself alone in the world and helpless. You might even have to marry another man, whom – possibly – you wouldn't be able to care for either.

BOLETTA: Yes . . . I do see. Everything you say is perfectly true. But still . . . And yet –

ARNHOLM [*quickly*]: Well?

BOLETTA [*undecided, looking at him*]: Perhaps after all it's not completely impossible . . .

ARNHOLM: What, Boletta?

BOLETTA: That I might perhaps – agree – to what you propose.

ARNHOLM: Do you mean that perhaps you might . . .? That at least you'll give me the pleasure of helping you as a friend?

BOLETTA: No, no, I could never do that – *that* would be quite

320

impossible now. No, Mr Arnholm, I would rather come to you –

ARNHOLM: Boletta? You will, after all?

BOLETTA: Yes – I think I will.

ARNHOLM: You'll be my wife?

BOLETTA: Yes – if you still feel that – you want me.

ARNHOLM: If I feel . . .! [*Taking her hand*] Oh, Boletta, thank you – thank you! What you've told me – all your hesitation – it doesn't frighten me. Even if you don't love me now, I shall be able to win you. Oh, Boletta, I'll be so good to you!

BOLETTA: And I'm to see the world – and live in it? You promised me.

ARNHOLM: And I'll keep my word.

BOLETTA: And you'll let me learn all the things I long to?

ARNHOLM: I'll be your teacher myself – just as I used to be, Boletta. Remember our last year together . . .

BOLETTA [*quietly, wrapped up in herself*]: Just think . . . to know that I'm free – able to go out into the world. And not to have to worry about the future! No more wretched anxiety about money . . .

ARNHOLM: No, you'll never need to give a thought to anything like that. And that's quite a good thing too, isn't it, Boletta dear?

BOLETTA: Yes, it is – it certainly is!

ARNHOLM [*putting an arm round her*]: Oh, you'll just see how happily and cosily we'll settle down together, and how secure and contented we'll come to feel with each other, Boletta!

BOLETTA: Yes, I begin to think – I really believe that we might. [*She looks out to the right, and quickly disengages herself.*] Oh, don't say anything about this.

ARNHOLM: What's the matter, dear?

BOLETTA: Oh, that poor man – [*Pointing*] Look over there.

ARNHOLM: Is it your father –?

BOLETTA: No, it's that young sculptor. Walking down there with Hilde.

ARNHOLM: Oh. Lyngstrand. Why? What's the matter with him?

BOLETTA: Well, you know how delicate he is.

ARNHOLM: Yes – if it isn't just imagination.

BOLETTA: No, it's real enough – he hasn't very long to live. Though perhaps that's the best thing for him.

ARNHOLM: The best thing, my dear – why?

BOLETTA: Well, because – because his talent would certainly never amount to much anyhow. Let's go before they get here.

ARNHOLM: Yes, my dear Boletta, I'd like to.

[HILDE *and* LYNGSTRAND *come from beside the pond.*]

HILDE: Hi there! Are you too grand to wait for us?

ARNHOLM: Boletta and I rather want to go on ahead.

[*He and* BOLETTA *go out to the left.*]

LYNGSTRAND [*with a little laugh*]: Isn't it funny how everyone here's going about in pairs these days – always two by two?

HILDE [*looking after them*]: I could almost swear that he's gone and fallen in love with her.

LYNGSTRAND: Oh? What makes you think so?

HILDE: Well, it's pretty obvious – if you keep your eyes open.

LYNGSTRAND: But Miss Boletta won't have him – I'm quite sure of that.

HILDE: No, she thinks he's got terribly old-looking. Besides, she thinks he's getting bald.

LYNGSTRAND: Oh, I don't mean only *that*. She wouldn't have him, anyhow.

HILDE: How do you know?

LYNGSTRAND: Well, there's someone else that she's promised to keep in mind.

HILDE: Only to keep in mind?

LYNGSTRAND: While he's away – yes.

HILDE: Oh, then, it must be *you* that she's going to keep in mind.

LYNGSTRAND: Perhaps.

HILDE: Did she promise?

LYNGSTRAND: Yes, just fancy! She promised me she would. But you mustn't ever let her see that you know about it.

HILDE: Oh, I can hold my tongue – I'm as silent as the grave!

LYNGSTRAND: I think it was very nice of her.

HILDE: And when you come back here again, are you going to get engaged? Are you going to marry her?

LYNGSTRAND: No, that wouldn't be at all a good idea. You see, I daren't think of anything of the sort for a year or two, and then by the time I'm well enough off, I expect she'll be too old for me.

HILDE: Yet you still want her to go on thinking of you?

LYNGSTRAND: Yes, it'd be such a help to me – as an artist, I mean. And it's so easy for her, seeing that she has no real vocation of her own. Still, it's nice of her, all the same.

HILDE: So you feel you'll get on better with your master-piece if you know that Boletta's thinking about you here?

LYNGSTRAND: Yes, I fancy I shall. You see, the secret know-ledge that somewhere in the world there's a lovely young woman quietly dreaming of one ... I think that must be so – so – Well, I don't quite know what to call it.

HILDE: I suppose you mean 'inspiring'.

LYNGSTRAND: Inspiring? Yes, that's it. Inspiring's just what I meant – or very nearly. [*Looking at her for a moment*] You're so clever, Miss Hilde – yes, you're really very clever. When I come back again, you'll be just about the age that your sister is now – you'll probably look very much the same as she looks now. Perhaps you'll have grown like her in mind, too. You could almost be yourself and her too – rolled into one, as the saying goes.

HILDE: Would you like that?

LYNGSTRAND: I don't quite know ... yes, I rather think I

would. But *now* – just for this summer – I'd rather you were like yourself – exactly as you are.

HILDE: You like me that way best?

LYNGSTRAND: Yes, I like that way very much.

HILDE: Hm! . . . Now tell me, as an artist, do you think I'm right to wear these light-coloured summer dresses all the time?

LYNGSTRAND: Yes, I think you're perfectly right.

HILDE: You think bright colours suit me, then?

LYNGSTRAND: Yes, to my way of thinking you look charming in them.

HILDE: But tell me – as an artist – how you think I'd look in black?

LYNGSTRAND: In black, Miss Hilde?

HILDE: Yes, all in black . . . do you think that'd suit me?

LYNGSTRAND: Well, black isn't exactly suitable for the summer . . . but apart from that, I think you'd look very nice in black too – especially with your figure.

HILDE [*looking into space*]: In black right up to my neck . . . with a black frill all round, black gloves, and a long black veil at the back.

LYNGSTRAND: If you were dressed like that, Miss Hilde, I'd want to be a painter, so that I could paint you as a lovely young widow all in mourning.

HILDE: Or a young girl mourning for her fiancé?

LYNGSTRAND: Yes, that would be better still. But you don't want to dress like that, do you?

HILDE: I'm not sure – but I think it'd be inspiring.

LYNGSTRAND: Inspiring?

HILDE: Yes, it's an inspiring thought. [*Suddenly pointing to the left*] Oh, look there!

LYNGSTRAND [*looking*]: The big English ship – right at the pier too!

[WANGEL *and* ELLIDA *come from beside the pond.*]

WANGEL: No, Ellida my dear, I'm sure you're wrong. [*Seeing the others*] Ah, you two – she hasn't been sighted yet, has she, Mr Lyngstrand?

LYNGSTRAND: The big English ship?

WANGEL: Yes.

LYNGSTRAND [*pointing*]: There she is already, Doctor!

ELLIDA: Ah – I knew it.

WANGEL: Already?

LYNGSTRAND: Like a thief in the night, as you might say – softly, without a sound . . .

WANGEL: Why don't you take Hilde down to the quay? You'd better hurry – I'm sure she'll want to hear the music.

LYNGSTRAND: Yes, Doctor, we were just going.

WANGEL: We may join you later – in a minute or two.

HILDE [*whispering to* LYNGSTRAND]: Another couple!
    [*She and* LYNGSTRAND *go out through the garden to the left. During the following, the distant music of a brass band can be heard from the fjord.*]

ELLIDA: He has come! Yes, yes, he is here, I can feel it.

WANGEL: You'd much better go indoors, Ellida. Let me see him alone.

ELLIDA: No, no, that's impossible, I tell you. [*With a cry*] Oh look, Wangel, here he is!
    [*The* STRANGER *comes in from the left and stops on the foot-path outside the fence.*]

STRANGER: Good evening. I've come back, Ellida.

ELLIDA: Yes . . . the time has come.

STRANGER: Are you ready to leave? Or not?

WANGEL: You can see for yourself that she's not.

STRANGER: I'm not talking about travelling-clothes or packed trunks, or anything of that sort. I have everything that she needs for the voyage on board, and I've taken a cabin for her. [*To* ELLIDA] So I ask you: are you ready to come with me – to come with me of your own free will?

ELLIDA [*imploringly*]: Oh, don't ask me! Don't tempt me so!
    [*A ship's bell is heard in the distance.*]

STRANGER: That's the first bell to embark. Now you must say yes or no.

ELLIDA [*wringing her hands*]: I can't decide – decide for my whole life. There'd be no turning back!

STRANGER: None. In half an hour it'll be too late.

ELLIDA [*looking at him shyly and searchingly*]: Why do you hold so fast to me?

STRANGER: We belong together – don't you feel that too?

ELLIDA: Because of our vow, you mean?

STRANGER: Vows hold no one – man or woman. If I cling to you so fast, it's because I cannot help myself.

ELLIDA [*softly, trembling*]: Why didn't you come before?

WANGEL: Ellida!

ELLIDA [*violently*]: Oh, this temptation that lures me into the unknown! It has all the power of the sea itself!

[*The* STRANGER *climbs over the fence.*]

ELLIDA [*shrinking behind* WANGEL]: What – what do you want?

STRANGER: I can see it, and I can hear it in your voice. You will choose me in the end, Ellida.

WANGEL [*advancing on him*]: There is no question of choice for my wife. I am here to choose for her and to protect her – yes, protect her.[15] Unless you go away – leave the country and never come back – do you realize what will happen to you?

ELLIDA: Oh, Wangel, no – no!

STRANGER: What will you do to me?

WANGEL: I shall have you arrested as a criminal – at once, before you go back on board. I know all about the murder out at Skjoldvik.

ELLIDA: Oh, Wangel, how can you?

STRANGER: I was expecting that, so [*bringing a revolver from his breast pocket*] I've provided myself with this.

ELLIDA [*throwing herself in front of* WANGEL]: No, no, don't shoot him! Shoot me instead!

STRANGER: Don't be afraid – I shan't shoot either of you. This is for myself. I mean to live and die a free man.

ELLIDA [*with rising agitation*]: Wangel, there's something that I must say – and I want him to hear. I know that you can keep me here – you have the power and the right, and no doubt you will use them. But there's my *mind* – all my thoughts and my longings and desires – you have no hold over *them*. They will reach out and yearn for the unknown that I was created for, and that you have kept me from!

WANGEL [*in quiet grief*]: I realize that, Ellida. Step by step you're slipping away from me. Your longing for the boundless and the infinite – for the unattainable – will, in the end, carry your soul out into the darkness.

ELLIDA: Yes, yes, I can feel it – like black soundless wings hovering over me.

WANGEL: It shall not come to that. There's no other possible salvation for you – at least, none that I can see. . . . So – so I cancel our bargain here and now. You are free to choose your own path. Completely free. . . .

ELLIDA [*gazing at him for a while as if speechless*]: Is that true? Is it true what you say? Do you really mean it – in your heart of hearts?

WANGEL: Yes, I mean it – from the bottom of my sorrowing heart.

ELLIDA: But *can* you do it? Could you let it happen?

WANGEL: Yes, I could – I could because I love you so much.

ELLIDA [*softly, trembling*]: Have I come to mean so very much to you?

WANGEL: Our years of marriage have accomplished that.

ELLIDA [*clasping her hands*]: And yet I never saw it!

WANGEL: Your thoughts were elsewhere. . . . But now – now you are completely free from me and mine. Now your own innermost life can take its true path again, because now your choice is free – and the responsibility is yours, Ellida.

ELLIDA [*staring at* WANGEL, *with her hands to her head*]:
Free – and with full responsibility! Oh, that changes
everything!

   [*The ship's bell rings again.*]

STRANGER: You hear that, Ellida? It's the last bell. Come
with me.

ELLIDA [*turning to him, she looks full in his face and says re-
solutely*]: I can never go with you now.

STRANGER: You will not?

ELLIDA [*clinging to* WANGEL]: Oh, Wangel, I can never leave
you after this.

WANGEL: Ellida – Ellida!

STRANGER: Is it all over, then?

ELLIDA: Yes, for ever.

STRANGER: I see that there's something here that is stronger
than my will.

ELLIDA: Your will hasn't the slightest power over me any
more. To me you are a dead man – who has come from the
sea, and will return to it. You hold no terror for me any
more – nor any fascination.

STRANGER: Good-bye. [*He vaults over the fence.*] From now
on, you are no more to me than – than a shipwreck that I
have come safely through.[16] [*He goes out to the left.*]

WANGEL [*looking at her for a moment*]: Ellida, your mind is like
the sea, it ebbs and flows. What made you change?

ELLIDA: Oh, don't you see? The change came – as it had to
come – when I could choose freely.

WANGEL: And the unknown? That has no fascination for
you now?

ELLIDA: No fascination and no terror. I could have faced it –
become a part of it – if I had only wished to. Now that I
could choose it, I could also reject it.

WANGEL: I'm slowly beginning to understand you. You
think and reason in pictures – in visual images. This longing of yours – this yearning for the sea, and the fascination

that *he* – this stranger – had for you, were really only the expression of a new and growing urge in you for freedom. . . . That's all.

ELLIDA: Oh, I don't know what to say to that. . . . But you have been a good doctor to me. You found – and you had the courage to use – the right remedy . . . the only one that could have helped me.

WANGEL: Well, in critical cases, doctors must have courage. But now, Ellida – you *will* come back to me?

ELLIDA: Oh, my dear, faithful husband. Now I will come back to you. *Now* I can, because I come to you freely – of my own free will – on my own responsibility.

WANGEL [*looking at her tenderly*]: Ellida – Ellida . . . Oh, to think that now we can live entirely for each other –

ELLIDA: – with all our aims in common – yours as well as mine.

WANGEL: Yes, that's true, my dear.

ELLIDA: – and for our two children, Wangel.

WANGEL: You call them *ours*?

ELLIDA: They're not mine yet, but I shall win them.

WANGEL: Ours! [*Quickly giving her hands a joyful kiss*] Oh, I can't tell you how grateful I am for that word!

[HILDE, BALLESTED, LYNGSTRAND, ARNHOLM, *and* BOLETTA *come into the garden from the left. At the same time, a number of young townsfolk and summer visitors pass along the footpath.*]

HILDE [*under her breath, to* LYNGSTRAND]: Well, look! She and Father look just like an engaged couple.

BALLESTED [*overhearing*]: It's summertime, little Missie!

ARNHOLM [*looking at* WANGEL *and* ELLIDA]: The English ship's just sailing.

BOLETTA [*going to the fence*]: Here's the best place to watch her.

LYNGSTRAND: The last trip of the season!

BALLESTED: 'Soon the ice will bar the way', as the poet says.

How sad, Mrs Wangel, and now we're going to lose *you* for a while, too; I hear you're off to Skjoldvik tomorrow.

WANGEL: No, she's not going now. We changed our minds this evening, she and I.

ARNHOLM [*looking from one to the other*]: Ah – really?

BOLETTA [*coming forward*]: Father – is this true?

HILDE [*going to* ELLIDA]: Are you going to stay with us after all?

ELLIDA: Yes, Hilde dear – if you'll have me.

HILDE [*struggling between tears and laughter*]: If I'll have you! Oh, of course!

ARNHOLM [*to* ELLIDA]: This is quite a surprise. . . .

ELLIDA [*smiling gravely*]: Well, you see, Mr Arnholm – you remember what we were saying yesterday: once you have become a land animal, there's no going back to the sea again – nor to the life of the sea.

BALLESTED: Why, that's just like my mermaid.

ELLIDA: Yes, it is rather.

BALLESTED: Except that the *mermaid* – dies. Human beings, on the other hand, can acclam – acclimatize themselves.

ELLIDA: Yes, they can if they're free, Mr Ballested.

WANGEL: And have full responsibility, Ellida dear.

ELLIDA [*quickly, giving him her hand*]: Yes, *that's* the secret.
   [*The great steamer glides silently out over the fjord. The music is heard from nearer in shore.*]

NOTES

1. *Chamberlain:* Norway abolished hereditary titles in 1821. Chamberlain is a title conferred by the King on prominent men.

2. *Independence Day:* Ibsen has merely '17 May'. His stage directions here are much more terse than they became in his later plays, where he goes into great detail. What he has written here is literally: '17 May. Evening. Public fête. A clearing in the Great Park. Music in the background. Coloured lights in the trees . . .', etc.

3. *Lundestad:* 'Farmer Lundestad', in accordance with the Norwegian custom; but this would give English readers a wrong picture of his status as a Member of the Storthing.

4. *'our local conditions':* A political catch-phrase from 1857, a gibe at the Conservatives. In the theatre of that day it would have got the same easy laugh as 'never had it so good' might get today.

5. *the Storthing:* The Norwegian Parliament.

6. *the Preliminary Election:* This was the *Valgdmandsvalg* – the election of electors, where the voters would elect a College of Electors who were to choose the Members of the Storthing.

7. *[rising]:* In some embarrassment – Aslaksen knows all too well what Hejre is about to say.

8. *naufragium:* Ibsen makes him say *skibbrud*, 'shipwreck', which makes the pun, such as it is, even more obscure.

9. *Conciliation Court:* The preliminary hearing by an Arbitration Commission to decide if a case should come to open Court.

10. *happy brothers and sisters:* A parody of the style of the less-gifted followers of the great Liberal leader Sverdrup.

11. *[He whispers . . .]:* In the first draft, Fjeldbo said outright, 'Monsen of Storli', and a line or two later Brattsberg repeated it. This made the Chamberlain's mistake much clearer, and it is hard to see why Ibsen should have changed it. Years later, when Shaw accused Ibsen of wilful obscurity, Ibsen replied, 'What I have written, I have written.' Shaw retorted, 'Yes, and what you haven't written, you haven't written.'

Though Thora's aside to Fjeldbo would be clear to an audience, it might puzzle a reader. She is thanking Fjeldbo for sparing her father the truth.

12. *tread on a worm:* We do not learn till Act Five what had happened earlier in the day between Thora and Fjeldbo to make him so happy.

13. *sisters:* Unfortunately we have no English equivalent for *søsken* – a convenient word that means both brothers and sisters. The psychiatrist's 'siblings' – even if it could be admitted as an English word – would be out of period.

14. *Hassan:* Ibsen has 'Jeppe'. This was a character in one of Holberg's comedies who would be familiar to a Norwegian audience. Like Hassan and Christopher Sly, he was granted a single day of luxury.

15. *Now there's someone:* Ibsen does not explain the Chamberlain's sudden change of attitude towards Fjeldbo till the very end of the play.

16. *The late King:* King Karl Johann.

17. *elegible:* What Lundestad actually says (*'du har skaffet Dem Stemmerett'*) would be obscure to anyone not familiar with the Norwegian political system. In fact, it turns out later that Stensgård lacks the 'Property Qualification'.

18. *grouse: tiur* is really 'woodcock'.

19. *a stork or a –:* In the first draft, Stensgård said '. . . and there were ravens and woodpeckers and herons [*hejre*] –'; to which Erik asked, 'Herons too?' and Stensgård replied, 'Well, one specimen at any rate.'

20. *a steep crag: Et bratt fjeld,* a play on 'Brattsberg'.

21. *dollars:* The Specie dollar was still the unit of currency in Norway when this play was written. It was worth about four shillings and sixpence.

22. *as the poet says:* Henrik Wergeland in his 'To Herman Foss' (1837). It is the opening and closing line of the poem.

23. *old man:* Bastian now uses the familiar 'thou' to Stensgård.

24. *a split in his personality:* This looks like an anachronism now that 'split personality' has become such a part of our fashionable psychological jargon, but *'splittelse i personligheden'* is just what Ibsen wrote.

25. He assumes his Property Qualification at last.

26. *Fjeldbo, you mean:* According to the Norwegian custom of addressing people by their occupation, the original dialogue runs:

> MADAM: Congratulations, Mr Lawyer.
> FJELDBO: 'Doctor', you mean.

27. *on the balcony . . . behind that curtain:* This is rather hard to visualize. Ibsen's first draft had: '. . . less voice on the balcony when I'm inside', which seems clearer than his second thoughts. Archer cleverly gets out of the difficulty by making the Chamberlain snooze 'in the bay window', but *karnapp* is literally 'balcony'.

28. *perhaps both at once:* In *A Public Enemy*, written thirteen years later, Aslaksen refers to him as 'Councillor Stensgård'. At the time this play was written, Ministers did not sit in the Storthing, but Ibsen's prophesy was remarkably accurate – the change came some thirteen years later when the Liberals came to power.

29. *theologian:* On the stage, either a gesture or Helle's costume would make it clear whom Ibsen means by this.

A DOLL'S HOUSE

1. *fifty øre:* The equivalent of a sixpence. A hundred øre equals one krone, then worth just over a shilling.

2. *Torvald:* Almost alone among Ibsen's married women, Nora always calls her husband by his Christian name. It would have been more usual for her to call him simply 'Helmer'.

3. *dollars . . . kroner:* Specie dollars were the old Norwegian unit of currency. They were changed to kroner soon enough before this play was written for Nora to think in both currencies – rather as in 1964 the English weather forecasts give temperatures in both Centigrade and Fahrenheit.

4. *'Well I'm damned!':* literally is *død og pine*, 'death and torment', a surprisingly mild expletive in Norwegian. In these more outspoken days it sounds rather an anticlimax after all Nora's preparation.

5. *stripped:* In Scandinavia the Christmas tree and its presents are enjoyed on Christmas Eve.

6. *Christian-name terms:* The English translator's hurdle again. What

Helmer actually says is *vi er dus* – 'we were thous' – that is, they used the familiar second person singular.

7. *Krogstad's footsteps are heard:* One of the rare occasions where Ibsen's practical stagecraft deserts him. If he had remembered his days as stage manager at Bergen, he would have realized how heavy-footed Krogstad would have to be if the audience were to hear him. In Act Three Ibsen even specifies that they are 'soft footsteps'.

8. *Nils:* Mrs Linde calls him 'Krogstad' throughout, but in English this would seem stilted in so intimate a scene.

9. *Mr Helmer:* Actually, as a new employee of the Bank, she calls him *Herr Direktor* – 'Mr Manager'.

10. *S. Rank,* M.D.: 'Doktor Medecinæ Rank', according to the Norwegian custom. To translate the card into English there must be an initial, but nowhere in the text or in the earlier drafts has Ibsen given Rank a Christian name, so an initial had to be picked at random.

11. Under protest, Ibsen rewrote the closing lines for the German production. His altered ending ran:

> NORA: . . . that our life together could become a real marriage. Good-bye. [*She starts to go.*]
>
> HELMER: Go then! [*He seizes her arm.*] But first you shall see your children for the last time.
>
> NORA: Let me go! I will not see them. I cannot!
>
> HELMER [*dragging her to the door on the left*]: You shall see them! [*He opens the door and says softly*] Look – there they are, sleeping peacefully and without a care. Tomorrow, when they wake and call for their mother, they will be . . . motherless!
>
> NORA [*trembling*]: Motherless!
>
> HELMER: As you once were.
>
> NORA: Motherless! [*After an inner struggle, she lets her bag fall, and says*] Ah, though it is a sin against myself, I cannot leave them! [*She sinks almost to the ground by the door.*]
>
> The curtain falls

Not surprisingly, Ibsen described this as a 'barbaric outrage'; and in the following year he refused to allow the altered ending to be used in Italy.

THE LADY FROM THE SEA

1. *lunch*: *Frokost* is more properly 'breakfast', cf. the French (*petit*) *déjeuner*, but this would suggest that the scene takes place earlier in the day than it actually does.

2. *Isn't she well, then?*: This seems strange to us in these days when we bathe rather for pleasure than for health, and when a daily bathe suggests an almost aggressive fitness.

3. *Skjoldvik*: Pronounced *Shol'-veek*. The picture is of a sparsely populated and isolated island with a lighthouse, out at the mouth of the fjord.

4. *Are you there, Wangel?*: According to the Norwegian custom of the period, the wife addresses her husband by his bare surname.

5. *called you after a ship*: The name Ellida (pronounced Ell-*ee*-da) was a brilliant afterthought. It is the feminine form of *Ellidi* – the 'Storm Rider' – the troll-haunted ship in the saga of *Frithof the Bold*.

6. *your – your birthday*: He starts to say *geburtsdag*, but changes it to the more formal *födelsdag* – a distinction that does not exist in English.

7. *in French*: In the original, he goes on in English.

8. *so fascinating*: This is the child who will grow up to send Master Builder Solness to his death.

9. *Finnmark*: The northernmost part of Norway bordering on Finland. *Kvæn* is another word for Finn, but to translate it 'Finnlander' would make Ellida's next line pointless.

10. *the two rings*: A memory of an incident in Ibsen's own early life in Bergen when he was in love with a girl named Rikke Holst.

11. *live on the sea*: In a letter at this time Ibsen wrote: 'We ought to avail ourselves of the sea, building floating cities on it so that we can move southward or northward according to the time of year. . . . Some such happy state will come one day, though we shall not live to see it.'

12. *here you are at last*: On the stage, the tone of her voice would make it clear that she thinks it is Wangel she is speaking to.

13. *my dear*: The Stranger is using the familiar pronoun *du* throughout the scene. Ellida uses the formal *De*.

14. *of my own free will*: The phrase is to become of enormous im-

portance in the later scenes. Ellida has given up her freedom by marrying Wangel for security rather than for love; only the return of it can release her. As early as 1862, in *Love's Comedy*, Ibsen had attacked marriages not based on complete freedom.

15. *choose . . . and protect:* An untranslatable play on the words *værge* and *vælge*.

16. *you are no more to me:* Here, for the first time, he uses the formal *De*.